Origins of
Sexuality and Homosexuality

Origins of Sexuality and Homosexuality

Edited by
John P. De Cecco
Michael G. Shively

Origins of Sexuality and Homosexuality was originally published in 1984 by The Haworth Press, Inc., under the title *Bisexual and Homosexual Identities: Critical Theoretical Issues.* It has also been published as *Journal of Homosexuality*, Volume 9, Numbers 2/3, Winter 1983/Spring 1984.

Harrington Park Press
New York • Binghamton

ISBN 0-918393-00-0

Published by
Harrington Park Press, Inc.
28 East 22 Street
New York, New York 10010

Harrington Park Press, Inc., is a subsidiary of The Haworth Press, Inc., 28 East 22 Street, New York, New York 10010.

Origins of Sexuality and Homosexuality was originally published in 1984 by The Haworth Press, Inc., under the title *Bisexual and Homosexual Identities: Critical Theoretical Issues.* It has also been published as *Journal of Homosexuality,* Volume 9, Numbers 2/3, Winter 1983/Spring 1984.

Library of Congress Cataloging in Publication Data

Bisexual and homosexual identities, critical theoretical issues.
    Origins of sexuality and homosexuality.

    Reprint: Originally published: Bisexual and homosexual identities, critical theoretical issues. New York : Haworth Press, c1984.
        1. Homosexuality—Addresses, essays, lectures. 2. Bisexuality—Addresses, essays, lectures. 3. Sex (Psychology)—Addresses, essays, lectures. 4. Identity (Psychology)—Addresses, essays, lectures. I. De Cecco, John P. II. Shively, Michael G.
HQ76.25.B57   1985   306.7'66   84-22563
ISBN 0-918393-00-0 (pbk.)

CONTENTS

THE HOMOSEXUAL CONTEXT

THE BIOLOGICAL CONTEXT

The *Journal of Homosexuality* is devoted to theoretical, empirical, and historical research on homosexuality, heterosexuality, sexual identity, social sex roles, and the sexual relationships of both men and women. It was created to serve the allied disciplinary and professional groups represented by psychology, sociology, history, anthropology, biology, medicine, the humanities, and law. Its purposes are:

   a) to bring together, within one contemporary scholarly journal, theoretical, empirical, and historical research on human sexuality, particularly sexual identity;
   b) to serve as a forum for scholarly research of heuristic value for the understanding of human sexuality, based not only in the more traditional social or biological sciences, but also in literature, history and philosophy;
   c) to explore the political, social, and moral implications of research on human sexuality for professionals, clinicians, social scientists, and scholars in a wide variety of disciplines and settings.

RICHARD HALL, MA, *Writer, New York City*

JOEL D. HENCKEN, MA, *Private Practice, Boston; PhD Candidate in Clinical Psychology, University of Michigan*

EVELYN HOOKER, PhD, *Retired Research Professor, Psychology Department, University of California, Los Angeles*

RICHARD J. HOFFMAN, PhD, *Associate Professor, Department of History, San Francisco State University*

FRED KLEIN, MD, *Clinical Institute for Human Relationships, San Diego*

MARY RIEGE LANER, PhD, *Associate Professor of Sociology, Arizona State University, Tempe*

ELLEN LEWIN, PhD, *Medical Anthropology Program, University of San Francisco*

DON LILES, MA, *Instructor in English, City College of San Francisco*

A. P. MACDONALD, JR., PhD, *Acting Director and Associate Professor, Center for the Family, University of Massachusetts, Amherst*

WILLIAM F. OWEN, MD, *Private Practice, San Francisco*

L. ANNE PEPLAU, PhD, *Associate Professor of Psychology, University of California, Los Angeles*

KENNETH PLUMMER, PhD, *Department of Sociology, University of Essex, England*

SHARON RAPHAEL, PhD, *Associate Professor of Sociology, California State University, Dominguez-Hills*

KENNETH READ, PhD, *Professor of Anthropology, University of Washington, Seattle*

MICHAEL ROSS, PhD, *Senior Demonstrator in Psychiatry, The Flinders University of South Australia, Adelaide, Australia*

DOROTHY SEIDEN, PhD, *Professor, Department of Home Economics, San Francisco State University*

G. WILLIAM SKINNER, PhD, *Professor of Anthropology, Stanford University*

RICHARD W. SMITH, PhD, *Professor of Psychology, California State University, Northridge*

JOHN P. SPIEGEL, MD, *Director, Training Program in Ethnicity and Mental Health, Brandeis University; Current President, American Academy of Psychoanalysis*

FREDERICK SUPPE, PhD, *Chair, Committee on the History and Philosophy of Science, University of Maryland, College Park*

JOHN UNGARETTI, MA, *Classics; MA, Literature; San Francisco*

JEFFREY WEEKS, PhD, *Research Fellow, Department of Sociology, University of Essex, England*

JAMES WEINRICH, PhD, *Psychiatry and Behavioral Sciences, Johns Hopkins University*

JACK WIENER, MSW, *Retired, National Institute of Mental Health, Bethesda, Maryland*

DEBORAH WOLF, PhD, *Institute for the Study of Social Change, University of California, Berkeley*

WAYNE S. WOODEN, PhD, *Assistant Professor, Behavioral Science, California State Polytechnic University, Pomona*

Foreword

The notion that individuals have a sexual identity—bisexual, heterosexual, or homosexual—has a history extending well over a century. Until recently this idea was rarely called sexual identity. It was usually labeled in terms of the sexual variation that absorbed the interest of the investigator. The homosexual identity, for example, has been called the third sex, antipathetic sexual instinct, perversion, inversion, homosexuality, homosexual outlet, homosexual orientation (or preferences), and, more recently, the gay or lesbian lifestyle and the socially constructed gay identity. The bisexual identity, more obliquely, has been labeled sexual perversity (as opposed to sexual perversion), psychical hermaphroditism, acquired (as opposed to congenital) perversion, situational or episodic homosexuality, and, of course, simply bisexuality. The heterosexual identity has rarely been assigned any other name since it has been conceived as the "natural" or "normal" identity—the product of a biological or psychological process of development that squared with moral and institutional prescriptions for sexual relationships.

Whatever the designation, the underlying assumption has been that the individual's sexual identity constituted a core ingredient of spirit, body, mind, personality, or social relations. This personal essence was variously cast in biological, psychological, or socio-cultural forms, depending on what particular theoreticians believed were its chief determinants. Yet the biological form has been the most basic because all three conceptualizations of sexual identity make the biological sex of partners in sexual relationships the attribute that consistently distinguishes one identity from another.

Theories of sexual identity have embodied unacknowledged moral dicta, implicit philosophical conceptions of biology, individuals, and society, and assumptions about the applicability of the scientific method to social science research. Any analysis of sexual identity, if it is to represent a significant advance in knowledge, must expose and examine the premises upon which the idea has been erected. In this critical process some tender areas of conviction and commitment will undoubtedly be probed, and this could lead to illuminating debate.

So that all sides of any ensuing debate on sexual identity can be aired, the editor is planning to devote a future issue of the *Journal* to extended and detailed reactions to the articles contained in the present collection. Some of these critiques will be solicited from the theoreticians and investigators who approach the issue of sexual identity from perspectives that are significantly different than those presented here. It is also anticipated that other critiques will be volunteered. These, we hope, would deal with possible inaccuracies and misconceptions in the present monograph and cogently defend alternative positions. In those cases in which clarity and knowledge would be served, the authors in this collection will be invited to reply. Readers who are moved to prepare critical essays should send them to the editor no later than March 1984.

The present theoretical collection will be followed by another (Volume 9, Number 4) that focuses more specifically on clinical issues and also subjects the hormonal research on homosexuality to a more extensive analysis than was possible here.

In presenting this monograph the editors of the *Journal* hope to join the current effort to scrutinize the idea of sexual identity. Mary McIntosh, perhaps, spawned this inquiry which now has been notably joined in Europe by Martin Dannecker, Michel Foucault, Guy Hocquenghem, the late Mario Mieli, Kenneth Plummer, and Jeffrey Weeks, and, in the United States, by Dennis Altman and Jonathan Katz. It is the editors' hope that this monograph will contribute to the current discourse in the social sciences and historiography by delineating assumptions and problems inherent in the idea of sexual identity and, in the process, provide new theoretical directions for inquiry into sexual relationships.

It is not possible to thank everyone who contributed to this monograph, but surely the major portion of our gratitude goes to the authors, who weathered the almost interminable process of delay, review and revision, in some cases extending over a period of countless months. We are deeply indebted to them for their outstanding contributions and for their stoic forebearance and generosity of spirit. We also wish to thank the referees who read the articles in their protean forms, were quick to recognize their merit, and also quick to suggest emendations. Among the reviewers we express our deep appreciation to Dennis Altman, Philip Blumstein, William Bonds, Eli Coleman, Louis Crompton, John Gonsiorek, Joel Hencken, Stuart Kellogg, A. P. MacDonald, Wendell Ricketts, John Spiegel, and Fred Suppe. Finally we wish to thank our publisher, The Haworth Press, for their magnificent warm assistance and advice in moving this project to fruition.

John P. De Cecco
Editor

                                           Michael G. Shively
                                             Associate Editor

From Sexual Identity to Sexual Relationships: A Contextual Shift

John P. De Cecco, PhD
Michael G. Shively, MA
San Francisco State University

ABSTRACT. The article has three major purposes. First, it adumbrates four contexts within which the discourse on sexual identity has been carried on: the historical, bisexual, homosexual, and biological. Within these contexts sexual identity has been conceived in three general forms: the biological, psychological, and socio-cultural. The biological form is the most basic since all conceptualizations of sexual identity make the biological sex of partners in sexual relationships the criterial distinction. Second, the article addresses problems that have arisen in each of the contexts: the uncritical use of popular concepts and explanations of sexual identity, the incorporation of unacknowledged moral judgements, and the misapplication of the scientific method. Third, it identifies conceptual, methodological, and moral advantages in redirecting the discourse on sexual identity so that the focus of inquiry is on sexual relationships: (a) The focus is shifted from isolated individuals to their mutual associations. (b) Social scientists could conceive of sexual relationships in other than biological terms or metaphors. (c) The shift would capitalize on the advantages of the psychoanalytic method (the exploration of personally constructed meanings) and symbolic interactionism (the identification of socially constructed meanings) while avoiding the pitfalls of relying on one of these approaches to the exclusion of the other. (d) The shift would allow investigators to view sexual relationships from the vantage point of a morality of individual choice rather than a traditional morality of externally imposed obligation.

The idea of sexual identity has many diverse meanings which derive from the scientific discourse within which it developed. The discourse occurred chiefly in European and American psychiatry, medicine, and the

Besides being respectively Editor and Associate Editor of the *Journal*, the authors are also Director and Associate Director of the Center for Research and Education in Sexuality (CERES) at San Francisco State University. As founders of CERES in 1975, they have directed federally funded research on discrimination, aging, and jail assault. The senior author is Professor of Psychology and Human Sexuality at San Francisco State University. The authors have been investigating the history of the idea of sexual identity and its implications for sexual relationships. Reprint requests should be addressed to the authors at CERES, San Francisco State University, San Francisco, CA 94132.

social sciences from the middle of the nineteenth century to the present.

The purpose of this article is, first, to adumbrate four contexts within which that discourse has occurred: the historical, bisexual, homosexual, and biological. The second purpose is to address research problems that have arisen in each context: the uncritical use of popular concepts and explanations of sexual identity, the incorporation of unacknowledged moral judgements, and the misapplication of the scientific method. Third, the article identifies possible conceptual advantages in redirecting the discourse on sexual identity so that the focus of inquiry is on sexual relationships. Finally, it shows how the articles in this monograph contribute to the understanding of sexual relationships.

The key concepts in this analysis are *sexual identity* and *sexual relationships*. In the various contexts, sexual identity is conceived as an essence, interiorly lodged within the individual, one which determines whether the individual has only female or only male sexual partners or both females and males. If the partners are of the opposite biological sex, the individual's identity is called heterosexual. If partners are of the same biological sex, the identity is designated as homosexual. If partners are of both sexes, it is bisexual.

A sexual relationship can be defined by its structure, the constituent elements of which are the attitudes of partners that inform their treatment of each other. These attitudes may, for example, include beliefs about biological sex, femininity and masculinity, complementarity, exclusivity, sensuosity, intimacy, and permanency. The structure of a sexual relationship consists of the implications or consequences of partners' having various attitudes. For example, partners may view a relationship as a network of externally prescribed obligations or they may view it as consisting of both negotiated and personal choices. These differing views of relationships would probably have sharply contrasting structural implications or consequences. As such, the structure is unknown to the partners because it is the conceptualization of the social scientist who notes the implications of partners' holding similar or dissimilar sets of beliefs. As noted by F. A. Hayek (1952/1979): "It is important to observe that . . . the various types of individual attitudes are not themselves the object of our [the social scientists'] explanation, but merely the element from which we build up the structure of possible relationships between individuals" (p. 68).

Still unanswered is the question of what distinguishes a relationship that is *sexual* from one that is not sexual. A relationship can be considered sexual from two vantage points: that of a shared moral tradition and that of the individual. Because traditional sexual morality has been chiefly concerned with regulating physical contact between individuals, particularly when it involves the genitalia, a relationship can be viewed as sexual whenever it falls within the purview of strictures placed on such conduct.

Sexual conduct, however, is not a static reality. Although the Judaeo-Christian tradition proscribed forms of sexual conduct such as sodomy and bestiality, it did little to elucidate what particular behavior was forbidden. The institutional fear of fostering the forbidden sexual conduct resulted in only elliptical references to specific behavior. The individual, therefore, was the unwitting heir of the freedom to determine which specific acts were forbidden.

Therefore, a relationship can also be considered sexual because of the individual's understanding of traditional morality and independent beliefs about what constitutes sexual conduct. Moral principles are not ingested or applied by individuals as irreducible substances. They are ideas that are modified by the individual on the basis of conscious and unconscious knowledge and are applied as the individual deems necessary or appropriate.

THE HISTORICAL CONTEXT

Several historians who have joined the discourse on sexual identity have assumed that it is a biological essence that transcends history. In 1955, for example, Derrick Sherwin Bailey (1955/1975), in his exploration of biblical and ecclesiastical attitudes toward homosexual practice, referred to "the true male invert" and to inversion as "an inherent condition . . . [that] cannot be institutionalized" (p. 171). He defined inversion as a *"condition* due to biological, psychological, or genetic causes" (p. 173). He distinguished the invert from the pervert, for whom homosexual practice was only a single ingredient in a life filled with debauchery and sexual dissipation. Vern Bullough (1976), in his historical survey of sexual variance in Eastern and Western history, assumed that an individual could be classified on the basis of one sexual identity or another as "a homosexual" (e.g., pp. 573, 593, 606), "a transsexual" (e.g., p. 598), or "a transvestite."

A historian who fully embraced and defended the notion of sexual identity as essentiality was John Boswell (1980). In his history of attitudes toward "gay people" in medieval Europe, he defined sexual identity as an "involuntary sexual preference" (p. 45, n. 10). Leaning heavily on sociobiological theories of the genetic basis for homosexuality, Boswell adopted the concept of a biologically predetermined sexual identity as an entity distinguishable from sexual behavior (see Boswell, pp. 8–10; 41–59). Apparently Boswell believed that social attitudes in history could restrict sexual behavior but that only biology could determine sexual identity. He could therefore refer to "homosexual acts committed by apparently heterosexual persons" (p. 109).

Boswell (1982/1983) later explicated his position on sexual identity by distinguishing between a "nominalist" theory that all individuals are capable of "erotic and sexual attraction with either gender" (p. 97) from a "realist" theory that individuals fit into only one "native" sexual category (i.e., either bisexual, heterosexual, or homosexual) "though external pressures or circumstances may induce individuals in a given society to pretend (or even to believe)" (p. 97) that they belong to another category. The first theory was "nominalist" because it regarded "heterosexual" and "homosexual" as mere labels applied by society to an undifferentiated sexual reality. The second was "realist" in two senses: It was predicated on categories that undergird human sexual experience "even when obscured by social constraints or particular circumstances" (p. 99). Moreover, the second theory was that which Boswell believed was endorsed in ancient society as well as in "popular modern conception": "Some people prefer their own gender; some the opposite; some both" (p. 99). Assuming that "gayness" was an essential physical ingredient of a particular group of individuals, Boswell (1980, Chapter 9, pp. 243–266) searched for evidence that everything they thought and did had a "gay" form. He therefore spoke of a "gay subculture," "gay love," and a "gay minority."

These historians have uncritically incorporated into their work theories and concepts that are currently popular. In the main they have accepted the popular notion of sexual identity as a biological essence. It is biological because it rests on the identification of the biological sex of partners in sexual relationships. Thus Bailey wrote of the "true" homosexual and Boswell of the individual possessing a "native" sexual identity. The idea that individuals possess an "identity" is a product of medicine and the social sciences. That individuals possess a *sexual* identity, as Michel Foucault (1976/1978) and Jeffrey Weeks (1977) have shown, is an idea of nineteenth century vintage. The idea of their having a *social* or *psychological* identity is still newer (Erikson, 1959; Mead, 1934).

What is most striking was the willingness of historians to make a *biological* concept the foundation of a *historical* inquiry that has consisted of describing the circumstances under which this identity existed in the past. Sexual identity is accepted as a commonsense assumption that requires no historical or theoretical analysis of its own. In effect, the historical investigation of the past is reduced to a retrospective reconstruction of history which corroborates currently popular notions of sexual identity.

In subscribing to these popular ideas, historians have also embraced the associated, contemporary stereotypes. Thus Bailey (1955/1975) adopted the medical theory of the fifties that the homosexual identity represented a congenital and psychological pathology. Boswell (1980) endorsed the portrayal of gay people fostered by the Gay Liberation movement in the seventies. Randolph Trumbach (1977/1978) and Alan Bray (1982) searched for the historical origin of the "gay community" in the "sodomite subcultures" and "molly houses" of late seventeenth-century England.

Recent historiography on sexual identity has often reflected the writers' unacknowledged moral judgements about sexual relationships. One widely held moral belief is that relationships involving younger and older men should not include having sex. This moral stricture was reflected in K. J. Dover's (1978/1980) conclusion that the erastes (the older male partner) did not obtain physical pleasure from the eromenos (the younger male partner), nor ever penetrated any orifice of the eromenos' body in Greek pederastic relationships. The variety and breadth of sexual relationships in classical Greece, however, makes Dover's conclusion extremely dubious (Ungaretti, 1982).

There is also the Judaeo-Christian prescription for marital fidelity. This belief surfaces in Dover's assertion that the pederastic relationship with the eromenos ended with the marriage of the erastes. There is, however, evidence that extramarital homosexual relationships were commonplace among the Greeks (Ungaretti, 1982). It is also possible that a belief in the paternal role made it difficult for Dover to accept the possibility that a father who had responsibility for the rearing of his own sons could also have sexual relationships with the sons of other fathers.

The belief that sexual relationships should involve partners of similar ages is a recent moral stance, perhaps reflecting the fear and suspicion that a wide disparity of ages leads to the sexual exploitation of the younger by the older, more powerful partner. Also, the issue of "man-boy love" was a moral embarrassment for those leaders of the Gay Liberation movement in Europe and America who publicly portrayed gay relationships as primarily affectional rather than physical, and egalitarian rather than hierarchical. In describing gay romantic relationships in Imperial Rome, Boswell (1980) claimed that they usually involved partners of similar ages. Literary references to "boys," he asserted, were intended to suggest "youthful beauty rather than chronological minority" (p. 81). Boswell's claim that homosexual relationships were more often androphilic than pedophilic does not square with historical accounts of pederasty in the ancient and early medieval world, at least since Bloch (1910) and Westermarck (1926).

The discourse on sexual identity, within the historical context, purports to be an objective account of sexual relationships, based on the known, extant, and available documents. In fact, the amount and quality of the documentation of sexual attitudes and conduct, as well as the investigative ingenuity in uncovering them, have been truly impressive. What is lacking, however, in this already prodigious effort to illuminate the sexual relationships of the historical past, has been a theory of the structure of sexual relationships. Such a theory would identify structural similarities and dissimilarities in terms of sets of attitudes held by partners and the implications of these attitudes for their treatment of each other. Equipped with such a theory the historian would then be able to show how (1) the structures of sexual relationships in the past compared with present structures and (2) the fortuitious consequences of earlier for subsequent structures.

Although social historians cannot be held responsible for the absence of theory, they are responsible for substituting merely popular notions or personal convictions about sexual identity. Such avoidance of the theoretical issues exposes them to charges that their historiography is political advocacy, religious apologetics, or a veiled defense of or an attack on moral tradition.

THE BISEXUAL CONTEXT

The discussion of sexual identity within the bisexual context has been pursued as a biological concept. As in the case of the heterosexual and homosexual identities, its distinguishing feature has been the biological sex of partners in sexual relationships. There are several popular formulations of the bisexual identity that occur in the scientific discourse on sexual identity. It has been popularly conceived in at least four ways: as a biological essence; as a transitional state that lies between the achievement of an exclusive heterosexual or homosexual identity; as a corrupted heterosexual identity; or as a corrupted homosexual identity.

The view of the bisexual identity as a biological essence, clearly distinguishable from the heterosexual and homosexual identities, has rapidly gained currency (e.g., Klein, 1978; MacDonald, 1981; Rubenstein, 1982). A. P. MacDonald (1981), for example, identified this view as the belief that bisexuality is a "real [sexual] orientation" (p. 29), a natural human capacity that existed throughout history and in most societies. He defined that bisexual identity as an individual phenomenon that "may or may not change" like being "a waiter, a Democrat, or an agnostic" (p. 33, n. 4). He suggested that bisexuals were an identifiable group, possessing a distinctive lifestyle and facing problems of discrimination and social acceptance by both heterosexuals and homosexuals.

Other views of the bisexual identity have questioned or denied its existence. They share the common assumption that there exists only the heterosexual or the homosexual identity. They differ, however, in the ways in which they explain the fact that some men and women form sexual relationships with partners of both biological sexes.

The transitional explanation questions the validity of the bisexual identity by viewing the individual as being in a state of flux from one identity to the other. Although the period of transition may be characterized by the individual forming sexual relationships with both females and males, it is assumed that eventually one biological sex will be completely surrendered for the other. This transitional explanation can be traced historically to conceptions of bisexuality that prevailed in psychiatric circles in the late nineteenth and early twentieth centuries.

Albert Moll (1897/1933), the German sexologist and psychiatrist, believed that the sexual instinct evolved through a process consisting of three stages: (a) an *asexual* stage in which the sex organs were undifferentiated; (b) a *bisexual* stage in which both female and male sex organs were present; and (c) a *monosexual* stage from which the "heterosexual reaction capacity" emerged. In bisexual individuals, Moll believed, the heterosexual reaction capacity, as a biological trait like seeing and hearing, was flawed either because of some congenital weakness or because the individual's sexual development was inhibited during childhood. Krafft-Ebing (1906/1935) and Havelock Ellis (1897/1936) believed that embryonic development started with an initial bisexual state and normally proceeded to a monosexual state in which the organs of one sex vanquished those of the other. In the bisexual, as in the homosexual, they speculated, this sexual conquest was incomplete so that remnants of the conquered sex remained.

To the degree that these theories lean on congenital factors, the bisexual "transition" in the adult female or male was viewed as a frozen state. They implied that when men and women, caught up in such a state, turned to their own biological sex to form sexual relationships, they were compensating for ingredients that never fully emerged in their own sexual development. When they turned to persons of the opposite sex, they were acting in conformity with nature's design.

Other psychiatric theorists of psychosexual development viewed the transition from homosexuality to heterosexuality as a necessary stage in childhood or adolescent development. Sigmund Freud (1923/1961, p. 33) believed that boys and girls faced the dissolution of both the positive and negative Oedipus complexes. The dissolution of the positive complex involved the surrender of the opposite-sex parent as a lover. The dissolution of the negative complex, about which Freud wrote little in adumbrating the normal course of heterosexual development, required the child to surrender incestuous love for the same-sex parent. For both little boys and little girls to develop a heterosexual identity, the dissolution of the negative complex had to precede the dissolution of the positive. For both Freud and Harry Stack Sullivan, passing through the homosexual stage was a prerequisite for achieving the heterosexual identity. Sullivan (1965) claimed that homosexual relationships between adolescent chums was a phase of normal heterosexual development. He suggested that adult homosexuals were those people who, as adolescents, failed to develop solid peer relationships. However, no theorist of sexual identity has suggested a heterosexual stage as a transitional requirement for the development of the homosexual identity.

Most theories of the bisexual identity view it as a corrupted heterosexual or homosexual identity. In a number of theoretical stances it was held that bisexuality emerged when the individual's primary heterosexual identity was corrupted or spoiled by engaging in homosexual relations. These theories rested on the assumption that there was a distinction between sexual identity and sexual behavior. Although the behavior was homosexual, even in a virulent form, the identity, as a biological entity, remained heterosexual.

According to psychiatric speculations in the nineteenth century, the heterosexual identity could be corrupted when the individual was exposed to temptation. For example, Benjamin Tarnowsky (1886/1898), the Russian forensic psychiatrist, wrote about the "acquired inversion" in boarding schools for boys. Tarnowsky believed that it took only one boy with already "perverted sexual instinct" (p. 91) to become the "source of contamination" (p. 91) for his schoolmates. Besides boarding schools, Tarnowsky warned of "sailing vessels on long voyages, prisons, [and] barracks with schools for soldiers' boys" as situations for the "spread and development of acquired pederasty" (p. 96).

It was also possible to corrupt a basically sound heterosexual identity by moral depravity, what Johann Casper (1857–1858/1864) called a vice acquired "as a result of the satiety of the natural sexual pleasures" (p. 330). One of the earliest taxonomists of sexual "parasthesia," Richard von Krafft-Ebing (1906/1935) distinguished between "perversion," innate degeneracy, and "perversity' (pp. 79–80), acquired vice. Perversity, he believed, was caused by masturbation, sexual excess, or the environmental impossibility of having "natural" coitus. As a form of moral depravity, prolonged practice of homosexual behavior for the sexual rake could become a permanent trap, weakening the desire for heterosexual coitus and becoming the ruling mode of sexual gratification.

In more recent theories, bisexuality surfaced as a reparative homosexuality. The psychoanalysts in the Bieber group (1962) disavowed the idea of an innate homosexual identity. They conceived of the heterosexual identity as the "biologic norm." Homosexual relationships were the vain effort of males to repair a badly damaged masculinity. The injury or traumas were psychological and difficult to repair because they occurred in the earliest years of childhood. However, the Bieber group did identify "bisexuals" in their homosexual sample, men who had sexual relationships with both sexes. In these men the damage to the heterosexual identity stood the best chance of therapeutic repair because it was less compromised by the parental treatment they received as children.

In more recent speculations, bisexuality has been viewed as a corrupted homosexual identity. Although the individual's behavior was preponderantly heterosexual, the identity was called homosexual. Joseph Harry and R. Lovely (1979), for example, believed that the vast majority of men who claimed equal attraction to both biological sexes were not bisexuals "but use this label as a means of avoiding the full stigma of a homosexual label" (p. 183). Even though the individual sustained heterosexual relationships into middle and late adulthood, the first public disclosure and embracing of a homosexual relationship was believed to erase past deception and restore unity between their sexual behavior and homosexual identity.

There were several unacknowledged moral assumptions in these conceptions of bisexuality. For those who conceived it as a biological essence there was the implicit assumption that it deserved personal understanding and social tolerance equal to that accorded the heterosexual and homosexual identities. The transitional view of bisexuality contained the mandate that the individual should complete the process of psychosexual development by surrendering the lustful fantasies of childhood and thereby achieve full manhood or womanhood. Bisexuality as a corrupted heterosexual identity implied the moral dictum to surrender licentiousness for normal coitus, preferably within the bosom of marriage. Forming sexual relationships with both biological sexes was seen as open defiance of the tradition of sexual fidelity, held in high esteem by the moral defenders of romantic love and monogamy. As a corrupted homosexual identity the moral preachment to bisexuals was for them to drop the cloak of heterosexuality and disclose their true homosexual essence. In this way they could experience the rewards of a unified self while stoically bearing up under the stigma attached to homosexuality.

All four conceptions of the bisexual identity laid claim to the authority of science. As a biological essence it could be operationally defined as the middle ratings on the Kinsey heterosexual-homosexual rating scale (MacDonald, 1981). As a transitional stage it had the authority of evolutionary biology buttressed by parallel theories of psychological development. As a corrupted heterosexual or homosexual identity it could lay claim to the clinical authority of those psychiatrists and psychologists who documented the unhappiness of those whose lives departed from their sexual essence.

THE HOMOSEXUAL CONTEXT

The idea of sexual identity was first formulated within the homosexual context. The homosexual identity was created by Karl Heinrich Ulrichs and the forensic psychiatrists of the nineteenth century, who assumed the existence of an unarticulated heterosexual identity that stood as its counterpart. Sigmund Freud, viewing both sexual identities as problematic, went on to create a fully explicit notion of the heterosexual identity. In one hundred-thirty years of discourse on the origin, basis, or etiology of the homosexual identity, it has assumed three general forms: biological, psychological, and socio-cultural.

The initial conceptualization of the homosexual identity as a biological essence was based on the assumption that sexual relationships could only consist of female and male partners. The various biological theories of the homosexual identity were attempts to adapt it to this basic male-female design. Ulrichs (1868), for example, postulated the existence of feminine and masculine sex drives that were independent of the biological sexes of the partners. Magnus Hirschfeld (1947) theorized the existence of female and male sex hormones that controlled the strength, direction, and periodicity of sexual desire. A preponderance of female hormones in the male or of male hormones in the female would produce a homosexual identity.

The most fully developed example of the psychological homosexual identity was provided by Freud as a by-product of his unwitting creation of the heterosexual identity. In Freud's formulation, sexual identity consisted of three sets of polarities: physical appearance (female or male sexual characteristics), mental characteristics (feminine or masculine attitudes), and object choice (attraction to female or male sexual partners). For each set the individual's biological predisposition and the contingencies of experience combined to determine whether sexual development leaned toward one pole or the other. The ideal heterosexual identity required the female, for example, to be wholly female in appearance, purely feminine in attitude, and to choose the male exclusively as her sexual object. The homosexual identity consisted of reversals chiefly in mental attitudes and object choice, a swing toward the feminine in males and the masculine in females and in both toward objects of their own sex.

The socio-cultural homosexual identity derived from forces and circumstances that · formed the individual from the outside. It was first described as a social amalgam by the ethnographers of the 1950s and 1960s—a subculture forced upon individuals occupying a sexually deviant status. The homosexual identity has also been conceived as socially constructed, that is, produced by encounter and interaction with heterosexual norms and existing as a sexual role, career, or script. It was constructed from ingredients outside the individual such as social intolerance, legal persecution, and the gay subculture as refuge and hospice. Finally, the homosexual identity was conceived by clinical psychologists as a gay identity achieved through a process of increasing awareness, acceptance, and disclosure and the consolidation of identity and behavior. The gay identity was a socio-cultural identity because the crucial developmental events in its acquisition required the individual to disclose it to ever-broadening circles of individuals who were presumably heterosexual in identity.

Each of these general forms of the homosexual identity contained implicit moral assumptions. Those who conceived it as a biological identity assumed that it was a product of nature. As ordained by nature, there were basic and complementary differences between the male and female sexes. These differences were thought to be essentially biological and most visible in genital anatomy. Because the homosexual identity was described as a variation of this male-female design, it too was conceived as a product of nature. The unacknowledged assumption was that if a phenomenon were natural, then it was above moral reproach.

Although the homosexual identity was believed to be "natural," the implicit assumption was that only the heterosexual was "normal," because it provided the perfect fit for the male-female design. It conceived of females and males as feminine or masculine counterparts ideally suited for the performance of their ordained procreative roles. Even in the defense of the homosexual identity by its staunchest advocates, there was the lingering suspicion that departures from feminine or masculine stereotypes and the absence of fecundity were marks of "abnormality." The unacknowledged moral assumption was that if a phenomenon were normal, then it was "better" than the abnormal.

In the psychological conception of the homosexual identity there was the implicit assumption that parents, along with nature, were responsible for the failure of the child to become a heterosexual. Although children were the central figures in Freud's Oedipal drama, they were the mere victims of the unfolding tragedy. Freud believed the proper moral stance for the psychoanalyst was understanding and compassion for individuals possessed of an identity that could not be reversed. If homosexuals accepted their identity and made the most of their gifts, which Freud thought were often not inconsiderable, then the cultural contributions they made exonerated them from the failure to insure the survival of the human race by begetting children of their own.

The socio-cultural form of the homosexual identity shifted the moral responsibility from biology and parents to the shoulders of society. Its conception echoed the note of civility and tolerance for the blameless afflicted. Just as homosexuals had no choice of biological endowment or parents, they had no choice of the moral traditions under which they were reared. The anthropologists argued that if these same individuals had lived in different ages and cultures, they may have occupied positions as prophets, priests, or saints rather than being social pariahs. Because homosexuals did not confer a deviant status on themselves, the most they could do was to recognize the social reality that had been constructed for them and band together with others like themselves and resist oppression.

All three forms of the homosexual identity were proposed and defended under the aegis of science. Those who viewed it as a biological essence laid claim to the authority of biological and medical research, particularly to the recondite research on hormonal and neural interactions. As a psychological phenomenon, the homosexual identity was based on Freud's "biology of the mind," to paraphrase Frank Sulloway (1979), the claim that psychoanalysis was a lawful science of mental apparatus and function. As a socio-cultural identity, it was based on a view of the social sciences as modeled after the natural sciences. Consequently, there were claims that the socio-cultural form of the homosexual identity could be theoretically conceived and empirically verified in the manner of physical phenomena. The achievement of the gay identity, for example, was based on the assumption that an underlying paradigm of homosexual development existed that predicted a sequence of basic, measurable stages the individual passes through on the road to full acceptance of self as a homosexual.

The moral judgements that pervaded these conceptions of the homosexual identity revealed that they were prescriptions for sexual behavior and relationships rather than theoretical conceptions of natural phenomena. To try to find the basis for the homosexual identity or, for that matter, the heterosexual, or why some females are seen as masculine while most are seen as feminine, are not scientific pursuits. The idea of sexual identity has been fostered by conceptions of human society based on the belief that people's biological sex is the brute reality before which all human relationships must bow.

THE BIOLOGICAL CONTEXT

The earliest formulations of the homosexual identity were biological. The essence that theoretically inhered in the homosexual was variously conceived as sex drives, brain centers, germ plasm, hormonal secretions, and genes. Krafft-Ebing (1906/1935), for example, held that the sexual instinct was lodged in the psychosexual centers of the cerebral cortex and located next to the visual and olfactory centers. These brain centers served as junctions where visual and olfactory responses to sexual stimuli were properly routed to the sex organs. Because the psychosexual centers of homosexuals were congenitally diseased, messages went out to "inappropriate" sexual stimuli.

Havelock Ellis (1897/1935) wrote mysteriously about female and male "germs" situated in the fertilized ovum, which later manifested themselves as organic sexual instinct. Normally the germ plasm of one sex obliterated the development of the other sex. In the "invert," however, this process remained incomplete so that the remnants of the "conquered" sex persisted.

More recently, Hirschfeld's explanation of sexual identity has been revived (e.g., Ehrhardt & Meyer-Bahlburg, 1981). For the female fetus to develop into a feminine child an excessive secretion of the male sex hormone had to be avoided. Conversely, the male fetus developed into a masculine child when adequate amounts of the male sex hormone were available. The to-be-homosexual female had been subjected to hormonal excess that "masculinized" the fetal brain. The to-be-homosexual male suffered a deficiency that "feminized" the fetal brain.

The sociobiologists posited the existence of heterosexual and homosexual genes transmitted through the evolutionary process of natural selection. In the realm of human sexuality, genes bestowed an entire identity on the individual whose behavior they presumably controlled. Wilson (1978) could speak, therefore, of the "fully heterosexual" and "fully homosexual" person as distinct human types. These speculations of the sociobiologists about the basis of the homosexual identity, as we have shown, were preceded by theories about quirks in the development of the embryo, the effects of hormones, and the working of the central nervous system.

The discourse on the homosexual identity, within the biological context, although parading as more scientific than that occurring within the other contexts, was equally rife with implicit moral assumptions. First of all there was the unquestioning faith that the male-female design constituted the fundamental order of human relationships: Males should be masculine and heterosexual, females feminine and heterosexual. Homosexuals were exceptions to the design, neither true females nor true males. True males, John Money and Patricia Tucker (1975, p. 38) wrote, "impregnate," while true females "menstruate, gestate, and lactate."

What homosexuals lacked in characteristics stereotypically associated with their own sexes was matched by characteristics associated with the opposite sexes. This was as true for experimental rodents as it was for humans. In examining reports on laboratory experiments designed to discover the hormonal basis for the homosexual identity, Lynda Birke (1981) noted that the rats called "homosexual" were those that fitted the prevailing stereotypes: the female rat who mounted another female and the male rat who was mounted by another male. However, both the "mountee" and "mounter" were homosexual in the sense that each sexual encounter consisted of two rats of the same sex.

By treating the homosexual identity as an involuntary physical condition, the biological theorists believed they were removing it from the realm of moral judgement. Yet, by portraying homosexuals as "intersexuals," unfinished exemplars of their biological sexes, they were assigning them to an inferior rank on the scale of social values, while resoundingly endorsing the prevailing sex-role stereotypes.

The failure to recognize the futility of attempting to resolve moral issues with the scientific methodology of the biological and physical sciences has reduced the biological research on sexual identity to ceaseless repetition. Although over a century of speculation and investigation has proved to be barren, the clinical and laboratory research has persisted (e.g., Dörner, 1976). For most problems in the biological and medical sciences such results would long ago have led to the abandonment of the research program. The argument for continuing this research in the face of repeated failure is that greater scientific rigor or advances in medical technology will finally solve the riddle of the homosexual identity. The issue, however, is not that of increased rigor or technical ingenuity but of the egregious misapplication of the scientific method to moral issues.

FROM IDENTITY TO RELATIONSHIPS

There are distinct advantages, we believe, in shifting the discourse on sexual identity, in its historical, bisexual, homosexual, and biological contexts, to an inquiry about the structure of sexual relationships. These advantages may be categorized as conceptual, moral, and methodological.

The initial conceptual advantage is that the focus of inquiry is shifted from isolated individuals to their mutual associations. The emphasis on individuals outside of their historical and social contexts is probably an unfortunate import by the social sciences from medicine and natural science. In biology, as well as medicine, a picture of the whole phenomenon is usually developed through a detailed analysis of its parts. In psychotherapy the attitudinal and behavioral structures of clients are probed for the purpose of individual insight and possible change. Social scientists, we believe, should be curious about the mental attitudes of the individuals they observe. However, the focus of their inquiry should not be isolated individuals but the structure of social relationships, be they economic, political, or sexual.

The second and, perhaps, major advantage would be to allow social scientists the opportunity to explore aspects of sexual relationships other than the biological. The chief conceptual difficulty posed by the idea of sexual identity is that it rivets attention on the biological aspects of sexual relationships almost to the exclusion of other considerations.

Sexual identity is basically a biological concept that makes the anatomical differences between females and males the pivotal analytical distinction. The biological penumbra that hangs over the idea of sexual identity ultimately leads to viewing sexual relationships as grounded in the genitalia of the partners. These simple anatomical differences are then symbolically elaborated as psychological properties of individuals, such as feminine and masculine attitudes, or as socio-cultural properties of sexual collectivities, such as the "straight lifestyle" or the "gay community." It may be asserted, perhaps rather boldly, that the long discourse on sexual identity has been essentially an exercise in exhaustively symbolizing the myriad ways in which sexual relationships can be described as extensions of the biological sex of partners.

Investigations of sexual relationships from other than a biological stance may discover structures based on motivations, attitudes, and expectations of partners that are unrecognized because there are no taxonomies or theories with which to describe or explain them. Since the eighteenth century Enlightenment bequeathed to individuals the ideology of personal choice, to be exercised in selecting partners or in sustaining or ending relationships, it is difficult to believe that these choices can be understood simply in terms of biological characteristics. The idea of sexual identity, with its aura of biological determinism, hardly provides a context broad enough to account for the complexity and consequences of choices that are conceived and exercised in sexual relationships.

A third conceptual advantage pertains to our definition of sexual relationships as a structure that is described by the social scientist who notes the consequences of partners holding particular sexual attitudes. Because these attitudes are unique amalgams of personal and societal knowledge and meanings, the shift in focus from sexual identity to sexual relationships capitalizes on the advantages but avoids the shortcomings of both psychoanalytic theory and symbolic interactionism (i.e., social constructionism). Psychoanalytic theory is exquisitely sensitive to the fact that individuals create personal meanings out of the vicissitudes of experience rather than simply importing them from the social milieu. It tends, however, to lose the individual in a world of private meanings that are only vaguely tied to historical or social contexts. Symbolic interactionism is acutely aware that the personal and social categories to which individuals assign themselves and others are largely imports from meanings handed down through society and history. However, it tends to surrender the individual to a world of social meanings that are minimally subject to personal criticism and interpolation. The structure of sexual relationships, as conceived here, exists as an intersection of both the uniquely personal meanings of the individual partners and a locus in history and society.

The moral injunctions implied by the scientific discourse on sexual identity have been essentially a perpetuation of Judaeo-Christian strictures. Relationships had to have an extrinsic, "higher," purpose, if not procreation and rearing of family, then some transcendental reembodiment of the individual in, for example, romantic love, poetry, painting, or altruism. In the discourse on sexual identity there has been the lingering note of discomfort with sexual relationships that are formed perhaps exclusively for the purpose of the happiness and satisfaction of the partners alone.

Judaeo-Christian doctrine had warned against sexual relationships that were formed outside of prescribed boundaries as seriously jeopardizing the individual's soul and salvation. Under the banner of science, medicine also warned people about the dangers of errant sexual behavior. If the warning was not heeded, the proscribed behavior constituted a serious threat to physical and mental health. Lust, the Church Fathers had sternly cautioned, could drive men and women to perdition. Their successors in the nineteenth and twentieth centuries, the fathers of medicine and the social sciences, zealously warned individuals that lustful indulgence could drive them to insanity, perversion, and loss of identity.

There are advantages in moral clarity that could be gained in shifting the discourse from sexual identity to a focus on the structure of sexual relationships. The underlying assumption has been that permissible relationships are prescribed for individuals rather than by them. The scientific discourse on sexual identity, because it has embodied the Judaeo-Christian morality, overshadowed the view of human relationships propounded by the philosophers of the eighteenth century Enlightenment. Their philosophy bequeathed moral choice to the individual where previously there had been only the moral authority of Church and State (Gay, 1954). Peter Gay (1954) drew this contrast between Christian and Enlightenment views of sexual morality:

> Whatever the rationalism of some Christian theologians, fundamental to Christianity was the enmity of passion and salvation: a sense of guilt was to hold back desire—the Fall of man at once created lust and gave man a weapon against it. In the Enlightenment, the dichotomy of lust versus guilt was softened into the opposition of reason to emotion, and with this softening rose the opportunity of achieving a view of man in which these opposites would be reconciled. (p. 154)

These moral prescriptions have been perpetuated in their biological, psychological, or sociological avatars. Biology prescribed the fundamental structure of sexual relationships because it was based on the anatomical differences between the two sexes. By extension, however, bisexual and homosexual relationships were conceived as adaptations within the design rather than basic modifications. Because psychiatry and, later, psychology, as the sciences of mental and behavioral processes, and sociology, as the science of collective processes, were modeled in part after evolutionary biology, it was possible to express the biological design for sexual relationships in psychological and sociological metaphors.

The awesome inevitability of biological, psychological, and social processes, presumably working in concert, placed most responsibility for sexual relationships well beyond the grasp of the partners involved in them. If any responsibility was left for the individual, then it was the "choice" to form relationships that were harmonious with the requirements of a stern reality. To ignore or flout this reality was to risk "punishment," visited in the form of biological incapacity, mental suffering, or social rejection.

The structural implications of individuals replacing a morality of obligation with a morality of choice in their sexual relationships has scarcely been explored in the social sciences. It is possible to theorize, however, about the changes that would transpire. First, and perhaps most obviously, decision-making within the relationship would be viewed as the prerogative of the partners themselves. Power would be exercised as if it resided in the relationship rather than in some authority external to it. Second, rules governing the relationship and establishing its boundaries would be created and modified through a process of negotiation in which each partner had a voice. Third, the structure of the relationship would reflect the attitudes and values of the individuals who comprised it regardless of how accurately or inaccurately these incorporated the prevailing morality.

There are important methodological advantages for historiography and the social sciences in shifting to a focus on sexual relationships. For one thing, the taxonomies and theories for describing and explaining relationships would be derived from the consequences of partners exercising particular choices as a reflection of personal attitudes and expectations. The proper subject matter of the social sciences, according to Hayek (1952/1979), is the mentality of the individuals whose relationships the investigator hopes to decipher. Furthermore, it would be possible to study a broad spectrum of relationships without prejudging them as natural, normal, or morally right. The structural similarities of particular sexual relationships, heterosexual and homosexual, for example, may go unrecognized because it is assumed that the sexual identity of partners requires dissimilar structures.

The uncharted territory in sexual relationships are those feelings, motivations, attitudes, intentions, and expectations held by the partners themselves. Approaching relationships as if they are governed by lawful forces, in the manner in which the physical universe is organized, the social scientist is blinded to the boundless ingenuity individuals can exercise in forming, maintaining, and even ending sexual relationships and to the fortuitous consequences that the reformulation of past relationships has for future ones. Projected against these possible discoveries, the concern with the sexual identity of partners appears to be a narrow preoccupation.

CONTRIBUTIONS OF THE ARTICLES
TO THE CRITIQUE OF SEXUAL IDENTITY

The articles in this volume provide theoretical critiques of the concepts of the bisexual and homosexual identities and, in several cases, also contribute to the understanding of sexual relationships within historical, bisexual, homosexual, or biological contexts.

Within the historical context, Richard Hoffman contrasts two systems of religious beliefs, the polytheistic and monotheistic cosmologies. Hoffman's article provides convincing evidence that the currently popular concepts of the heterosexual and homosexual identities have been far from universal. By showing how historical views of biological sex, social sex-roles, and sexual relationships have been linked to religious cosmologies, the unacknowledged moral judgements implicit in those concepts are clearly exposed.

Hoffman's argument is that religion, society, and sexuality interact very differently under the two systems. In the polytheistic cosmology, sexual categories in the realm of the supernatural reflect a conception of the universe as fluid and interconnected and full of unbounded and unregulated sexuality, one in which there is blurring of biological sex and social sex-roles. As for human sexual relationships, the polytheistic cosmic order did not preclude any particular form of sexual behavior nor did it rigidly separate the feminine from the masculine. Therefore, the segregation of individuals into rigid categories, such as heterosexuals and homosexuals, was unknown.

The monotheistic cosmology, according to Hoffman, stood in sharp contradistinction. Femaleness and maleness were rigidly delineated and played a major role in the conception of sexual relationships. This dichotomization of biological sex reflected a conception of the universe in which maleness and femaleness were reduced to the biological observations of genitalia and reproduction. All aspects of society, particularly sexual relationships, were regulated. Ambiguous categories were abominations. The only appropriate sexual relationship was one in which human males gave their seed to their wives.

Within the bisexual context, two articles provide trenchant criticism of the notions of the heterosexual and homosexual identities and, in the process, suggest new avenues for exploring sexual relationships. Jay Paul argues that a system of defining sexual identity as either heterosexual or homosexual, although alluringly simple for those who can apply it to themselves, is bewildering for those who feel sexual, emotional, and social attraction for both men and women. He asserts that it is necessary to recognize the bisexual option as a third identity. Any sexual identity ascribed to individuals, with its accompanying stereotypes, determines the role they play in society and can expose them to stigmatization.

Paul locates much of the basis for the dismissal, or suspicion of the bisexual in current notions of femaleness and maleness, social sex-roles, and sexuality, all of which are challenged by the idea of a bisexual identity. Perhaps most importantly, he suggests, the bisexual identity is perceived as a challenge to the institution of monogamy which, as commonly conceived, equates loyalty and fidelity with an exclusive attachment to one partner. Rather than question their emotional authenticity, Paul proposes that people view bisexuals as a spur to social change. Men and women who form relationships with both sexes may be paving the way to a broader perspective on sexual relationships than those who limit themselves to one sex. With the possibility of partners being of either sex, a new fluidity is added to a relationship, so that whether it starts at the point of affection or physical contact, as friend or lover, the alternative option remains open to further exploration.

Within the context of sexual relationships, Timothy Murphy's article shows how Freud's use of the concept of bisexuality was determined by moral judgements rather than dispassionate scientific inquiry. Freud's conception of bisexuality was that the individual was born with both heterosexual and homosexual capacity. However, his principal use of the idea of bisexuality, according to Murphy, was to explain the origin of homosexuality.

If bisexuality describes the native capacity to form sexual relationships with both females and males, it raises the theoretical question of how the individual enters into either heterosexual or homosexual relationships to the exclusion of the other. This question seems singularly appropriate if either form of exclusivity is viewed as a highly restricted use of sexual capacity.

Rather than pursue this challenging issue, Freud looked for the beginnings of homosexual desire in bisexuality, whereas he left the idea largely out of his account of heterosexual desire. To use bisexuality to account for homosexuality, Freud had to bend the idea. Originally it referred to a biological capacity. In his formulation of an etiology of homosexuality, Freud, however, added a host of psychological factors to the biological conception of bisexuality, centering around the dissolution of the Oedipus complex. In following this tack, Freud ended up by conceiving homosexual development as an early, usually irreversible disturbance of the psychosexual process. Murphy convincingly argues that Freud's unacknowledged endorsement of the professed sexual ethic in Western civilization led him to view, in our terms, homosexual relationships as flawed and heterosexual relationships as normal, despite his humanitarian disclaimers about "homosexuals" as potentially happy and creative individuals.

Three articles in this monograph constitute serious criticisms of the idea of sexual identity within the homosexual context. Within that context a fourth article adumbrates a developmental process for the acquisition of the gay identity. Taken as a whole, these four articles have at least broad implications for understanding sexual relationships.

The idea of a homosexual essence, according to Diane Richardson, is basic to all theories of homosexuality. It is the idea that homosexuality inheres in human biology, personality, and society. Richardson believes that the homosexual essence has had four different theoretical conceptions: a personal state of being, sexual desire, sexual behavior, and sexual identity. The idea of the homosexual essence, according to Richardson, originally came from medicine and psychiatry, which conceived of homosexuality as a personal state of being or a condition, what she calls the "homosexual person." Next, the homosexual essence was defined as sexual desire or "state of sexual being" by Freud and his followers. Then the Kinsey group defined this essence as "sexual behavior," fueled by an innate sex drive. Most recently it has been conceptualized as a "personal identity" by symbolic interactionists.

From our own perspective, we have viewed the idea of the bisexual, heterosexual, and homosexual essence as the individual's sexual identity. The idea of sexual identity, we believe, has been theoretically conceived in biological, psychological, and socio-cultural forms. All these forms, we have argued, are reducible to a biological essence because all define the individual's sexual identity in terms of the biological sex of partners in sexual relationships.

The dilemma of essentiality, which Richardson has cogently delineated, we believe cannot be resolved within any theory of homosexuality or, for that matter, of bisexuality or heterosexuality. The dilemma derives from a biological determinism implicit in all the theories, which keeps the focus of inquiry on the individual as a unit.

Henry Minton and Gary McDonald subscribe to the theory that the homosexual identity is "socially constructed," that is, derived from a pool of social categories that the individual selects and applies to the self. To this general notion they have added the psychological dimension of a developmental process wherein the individual, over the course of a lifetime, comes to recognize, incorporate, proclaim, and live harmoniously with the homosexual identity. The last stages in the developmental process involve the homosexual's grasp of the societal proscription of homosexuality and public disclosures of the homosexual identity. Disclosure is viewed by them as the vital requirement for integrating the homosexual identity into a broader personal identity and thereby achieving a whole sense of self. After acquiring the homosexual identity, what remains is learning how to "manage" it.

The psychological dimension of their essentially socio-cultural conception of the homosexual identity rests on the assumption that there is a homosexual ego. In the course of development, the ego moves from the egocentric stage of childhood and adolescence to the sociocentric stage of adulthood. In this process the individual replaces private perceptions and cognitions of the homosexual identity with social, cultural, and historical categories—those that are traditionally antipathetic as well as those supportive of a "gay identity."

Although Minton and McDonald never discuss the biological basis of their conceptualization of the homosexual identity, the biological essence is apparent. In describing the egocentric stage, for example, they refer to the individual becoming aware of a homosexual "bodily capacity," even before knowing about the "homosexual" label. In their developmental process biology provides the irreducible kernel of truth to which the individual must become reconciled—the core homosexual identity. Society and culture provide the experience and the reservoir of sexual meanings from which the individual comes to recognize a preordained homosexual identity as well as the barriers to be surmounted for full self-acceptance. With the acceptance of the gay identity, the structure of any sexual relationship is predetermined because the crucial beliefs and attitudes of the partners have been cognitively organized through a single process.

Vivienne Cass, in her contribution to this monograph, mounts a thorough-going critique of the idea of the homosexual identity as it is currently employed in psychological and sociological research. She attempts to restore a psychological dimension to what she believes have been the preponderantly socio-cultural conceptions of the homosexual identity. Identity, as defined by Cass, consists of two dimensions: a personal aspect, the representation of the self to the self; and a social aspect, the presentation of the self to others. Considerable disparity, she argues, can exist between the two aspects: Individuals can present an image of themselves (i.e., a social identity) that is at odds with the way they actually perceive themselves (i.e., their personal identity).

In the further elucidation of her theory, it appears as if Cass has grafted a psychological dimension to a basically socio-cultural conception of sexual identity. This becomes apparent when she considers what is essential to the homosexual identity. She argues that the homosexual identity is essentially psychological because it consists of a set of individual perceptions that are cognitively organized over time. Yet these cognitions appear to be unaltered imports by the individual of current notions of the gay identity. She asserts, for example, that the concept of the homosexual identity is an unavoidable part of reality, built into the cultural milieu of the present historical period as part of the "psychologies" of our time. It consists chiefly of "non-sexual" areas of awareness, such as the consciousness on the part of homosexuals that they constitute a minority and that their social circles are "gay."

In adding the psychological dimension to the socio-cultural form of sexual identity, Cass has attempted to steer clear of biology. She distinguishes, for example, between *homosexual* identity and *sexual* identity. Whereas homosexual identity refers to the individual's cognition of self as homosexual, sexual identity refers to patterns of sexual behavior. The true homosexual identity, she asserts, is more cognitive than behavioral. She argues that the sexual component of the homosexual identity becomes less central in its evolution over the course of an individual's lifetime.

Despite these disclaimers, there is the inevitable recrudescence of biology when she acknowledges, for example, that the conception of the self as a sensuous person can be a part of the individual's homosexual identity. Also, however defined, it remains a *homosexual* identity, unavoidably referring to partners of the same *(homo)* biological sex who are somehow *sexually* allied.

The report prepared by the editors of this monograph and their collaborator, Christopher Jones, provides empirical support for Cass' assertion that research on homosexual identity is plagued by serious definitional and terminological problems. This study was an analysis of the research on sexual orientation published mostly during the 1970s. Its major focus was to ascertain how sexual orientation was conceptually or operationally defined.

The definitional problems, it was discovered, were chronic. Rarely was sexual orientation conceptually defined and, even in those cases in which it was, the definitions were ambiguous, appearing outside of any explicit theoretical context. It was impossible to know how one conceptual definition stood in relation to another. Operational definitions were much more common, but they appeared in an astonishing variety of forms ranging from a credulous acceptance of the respondents' self-identification to asking them nothing about sexual orientation, relying instead on the identification of locales in which they were found.

The definitional problems, the authors conclude, stem from an underlying conceptual confusion. The idea of sexual orientation was popularized by the Homophile and Gay Liberation movements to identify homosexuals as a group victimized by institutional intolerance. During the 1970s the term was widely incorporated in the social science literature. It does not appear in the two Kinsey volumes, published in 1948 and 1953, which, instead, referred to heterosexual and homosexual "outlet."

Sexual orientation is a term with clear biological implications. It suggests the presence of a directional sex drive that "steers" or "orients" the individual either to sexual partners of exclusively one or the other sex or of both sexes. The conceptual confusion that pervades the studies surveyed, in large part, is attributable to the fact that a biological concept was pressed into the service of social science research.

Criticisms of studies that claim that sexual identity is biologically determined are provided in the final two articles. In the first, Thomas Ford

Hoult points to the basic assumption of biological research on human sexuality, that it is directly traceable to innate traits and processes. Hoult presents his broad critique within what he calls a "behavioral paradigm," that assumes a malleable sex drive that can be channeled by society, culture, and history in multitudinous directions. More particularly, he believes that individuals are not born with predetermined sexual orientations but acquire them through the process of conditioned learning. Most individuals learn what is socially deemed as "normal" behavior because the culture provides the most reinforcement for that behavior.

Because the studies he has examined are carried on within the tradition of biological and medical research, Hoult appropriately scrutinizes them for their methodological soundness and the relationship of methodology to conclusions. In his estimation almost none of the studies has observed the canons of scientific research. In the hormonal studies, he notes that the grandness of the claims stands in stark contrast to the meagerness of the data. In the twin studies the methodology has been inept and the conclusions are of questionable merit. Other researchers, in the course of long careers in research on human sexuality, have taken apparently contradictory positions, sometimes pressing for biological and at other times cultural explanations of the same behavior without any theoretical or empirical attempts to reconcile the disparity. Most strikingly, the latest claims that sexual identity is biologically determined have been boldly asserted by social scientists on the basis of psychological and sociological evidence.

Hoult, we believe, has convincingly demonstrated that the belief that sexual identity is biologically determined goes unsupported. In reaching this conclusion he is careful to include biology in his general portrayal of human sexuality. What biology provides, in his judgement, is sexual capacity or potential rather than the determinants of specific sexual identities, proclivities, or acts. While the evidence that individual sexual expression is controlled by biology is woefully lacking, he believes the evidence that it is a product of culture is abundant and persuasive.

The sociobiological belief that sexual identity, in particular homosexual behavior, is biologically determined is appropriately examined by two evolutionary biologists, Douglas Futuyma and Stephen Risch. According to these authors, the assertion that homosexual behavior is an evolved trait implies that there are genes that, under suitable environmental conditions, program individuals to develop that trait. Over the course of generations, these genes replace those that do not sponsor homosexuality.

In explaining homosexual behavior as an evolved trait, sociobiological theory faces the apparently insurmountable difficulty of showing how a gene for homosexual behavior would be passed on to succeeding generations if homosexuals do not reproduce (or do so at much lower rates) while heterosexuals do. To resolve this evolutionary dilemma, four hypotheses have been advanced by sociobiologists: heterozygous advantage, kin selection, parental manipulation, and homosexual behavior as an incidental by-product of an adaptive sex drive. After examining the plausibility of these hypotheses, as derivatives of evolutionary theory, and the evidence offered in their support, Futuyma and Risch conclude that the sociobiologists have entirely failed in the effort to explain homosexual behavior as an evolved trait.

Additionally, the authors raise an important moral issue. They question the extent to which appeals to biology by sociobiologists betray their misgivings about homosexual behavior as "healthy" or "normal." Such appeals, they believe, presume that what is natural is therefore good. But "nature," as victims of floods, famine, earthquakes, and fire know, is capable of a cavalier moral indifference. Moral standards and ethical progress, Futuyma and Risch remind us, cannot be based on biological theory.

What emerges from their astute criticism of sociobiological speculations about homosexual behavior is a view of human sexuality that contrasts sharply with the biological determinism that pervades the discourse on sexual identity. Because there is no evidence that, in our terms, the heterosexual and homosexual identities are genetically distinct, flexibility in human sexual behavior remains the likely biological endowment. Futuyma and Risch, like Hoult, propose that this flexible potential is shaped by social learning rather than prenatal determinants.

CONCLUSION

The biologist, Stephen Jay Gould (1983), has postulated two positions on the question of the relationship of human biology to human society: *biological determinism* and *biological potentiality*. In metaphorical terms, Gould suggests that whether one is a determinist or potentialist depends on one's estimate of the length and tautness of the leash with which genes hold on to culture. The determinist believes that the leash is short and tightly held. The potentialist believes it is loose and nonconstraining.

Although expressed in quantitative terms, Gould believes the two views result in *qualitatively* different conceptions of society. The determinist, in dealing with human culture, tends to be reductionist, squeezing its complexity to make it fit the confines of a few biological universals (e.g., the universality of certain facial expressions, the preference of newborns for sugar over water). Although future investigation will probably extend the list of universals, Gould believes they will never account for cultural diversity. The biological universals, he asserts, exert "little constraint upon the incredible richness of detail that so fascinates us and *is* the subject matter of the social sciences" (p. 6).

In redirecting the discourse on sexual identity, within its historical, bisexual, homosexual, and biological contexts, so that the focus of inquiry is on sexual relationships, we believe that the potentialist view of human sexuality would replace the determinist position that has dominated the discourse for well over a century. Within the context of sexual relationships, even human biological sexual potential itself would no longer have to be viewed as a set of constraints, as if it operated under its own physical laws, independently of the will of partners.

Our historical beliefs about sexual behavior and relationships have often been clothed in biological metaphor to lend them scientific authority. Now that we can distinguish more clearly between biology and human invention, speculation on the constraints imposed on sexual relationships by the sexual identity of partners can be replaced in the social sciences and historiography with attention to the rich diversity we believe can be discovered in those relationships.

REFERENCES

Bailey, D. S. *Homosexuality and the western Christian tradition.* London: Longmans, Green, 1955. [Reprinted by Archon Books, 1975.]

Bieber, I., Dain, H. J., Dince, P. R., Drellich, M. G., Grand, H. G., Gundlach, R. H., Kremer, M. W., Rifkin, A. H., Wilbur, C. B., & Bieber, T. B. *Homosexuality: A psychoanalytic study of male homosexuals.* New York: Basic Books, 1962.

Birke, L. I. A. Is homosexuality hormonally determined? *Journal of Homosexuality,* 1981, *6,* 35-49.

Bloch, I. *Sexual life of our time in its relations to modern civilization.* (6th edition). New York: Allied Books, 1910.

Boswell, J. *Christianity, social tolerance, and homosexuality: Gay people from the beginning of the Christian era to the fourteenth century.* Chicago: University of Chicago Press, 1980.

Boswell, J. *Rediscovering gay history: Archetypes of gay love in Christian history.* The fifth Michael Harding memorial address. London: Gay Christian Movement, 1982 (in xerox).

Boswell, J. Revolutions, universals, and sexual categories. *Salmagundi,* 1982/1983, No. *58-59,* 89-113.

Bray, A. *Homosexuality in Renaissance England.* London: Gay Men's Press, 1982.

Bullough, V. *Sexual variance in society and history.* New York: John Wiley, 1976.

Casper, J. L. *A handbook of the practice of forensic medicine based upon personal experience.* London: New Sydenham Society, 1864, *3,* 328-346. [Originally published in German in 1857-58.]

Dörner, G. *Hormones and brain differentiation.* Amsterdam: Elsevier, 1976.

Dover, K. J. *Greek homosexuality.* Cambridge, MA: Harvard University Press, 1978. [Reprinted by Vintage Books, 1980.]

Ehrhardt, A. A., and Meyer-Bahlburg, H. F. L. Effects of prenatal sex hormones on gender-related behavior. *Science,* 1981, *211,* 1312-1318.

Ellis, H. *Sexual inversion. Studies in the psychology of sex.* New York: Random House, 1936. [Originally published in England in 1897.]

Erikson, E. H. Identity and the life-cycle. *Psychological Issues,* 1959, *1,* 1-17.

Foucault, M. *La volonté de savoir.* Paris: Editions Gallimard, 1976. [Published in English as *The history of sexuality: An introduction.* New York: Vintage Books, 1978.]

Freud, S. *The ego and the id. The standard edition of the complete psychological works of Sigmund Freud,* *19,* 3-66. London: The Hogarth Press and the Institute of Psychoanalysis, 1961. [Originally published, 1923.]

Gay, P. *The party of humanity: Essays on the Enlightenment.* New York: Alfred A. Knopf, 1954.

Gould, S. J. Genes on the brain. *The New York Review of Books,* 1983, *30*(11), 5-10.

Harry, J., & Lovely, R. Gay marriages and communities of sexual orientation. *Alternative Life-styles*, 1979, *2*, 177-200.

Hayek, F. A. *The counter-revolution of science: Studies on the abuse of reason.* Indianapolis, IN: Liberty Press, 1979. *[Originally published, 1952.]*

Hirschfeld, M. *Sexual pathology: A study of derangements of the sexual instinct.* New York: Emerson Books, 1947. [Originally published in three volumes, in German, n.d.]

Klein, F. *The bisexual option.* New York: Berkley Books, 1978.

Krafft-Ebing, R. von. *Psychopathia sexualis.* Rebman, F. J. (Transl.) New York: Physicians & Surgeons Book Co., 1935. (12th German edition, 1906.)

MacDonald, A. P. Bisexuality: Some comments on research and theory. *Journal of Homosexuality*, 1981, *6*, 21-35.

Mead, G. H. *Mind, self, and society.* Chicago: University of Chicago Press, 1934.

Moll, A. *Libido sexualis: Studies in the psycho-sexual laws of love verified by clinical case histories.* New York: American Ethnological Press, 1953. [Originally published in 3 volumes in German, 1897.]

Money, J., and Tucker, P. *Sexual signatures: On being a man or a woman.* Boston: Little, Brown, 1975.

Rubenstein, M. *An in-depth study of bisexuality and its relationship to self-esteem.* Unpublished doctoral dissertation, Institute for the Advanced Study of Human Sexuality, San Francisco, CA, 1982.

Sullivan, H. S. *Personal psychopathology.* Washington, D.C.: William Alanson White Psychiatric Foundation, 1965 (unpubl.).

Sulloway, F. J. *Freud, biologist of the mind: Beyond the psychoanalytic legend.* New York: Basic Books, 1979.

Tarnowsky, B. *The sexual instinct and its morbid manifestations.* Paris: Charles Carrington, 1898. [Originally published in Russian, 1886.]

Trumbach, R. London's sodomites: Homosexual behavior and western culture in the 18th century. *Journal of Social History*, 1977/1978, *2*, 1-33.

Ulrichs, C. H. Memnon. *Die geschlechtsnatur des mannliebenden urnings.* Leipzig: Max Spohr, 1868.

Ungaretti, J. R. De-moralizing morality: Where Dover's *Greek Homosexuality* leaves us. *Journal of Homosexuality*, 1982, *8*, 1-18.

Weeks, J. *Coming out: Homosexual politics in Britain, from the nineteenth century to the present.* London: Quartet Books, 1977.

Westermarck, E. *The origin and development of the moral ideas.* London: MacMillan, 1926.

Wilson, E. O. *On human nature.* Cambridge, MA: Harvard University Press, 1978.

Vices, Gods, and Virtues:
Cosmology as a Mediating Factor
in Attitudes toward Male Homosexuality

Richard J. Hoffman, PhD
San Francisco State University

ABSTRACT. Using historical and anthropological evidence, the article examines the relationship of the polytheistic and monotheistic cosmologies and attitudes toward sexuality, in particular, male homosexuality. The polytheistic cosmology included the ideas of the continuity of creation, the generative forces of the universe as a whole, and gender blurring in the realm of the supernatural. In the monotheistic cosmology the godhead (Yahweh) is unborn and does not father any generations, the universe is desexualized, and the conception of gender is rigidified. The author concludes that polytheism created the conditions for a wide variety of sexual expression and sex-role behavior and did not preclude any particular form of sexual activity. In contradistinction, the monotheistic cosmology was highly restrictive of permissible male and female behavior and sexual expression and conduct. Consequently, polytheism was able to embrace the crossing of gender lines and homosexual relationships while monotheism was incapable of making these accommodations.

In a brief ethnographic digression on the Jews, Tacitus once observed that "things sacred with us, with them have no sanctity, while they allow what with us is forbidden" (*Hist.*, 5.4). Good and evil, vice and virtue: From the very beginning of human organization, societies have prescribed standards of behavior to be followed by various segments of the community. As Tacitus noted almost two thousand years ago, however, a vice in one society may be a virtue in another. Nowhere is this more prominent than in the area of sexual *mores*. From among the varieties of human sexual experiences reported in the cross-cultural literature, it is

The author is a fellow in classics at the American Academy in Rome. He was the recipient of a fellowship from the American Council of Learned Societies to study Roman law at Boalt Hall, University of California at Berkeley, where he also received his doctorate in Roman history. He is presently Professor of History at San Francisco State University, where he occasionally teaches in the human sexuality program. He has contributed articles to the *Journal* on Greek and Roman concepts of homosexuality and is currently interested in researching male friendship groups. Reprint requests should be addressed to the author, Department of History, San Francisco State University, San Francisco, CA 94132.

27

clear that few are more controversial than male homosexuality. A sharp contrast can be seen in societal attitudes in this area. Ford and Beach (1951/1970, pp. 132-151) note, for example, that 64% of the 76 societies in their study approved of some form of male homosexual behavior. On the other hand, there are societies in which all forms of male homosexual behavior are considered opporbrious; penalties range from fines, through exile or ostracism, to death.

Gender roles, sexual behavior, and sexual attitudes are the products of many forces—economics, society, geography, age, time, and habit. Religion is another cultural force affecting sexual expression in any society. In its broadest sense, religion is the collection of ideas and acts concerning the powers that permeate the universe.[1] Thus, it is inevitable that on certain occasions religion, society, and sexuality coalesce. Furthermore, it might be expected that the macrocosm of the universe will be reflected to one degree or another in the microcosm of society.

The present examination of the relationship between belief systems and attitudes toward male homosexuality has been prompted by two recent historical works. The first is John Boswell's *Christianity, Social Tolerance, and Homosexuality* (1980). While searching for the roots of rise of intolerance toward homosexuality in the mid-twelfth century, Boswell comes to the frustrating conclusion that the change in attitudes cannot be adequately explained (1980, 334)—at least not by the factors he chose to examine. In contrasting Roman and Judeo-Christian attitudes, Boswell ignores the possibility that differences in belief systems might be relevant factors in the study of changing attitudes towards homosexuality in Europe. Indeed, consciously or unconsciously, the author, *qua* church apologist, rejects at the very beginning the idea that the source of intolerance may well lie within the very nature of Christianity itself.

In contradistinction to Boswell's work is Judith Ochshorn's *The Female Experience and the Nature of the Divine* (1981). Ochshorn documents and explains how the shift from polytheism to monotheism in the ancient Near East resulted in a dramatic change in concepts of gender and of femaleness. She carefully shows how the changes in the sexual conceptions of the universe resulted in changes in the ways in which human sexuality itself was viewed. While her purpose was not to examine all aspects of sexuality, the question naturally arises as to the possible effects that such a shift in cosmology might have had on attitudes toward male homosexuality as well.

This article will examine the linkage between cosmology and sexuality. The fundamental question addressed in this paper is: Do religion, society, and sexuality interact differently in polytheistic societies than in monotheistic ones, especially with regard to male homosexual behavior? I hope to demonstrate that the historical and cross-cultural evidence on human sexuality suggests that a basic connection does exist between cosmology and the societal acceptance of male homosexual behavior: Polytheism and the polytheistic universe create conditions whereby male homosexual behavior can be a part of the cultural norm of a society; in contrast, monotheism and the monotheistic universe are, *ab initio,* irreconcilably hostile towards male homosexuality in all of its forms.

THE POLYTHEISTIC COSMOLOGY

Ironically, the fundamental difference between polytheism and monotheism does not lie in the number of divinities within each system. If all of the gods in polytheism were reduced to one god, the result would be henotheism, not monotheism. The difference between the two systems lies far deeper, within the very concept of the nature of the universe itself. Gender and sexuality are an integral part of one belief system, but they play a very minor role in the other. Beginning with polytheism, it is necessary first to discuss the nature of the universe in general, and then to examine the implications of this type of universe for society and sexuality in particular.[2]

Among the various ways in which the polytheistic universe differs from the monotheistic universe, three features stand out: the continuity of creation, the generative forces of the universe as a whole, and gender blurring in the realm of the supernatural.

One of the principal ideas common to all polytheistic systems is the concept of the continuity of creation. This concept describes the very structure of the universe, a structure that is fluid and interconnected. Anterior to the existence of the gods, a realm of being exists that scholars like to call the primordial or metadivine realm. This realm is full of power, especially generative power. The primordial realm is also autonomous, subject only to its own laws. Among these are Fate or Destiny. In mythology the metadivine realm is often thought of as a watery, swampy, muddy place. It is from the "stuff" of this primordial realm that the first gods and goddesses emerge and bring into being the divine or supernatural realm of existence. These deities, composed as they are of the matter of a superior realm, are subject to that realm's laws and decrees. In addition to the supernatural realm there is the realm of mankind. The first human beings either emerge directly from the bodies of divinities or are fashioned by gods out of the bodies of divinities. As a result, human beings, like the gods, contain matter from the primordial realm and, like the gods, are subject to its laws. Ultimately, the very life force of a god, of a man, of a spear—indeed, of everything—has its origin in the primordial realm.

A second, and related, feature of this cosmic order is that the universe is full of unbounded sexuality: Sex and sexuality are powerful forces, motivating and permeating the entire universe. Deities produce the divine and nondivine alike from their bodies, either conventionally through copulation or unconventionally from their bodily substances, including tears, blood, spilled semen, and urine. In the divine realm all forms of sexuality occur. Bestiality, adultery, masturbation, homosexuality, and incest are practiced along side the ordinary form of marital coitus. An example of this diversity of sexual expressions can be seen in a god like Samba, the divine son of Krishna. Samda not only engages in homosexual acts, but he also dresses up as a woman in order to seduce the wives of other gods. Another god, Agni, took Shiva's semen into his mouth and deposited it in the mouths or vaginas of other divinities, an act that produced more deities (O'Flaherty, 1973). Numerous examples can be found in all mythologies. These unions produce other gods, from the Sun to the Ocean; monsters, like the Titans or Gorgons; or heroes, like Gilgamesh and Achilleus. In sum, the polytheistic universe is seen as a sexually potent place—everything that came into being within the cosmos did so through a sexual process.

While all polytheistic myths provide examples of the continuity of creation and of the sexual nature of the universe, a simple and graphic example of how these two factors work together comes from ancient Egypt. (See Budge, 1967, 1969 for details.) Here the primordial realm was conceived of as a watery swamp, akin to the Nile during the fertile flood stage. At one point a mound of clay emerges from the swamp, and from that mound emerged Ra. Ra masturbated, swallowed his semen, and then, self-fertilized, produced life: He spit to produce the god Shu; he urinated to produce the goddess Tefnut; he cried to produce human beings. The other stories of the gods and their intrigues take off at this point; the gods eventually populate the entire universe. In addition to creation, Ra was also essential in completing the continuum of being: In the cult of the dead the spirit of the deceased sought out Ra in order to secure a place in the divine realm. The Egyptian myth reveals the interconnectedness of the universe, one that reaches back to the primordial realm. The myth also reveals the sexual nature of the universe with reference to cosmogony (i.e., the theory of creation) and to the everyday functioning of the cosmic order.

Gender as another aspect of sexuality is connected with the polytheistic universe: In the realm of the supernatural, gender is often blurred. Male deities, for example, can have female parts (especially breasts) or a female aspect integrated with the male part of their being. The Egyptian Hapi, the Hindu Shiva, and the Mesopotamian Anu are often pictured with female breasts. Ovid tells how Salmacis, the son of Hermes and Aphrodite, became united with a water nymph, so "these two joined in close embrace, no longer two beings, no longer man and woman, but neither, and yet both" (Metamorphosis, 4.287ff). Even Zeus is described as possessing a male womb—the god Dionysos was born a second time from that womb (Eurip., *Bacchae*). Similarly the Assyrian god Sin is described in a hymn as having a womb (Ochshorn, 1981, pp. 32–33).

Another form of gender blurring can be seen in the area of procreation itself: Giving birth is not necessarily a uniquely female function. Among the Greeks, for example, Aphrodite was born of a union between the male Salt Sea and the genitals of Ouranos; Athena and Dionysos were born of Zeus. Ra reproduced through masturbation and self-fertilization, Shiva by spilling his semen. In an African cosmogony, the male deity Bumba underwent labor pains, and by vomiting produced not only the Sun, but also all living creatures, including human beings (Eliade, 1967, p. 91). Among the Sambia of the Eastern Highlands of Papua New Guinea, the males have a myth that "men begat humanity through homosexual fellatio" (Herdt, 1981, p. 255). The Mesopotamian moon god, Nanna, also gave birth (Ochshorn, 1981, p. 32). Lastly, men giving birth can also be found in Hindu mythology separate from Siva (Satapatha-Brahmana, 11.1, 6, 1–11).

Finally, a lack of rigid gender identification can be seen in still another way. In some cosmologies all male deities have a female aspect as a part of their being (as in Hinduism). In other cosmologies every divinity has a corresponding divinity of the opposite gender. In Greece, the deities of war are the male Ares and the female Athena. In Egypt, Seb and Nut are counterparts of one another, and even Ra has his counterpart in Rat, the female sun. The Pharaoh Hatshepsut had no difficulty in calling herself "the female Horus." Indeed, this condition of two deities for the same phenomenon is common throughout the ancient Near East (Ochshorn, 1981, pp. 30 and 57ff.). Depending on the society, few things in the universe typically belong to one gender: neither wisdom nor war, not even the moon or the earth. Thus, just as there is a blurring among the realms, so there is blurring between the genders, a blurring which was considered a part of the natural order of the cosmos.

While the world of the gods abounds in what appears to be unregulated sexuality, the world of mankind is quite a different place. Limitations on sexual access and definition of gender roles are a part of every society. Nonetheless, under polytheism the cosmic order reflects three conditions that have an impact on society. First, the cosmic order itself does not preclude *any* one form of sexual behavior from being socially acceptable. Second, sex is a powerful and potentially dangerous force pervading the entire universe. And third, the cosmic order does not rigidly segregate what is masculine from what is feminine, even when it comes to giving birth. This cosmic order, in the form of polytheistic religion, is integrated with human sexuality and society in three ways: (1) in a positive fashion through ritual; (2) in a negative fashion through sexual pollution; and (3) in a neutral fashion, e.g., a wide range of sexual attitudes and behavior can exist independent of religion altogether. For most, if not all, polytheistic societies, all three of these conditions exist simultaneously, helping to define and regulate different aspects of sexuality within the community.

Ritual and ritual practices present one of the most common circumstances where sexuality and religion come together. Not only do priesthoods usually require their membership to be of a specific gender, but the sex life of these individuals is also the subject of regulation: the priestess of the Pythian Apollo had to maintain her virginity (usually fictive), and the Flamen Dialis could not divorce or, as a widower, remarry. Sexual acts can also be a part of the rite itself. Among the Keraki young initiates are sodomized by older males (Ford & Beach, 1951, p. 139; Herdt, 1981, p. 319). Sambia males undergo an extensive initiation rite which lasts from age 7 to age 30. For approximately thirteen of these years homosexual fellatio plays a major role in the "masculinization" of the young males (Herdt, 1981, pp. 54, 203-254). Male and female temple prostitutes were common among certain cults in Mesopotamia and Canaan (see Ochshorn, 1981, pp. 127-129). Erotic dancing is a key part of certain religious ceremonies in Polynesia (Ortner, 1981, pp. 383-384). Lewdness and obscene behavior—so-called "ritual license"—is often an important element in the religious life of a polytheistic community (Norbeck, 1967, pp. 215-218). In sum, sex and sexuality often play an important role in polytheistic religious activities. Furthermore, homosexual acts and expressions may be a part of these ritual encounters.

More important, however, is the role of the ambiguous—especially the sexually ambiguous—in ritual. In his study on Genesis, Edmund Leach (1969) notes how the ambiguous, or the anomalous, is often the focus of taboo and ritual observance (p. 11). People who mediate between different levels—between mankind and the gods in the case of priests, or between youth and adulthood in the case of initiates—are often made sexually ambiguous and, therefore, sacred. Indeed, part of their sacred quality results from this sexual ambiguity.

Sexual ambiguity can take several forms. One form is where the individual acquires a multiplicity of opposing sexual characteristics. For example, the Vestal Virgins in Rome were considered both matrons and virgins, both men and women (Beard, 1980). Opposing gender characteristics are the hallmarks of the female ritual leaders among the Bimin-Kuskusmin (Poole, 1981). A more common form of sexual ambiguity is ritual role reversal. Among the Gogo, for example, men and women exchange roles for purification rites (Rigby, 1968, p. 153). In the initiation rites of the Gururumba, the boys, while in a liminal state between boyhood and manhood, become women, even to the point of imitating menarche (Friedl, 1975, pp. 112-113). The list of examples is enormous (cf. Norbeck, 1967, pp. 200-205). Role reversal is not uncommon for priests as well. The shamans of the Siberian Chukchee acquire female characteristics, often marry other men, and have sexual intercourse with them (Ford & Beach, 1951, p. 138; cf. Krader, 1967, pp. 112-120). Similarly, the *berdache* of the Northern Plains Indians had an important sacred function within the tribe: "As half-man/half-woman he had powers to mediate or cross sexual boundaries and roles and, since he was a creation of a vision like other shamans, he mediated as well between the divine and human worlds" (Thayer, 1980, p. 292; cf. Whitehead, 1981, pp. 89, 107). In the Roman world certain semitic cults also involved ritual role reversal and homosexuality. Perhaps the most famous ancient priest in this context was Heliogabalus *(SHA, Hel.* 1-10).

To sum up, the blurring of genders is a sacral quality within polytheism, and it is this blurring of genders that helps to define sacred personages (Rigby, 1968, p. 173; Thayer, 1980, pp. 291-292). Two points should be made here. One is that the segregation of human beings into unbreachable, rigid categories is unknown: Conditions arise in the context of religion whereby genders become ambiguous and mixed. Second, while ritual, gender ambiguity, and role reversal do not necessarily involve homosexual behavior, they can, and often do, form a context within which acceptable forms of homosexual behavior can occur. The best examples here are the Keraki and Sambia initiation rites, the Chukchee shamans, and the Northern Plains *berdache.* Thus, the cosmic and sexual orders come together in a situation which, from a social point of view, is both positive and necessary.

The social reverse is also true: Sexual behavior and the cosmic order can intersect for evil. Hence the taboos involving pollution and the necessity for purification. Polluting sexual activities result from intercourse that takes place in a taboo spot (on an oxcart, in a garden), or during a taboo time period (during post partum or post-menstrual periods or an unpropitious time of year), or with a taboo person (incest, adultery). In each case the act is believed to be harmful to individuals or to the community as a whole (as in the case of Oedipus' incest). What tends to be a common link among all polluting sexual activity is that it is almost always heterosexual in nature. Avoidance of heterosexual contact has been variously explained by anthropologists as a means of birth control (if the taboo concerns your own wife) or as a means of reinforcing the social order (if the taboo concerns your neighbor's wife). In either case sex and sexuality are linked to cosmic forces—they are seen as powerful and dangerous and, therefore, to be avoided.

By and large, however, within these same societies homosexual acts are not considered polluting. Among the Etoro, for example, heterosexual intercourse with spouses is strictly limited to 135 days out of the year. While heterosexual contact is limited, homosexual fellation is not only common but mandatory: Fellatio is the means by which younger men get the force of life (semen) needed to function into old age (Brown & Buchbinder, 1976). A variation on this can be seen in Herdt's Sambia (1981, p. 238) where males are precluded from having sexual relations with males from families with which they are also forbidden to have heterosexual relations. Furthermore, sexual activity of all sorts is considered dangerous for men, both because of ritual taboos and because the loss of semen is linked to a loss of strength. Despite the various fears and taboos, including a homosexual incest taboo, male Sambians deem homosexual fellatio less dangerous than heterosexual coitus (Herdt, 1981, pp. 248-251).

Thus, in polytheistic societies a continuum of rules exists concerning sexual pollution. At one end are the Walbiri, who have no sexual pollution rules. Here, sexual conduct is strictly a social concern and prohibitions, such as adultery, are enforced by social sanctions alone (Douglas, 1966, pp. 141-142). Somewhat in the middle of the continuum are the Manus and Tikopia of Oceania (Firth, 1957; Fortune, 1934). At the other end are the Hindus.

The Hindus are the most difficult group to discuss because of the wide range of their beliefs, practices, and sects: Some believe in male chastity while others do not; some believe in female chastity, although others do not; some worship the male sex organ, others, the female.[3] Nevertheless, several things do emerge from a look at the Hindus. First their cosmology is par excellence a study of the potency of sex in the universe (O'Flaherty, 1973; Kaufmann, 1960, pp. 39-40). Second, every bodily orifice, every bodily fluid (especially semen) is sacred, sexual, and potent. The result is that bodily orifices and fluids are dangerous. The dilemma for the various Hindu sects is whether or not these powerful things should be preserved or spent. Third, despite the dilemma, all forms of sexual behavior are indulged in, and often raised to a high art. Among some Hindu groups, for example, fellatio includes twelve steps before orgasm.

A great divergence exists as a result of these beliefs. For some Hindu groups, the bodily fluids are not to be spent and the bodily orifices are not to be entered. Among these groups all forms of sexual activity are polluting to one degree or another. For example, for one group of Brahmin to engage in homosexual intercourse is equivalent to having heterosexual intercourse in the daytime or in water. The purification for such acts is to bathe with one's clothes on. In another group, anal intercourse could entail expulsion from one's caste, as could other forms of sexual activity. Thus, for these groups the eschewing of sexual activity was common to both heterosexual and homosexual acts. Other Hindu groups, however, with the same concepts of the potency of sex and sexuality, believe in action rather than in preservation. They feel that the sexual union is the reflection of the divine creation, and a high goal to be sought after, hence the Kama Sutra and Tantric groups. For all Hindus, however, sex is a part of the cosmic order, and it is a divine state: One can participate in that divine state either by abstinence (wherein every orgasm entails the release of dangerous and potent forces that require neutralization) or by indulgence (entailing a minimum of pollution rules).

Finally, in all polytheistic societies there is a wide range of sexual behavior than can be unconcerned with religion and the cosmic order. Here sex and sexuality are questions of societal and familial attitudes and enforcements (see Douglas, 1966; Selby, 1974). Moreover, concepts of masculinity and femininity, and their application in the everyday world, can also lie well outside the scope of religion. These conditions can be clearly seen in the ancient world. In Athens, for example, the choice of sexual partners for males was not related to concepts of manliness, though the choice of sexual position was. Nevertheless, neither the choice of sexual partner nor of position was related to religion in any way. Sexual boundaries and standards were the product of social custom rather than religious sanctions (Dover, 1978, p. 203; Hoffman, 1980, pp. 223–224).

This condition existed for heterosexual relations as well. Adultery in Athens and Rome did not unleash sacred forces, but it could (and did) unleash angry husbands and fathers. If anything, the cosmic order provided examples of, if not encouragement for, a broader range of sexual experience than might otherwise have been possible. This point was not lost on a poet like Ovid who, in fact, went beyond the bounds of Augustan propriety: for *carmen et error* he was sent into exile by the stern emperor. Even here, however, it was not a question of religion and cosmology, but of politics. Indeed, the actions of Augustus concerning sexual propriety were in themselves highly unusual for the ancient world, where legislation regulating sexual behavior was almost nonexistent. Unless public order or national dignity and decorum were involved, sexual behavior was the strict province of the family.

Similar patterns are also found throughout the contemporary world. Modern ethnographers describe societies where acceptable forms of male homosexual behavior occur in a strictly secular context. The male-male attachments formed by the Azande are a prime example (Evans-Pritchard, 1970). Other examples can be found in the *berdache* of some of the North American Indian tribes (Boswell, 1980, p. 34, n. 63; Devereux, 1937; Ford & Beach, 1951, pp. 137–138; Whitehead, 1981). There is, in fact, no lack of ethnographic examples of the development and existence of heterosexual and homosexual attitudes and behavior in an atmosphere unconnected with religion.

To conclude, the sexual force of the cosmos is reflected in polytheistic societies positively through ritual and negatively through pollution. The blurring of genders can be seen in everything from male pregnancies in New Guinea (Meigs, 1976) to cross-dressing in Siberia and Mongolia.

Furthermore, in the context of a sexually charged universe, no single sexual act is intrinsically inappropriate, excluded, or unknown, a condition related in the wide variety of sexual customs across the globe. Sexual customs are also formed through the interplay of many societal and environmental forces. Polytheism provides an atmosphere whereby male homosexual behavior in one form or another can exist without social opprobrium. Polytheism provides not only a positive context within religious practices but also a neutral one so that religion is irrelevant to certain aspects of sexual expression.

THE MONOTHEISTIC COSMOLOGY

Monotheism as developed by the Israelites was rather restricted in its sexual possibilities and was, from the very beginning, hostile to all forms of male homosexual behavior. The reasons for this hostility can be found in three areas: (1) the very nature of the monotheistic universe; (2) the intentional creation of a cult to Yahweh that was vigorously antipolytheistic in character; and (3) the historical realities of the movement of the Israelites into the land of Canaan.

Monotheism presents a universe that is the exact opposite of the polytheistic universe at every step. First, unlike polytheism, in monotheism there is no theogony, and as such, there is no cosmogony in the strictest sense of the word. Yahweh always was: He did not emerge out of a prior state of being. As a result, he is not limited by a higher, transcendent realm, nor does he share his power with other supernatural beings. It is Yahweh's will that is transcendent and totally unfettered. Furthermore, when it comes to the origin of the universe and its parts, Yahweh creates by his word rather than through any sort of sexual intercourse. Thus, not only is Yahweh unborn, but he also does not give birth or father any generations. The universe in monotheism is demythologized in the classical sense of what a myth is: the story of the births and lives of the gods. There are no such stories about Yahweh.

The demythologizing of the cosmos changes the conception of the universe and of gender. First, a gulf is formed between Yahweh and the universe. Rather than a continuity and a blurring of realms of being, a strict separation and distinction exists between the creator and created. Second, the universe becomes undeified and desexed. Yahweh may occasionally have human characteristics, but he never acts in a sexual way. Similarly, inanimate nature is nonsexual: The Salt Sea does not copulate with other aspects of nature to produce more creatures (See Kaufmann, 1960; Ochshorn, 1981.) Third, gender is reduced to the biological observations of genitalia and reproduction. In nature men and women exist as distinct and obvious forms, and there is no blurring. So too male and female roles in reproduction are perfectly clear, and are as distinct from each other as Yahweh is from his creation. In sum, neither Yahweh nor his cosmos is full of unbridled sexual forces. What sexuality that does exist, viz., among animals, is unambiguous in its dichotomy of male and female. A blurring of genders is unknown in the natural world of Yahweh.

The cult of Yahweh, from the beginning, reinforced in the most rigorous fashion the world-view of monotheistic separateness and distinction in all spheres: The close relationship between Yahweh and the children of Israel is a reaffirmation of the cosmic order. There are three spheres of belief and practice that emphasized the separateness of Israel.

First, the Israelites are made by Yahweh into a nation of priests (Ex., 19.6; cf. Lev., 11.44). This priestly quality of Israel has two ramifications. On the one hand it means that Israelites are separated from the human race. They are to be holy as a reflection of the holiness of their god. A gulf is thus created between the Israelites and the gentiles similar to the gulf between Yahweh and his creation—it is a gulf of sanctity and holiness. On the other hand, it also means that as a nation of priests, everyone in society becomes subject to all of the taboos, not just a small priestly caste. In Rome, for example, the Flamen Dialis was subject to a number of prescriptions and proscriptions, ranging from dress and food to marriage and bedroom furniture. Other Romans, however, were not subject to the same taboos. In Israel, however, every member of the community must live as if he or she were a priest, and, therefore, everyone is subject to a list of taboos, which elsewhere are usually meant for a few.

Second, and related to the first, since Israel becomes a priestly nation, the sacred totally subsumes the secular in a way not even present in Hinduism. In Hindu society, the lower one's caste, the fewer the taboos. Furthermore, in many polytheistic societies, taboos vary according to gender or age. This was not so for Israel, where all aspects of life had to be protected from the unholy for everyone: The nation as a whole had to be kept pure in every way in the sight of Yahweh. Thus, everything becomes a matter of sacred regulation: how to dress, how to do your hair, how to dispose of your excrement, how to eat, how to marry.

Third, and most interesting, concerns how the unholy, the forbidden is determined. At this point the observation of Tacitus should be recalled. That which was sacred in polytheism, the ambiguous and the anomalous, is never sacred for the Israelites. Everything that suggests ambiguity and the breaking down of distinctions is forbidden. Thus fields cannot be sown with two types of seed, yokes cannot be harnessed to two kinds of animals, the hybridization of stock cannot be done, and clothes are not to be made with cloth composed of two kinds of thread. The most famous prohibitions concern diet. Here, all animals anomalous for their class, or which seem to fall between two classes, are abominations and forbidden to be eaten. A clean animal had to possess all of the characteristics of its class. Thus, the pastoral model of the cloven-hoofed, cud-chewing ungulate was a standard for judging other animals. The rock badger was thought to chew its cud and, since it was not cloven-hoofed, it was forbidden. The infamous pig has cloven hoofs, but does not chew its cud—hence it was forbidden. Locomotive criteria are also included. For example, four-footed creatures that fly are unclean (Lev., 11.20–26), because such animals are supposed to walk on the earth. Fish have scales and swim; creatures without scales that live in water are unclean. All anomalies and ambiguities are abominations (see Douglas, 1966; 1975, pp. 276–316).

Just as with food and clothes, so too with sex: Ambiguous categories are abominations. Transvestitism is forbidden for both males and females (Deut., 22.5), as is bestiality. One is to act like one's kind, appropriate to one's class. Humans must dress according to their gender precisely because that *is* their gender. Unlike in polytheism, no occasion can exist for cross-dressing in the cult of Yahweh. So too, humans cannot have intercourse with animals, for nothing will come of it; humans are humans, and beasts are beasts, despite pagan myths to the contrary. Intercourse is to take place between animals of the same species for the purpose of reproduction. By extension, therefore, the giving of seed to one's own sex is also prohibited.

The proscription of male homosexual behavior goes beyond mere reproduction, however. The formulation of the prohibition is revealing: "Do not lie with a male as one lies with a woman" (Lev., 18.22). Since all of the sexual proscriptions in Leviticus 18 are addressed to men, unless otherwise noted, the passage need not have been phrased in that manner. The author might have said, "Do not have carnal relations with any man," as he said concerning beasts, or, "Do not uncover the nakedness of another man," as he does earlier in the chapter. Instead, the prohibition gives both the format for proper intercourse (i.e., men are to lie with women), and the rationale behind it: Women lie with men, and, therefore, for men also to lie with men confused gender distinctions. Any blurring of gender distinctions is abominable and, hence, taboo.

In the final analysis the only appropriate sexual form for human males is to give seed to their wives. All other forms are strictly prohibited. Incest, homosexuality, adultery, and fornication with a woman who cannot become the fornicator's wife are all punishable by death. As Douglas says in summarizing her analysis on diet in Leviticus, "all anomalies are bad and classed in a special sub-set expected to unleash disastrous chains of cause and effect" (1975, p. 306). One sub-set not mentioned by Douglas consists of men who do not act like others of their gender, either because they cross-dress or because they have sexual conduct with men. It is women who are expected to have sexual intercourse with men, not men.[4]

Some scholars, like Boswell (1980, p. 102), attempt to minimize the significance of the Leviticus prohibitions on homosexuality by reducing them to mere ceremonial uncleanliness. Scholars who do so commit two serious errors. First, they remove the prohibition from its proper context, viz., the morally reprehensible nature of the Canaanites. Yahweh expelled the Canaanites from their land because they had performed forbidden sexual acts: "Do not defile yourselves by any of these things, for by all of these the nations I am casting out before you defiled themselves; and the land became defiled, so I punished its iniquity, and the land vomited out its inhabitants" (Lev., 18.24–25). The tone and the intent are perfectly clear. The Canaanites were so iniquitous that they forfeited the land of their fathers. Second, these scholars fail to understand the importance of ritual and taboo. While in the twentieth century we might perceive the breaking of certain taboos in other cultures as a matter of "mere" ceremonial uncleanliness, this perception is anachronistic. Morality and taboo, for the Israelites, cannot be so separated. Not only do taboos highlight morally disapproved behavior, but a person who breaks a taboo becomes "a doubly wicked object of reprobation, first because he crossed the line, and second because he endangered others" (Douglas, 1966, pp. 129, 139). Morality and taboo are intimately linked, and one cannot reduce the moral significance of Leviticus 18 with modern philological scholasticism.

One final note should be made on the differences between polytheism and monotheism with reference to sexual prohibitions. In polytheism impurity is an active force that has to be neutralized. In monotheism the only active force is Yahweh—impurity displeases him, but it does not exist as a separate force to be reckoned with. Thus the purificatory sacrifices are commands of Yahweh, performed in recognition of his supremacy; these sacrifices symbolically make right what had been done wrong, either intentionally or unintentionally. In essence they have no magical efficacy as they do in polytheistic rites (Kaufmann, 1960, pp. 112–115).

Related to the question of the treatment of impurity is the difference in how the two systems deal with those who break sexual taboos. In polytheism there is always an expiation: Oedipus, even though guilty of patricide and incest, was not killed so that divine order might be restored in Thebes. Expiations of one sort or another are a part of the religious norm in polytheistic societies. Yahweh, however, is not so easily pleased. Involuntary sexual impurities can be righted (such as menstruation or nocturnal emissions), but voluntary sexual acts that cross prohibited lines are almost always punishable by death. In one case the punishment is reduced only slightly: Sex with a woman "having her sickness" is punishable by exile, a form of capital punishment in the ancient world. This extreme punitiveness for the breaking of sexual taboos is partly related to historical necessity, a factor usually absent in polytheistic societies.

History played an important role in reinforcing the sexual attitudes present in the Israelite cosmology and cult. As the Israelites crossed the Jordan River, they began to take away the land of the inhabitants, the Canaanites. The justification for the movement into Canaan was twofold. First, Yahweh had promised land to the descendents of Abraham as a reward for Abraham's faithfulness to his god. Second, the land to be given to the Israelites was that of the Canaanites because the latter had forfeited their right to it. As mentioned previously, this forfeiture was based specifically on the sexual crimes of the Canaanites. Twice in Leviticus Yahweh enumerates these crimes and tells the children of Israel that it was because the Canaanites practiced just such acts that he was expelling them from the land (Lev., 18.24–5; 20.23–24). Homosexual behavior was, of course, one of the abominable acts committed by the Canaanites.

Sexual "irregularities," especially of the male homosexual variety, are frequent occurrences in Genesis, and the Canaanites are often the most culpable. Just as Genesis in various stories points the reader down the road of righteousness from Adam to the Twelve Tribes, so too the reader can see the path taken by the unrighteous, particularly the Canaanites. The first hint of future attitudes toward homosexuality comes in the story of Cain and Abel. Cain is more than simply the murderer of his brother. As Leach shows (1969, p. 15), "Cain's sin was not only fratricide but also incestuous homosexuality." Cain's name derives from the Hebrew word Qanah: Qanah and Canaan are homophones, and the play on words was not lost on the ancient audience. The first time we meet Canaan, the protoancestor of the folk to bear his name, it is through his father Ham. In Genesis 9.22, Ham engages in incestuous homosexuality with his father Noah. The result is that Noah curses Ham's son, Canaan (Gen., 9.25). It comes as no great surprise, therefore, that three chapters later, when Abraham first comes to the land of the Canaanites, Yahweh promises to give that land to Abraham's descendents (12.7).

The Canaanites are a constant source of sexual problems for Yahweh from the very first time that Abraham sets foot in their land. Sodom and Gomorrah, on the periphery of the territory inhabited by the descendents of the accursed Canaan (Gen., 10.19), epitomize the problem. The Sodomites were sinners prior to Lot's sojourn among them (13.13), and Yahweh had decided to destroy them even before the visitation of the angels (18.20). When the Sodomites wished to gang rape the visiting angels, Yahweh strikes the offenders blind; shortly thereafter he utterly destroys the place. It is interesting to note that when the Sodomites chose to infringe on the hospitality extended by Lot, they did so in a sexual way.[5]

Individual Canaanites also cause sexual problems. Esau made the grievous mistake of marrying a Canaanite woman (26.34), an error not committed by his brother, Jacob (27.46 to 28.5). Dinah was seduced by the Canaanite prince of Shechem. The result was the destruction of the entire town by Simeon and Levi (34.1-31). Finally, Judah took a Canaanite wife. Their first son, Er, was "wicked in the sight of the Lord," and the Lord struck him dead (38.7). Their second son, Onan, did not fare much better. As a result of Onan's engaging in *coitus interruptus* with the wife of his dead brother, Yahweh struck him dead, too (38.10). There is a parallel here to the story of the Sodomites and the angels. Onan was being selfish in his refusal to complete intercourse with his sister-in-law: his selfishness, like the Sodomite inhospitality, was expressed in a sexual fashion, and appropriately punished by Yahweh with death. Ironically, the troublesome wife and sister-in-law was also a Canaanite, Tamar. She was later accused of temple prostitution, causing more difficulties for the troubled Judah (38.24; see Leach, 1969, pp. 58-59). In sum, the sexual track record of the Canaanites was not good, and the fact that they are singled out for particular abuse in Leviticus and Deuteronomy is to be expected. The homosexual behavior of the Canaanites was simply one ingredient in their general condemnation (Lev., 18.22, 24; Deut., 23.18).

To sum up, no room existed in the Israelite cosmology, cult, or historical experience for the development of acceptable forms of male homosexual behavior. It could not be a part of the cult, for as an ambiguous category it was intrinsically defiling to Yahweh. Furthermore, such behavior could not develop as an independent cultural phenomenon, as it could, say, in ancient Greece. The reason for this lack of development was that all aspects of society, especially the sexual aspects, were part of the sacred and, therefore, strictly regulated. With no true secular (or private) sphere, male homosexuality could not develop while escaping attack. The cult and customs of the Canaanites reinforced this negative picture: Canaan became a scandalous model of how not to act. The first monotheistic religion created a culture in which no form of male homosexuality could be tolerated or permitted.

COMPARISON OF THE POLYTHEISTIC AND MONOTHEISTIC COSMOLOGIES

In conclusion, an examination of the polytheistic and monotheistic cosmologies reveals two conflicting sets of attitudes concerning sex and sexuality. In polytheism, sex is a potent force, often considered dangerous, that has to be reckoned with. Furthermore, gender distinctions are not absolutes that cannot be broken—role reversal, especially in a ritual context, is practically universal. Polytheism creates conditions for a wider variety of sexual expression and behavior: In itself it does not preclude any particular activity. Homosexuality, for example, is in no way antithetical to the laws or nature of the universe. While not all polytheistic societies have approved forms of homosexual behavior, polytheism seems to predispose a society toward approval.

Monotheism presents a very different picture. Neither Yahweh nor his cosmos is sexually charged, and distinctions of all sorts are rigidly maintained. In ancient Israel, cosmology, cult, and history conspired together to provide an environment where sexual expression was rigidly controlled for all members of society, and where homosexual behavior could have no legitimate or approved place. The prohibitions of Leviticus persisted in Jewish religious writings, and continue to the present day. In reflecting the past, the modern state of Israel, under the influence of its religious parties, makes homosexual activity a criminal offense. Christianity and Islam were born directly from Judaism, and they share its world-view and hostilities when it comes to homosexuality. In monotheism, male homosexuality is presumed to be effeminate. Sex with men is an activity appropriate for women only, and those men who do have sexual contact with other men must be like women. Since crossing gender lines is fundamentally wrong and abhorrent, contrary to the nature of the cosmos of God, male homosexual behavior is equally wrong and abhorrent.

The contrast with polytheistic societies could not be greater. First, the choice by men of male sexual partners is not viewed by all societies as an act that crosses gender lines. Fellation among the Gururumba and Sambia, and sodomy among the Keraki are masculine activities, done with men by other men. The masculine hero, Hercules, did not cross gender lines in his acquisition of male lovers. Second, even when male homosexual behavior does include habits that a society might consider feminine (e.g., cross-dressing), these societies do not consider such actions inherently wrong. The *berdache* of North America and the male wives of the Azande warrior are not thought to be evil, abominable, or out of step with the universe or its gods. Indeed, individuals such as the Chukchee shaman and the Plains *berdache* are honored and powerful members of the community. Polytheism has no difficulty in accommodating male homosexual behavior.

Monotheism is incapable of making this accommodation. While homosexuality is sometimes tolerated, it is always sinful. Occasional toleration can easily evaporate into persecution. Such is precisely what happened in the middle of the twelfth century A.D.: Toleration of a forbidden sexual activity vanished, and homosexual behavior, which had been only one of the many sexual transgressions, was singled out for particular abuse. The problem lies in the nature of the cosmology in question—the world of polytheistic Rome was not the world of monotheistic Christians. Once the Roman emperor, Constantine, converted to Christianity, the basic view of the cosmos changed along with his religion.

NOTES

1. For a summary of the concepts and controversies concerning the anthropology of religion, see, for example, Douglas (1975) and Nottingham (1954).
2. The best exposition of the differences between polytheism and monotheism is found in Kaufmann (1960, pp. 7-121). The following brief discussion relies on his more detailed work. It should be noted, however, that Kaufmann does not discuss the sexual implications of the two systems as argued in this article. The ideas developed here formulated several years ago in conjunction with a lecture course on the history of sex and sexuality in Europe and the Mediterranean basin. Ochshorn's timely book, though not without its problems, fits in well with the work of Kaufmann and with this article.
3. This discussion of the Hindus is drawn from Bullough (1976, pp. 247-267), Douglas (1966), O'Flaherty (1973), and from the texts in Eliade (1967).
4. The avoidance of lesbianism in Leviticus is intriguing. Like Queen Victoria, did Yahweh refuse to believe that ladies did such things? Or were the male authors of the text simply unaware of what might be going on among women?
5. The Sodomites' behavior is an interesting reversal of hospitality. The extension of sexual favors to a guest was not uncommon in ancient times, and the practice persists to this day. Some Arab tribes still give their wives to guests, and among the Siwa sons are given (Ford & Beach, 1951, p. 139; Pitt-Rivers, 1977). The Sodomites wished to show their contempt for the messengers of Yahweh by sexually abusing them, the reverse of what ought to have been done.

REFERENCES

Beard, M. The sexual status of the Vestal Virgins. *Journal of Roman Studies*, 1980, *70*, 12-27.
Boswell, J. *Christianity, social tolerance, and homosexuality.* Chicago: University of Chicago Press, 1980.
Brown, P., & Buchbinder, G. *Man and woman in the New Guinea highlands.* Washington, D.C.: American Anthropological Association, 1976.
Budge, E. A. W. *The book of the dead.* New York: Dover, 1967.
Budge, E. A. W. *The gods of the Egyptians* (Vols. 1 & 2). New York: Dover, 1969.
Bullough, V. L. *Sexual variance in society and history.* New York: John Wiley, 1976.
Devereux, G. Institutionalized homosexuality of the Mohave Indians. *Human Biology*, 1937, *9*, 498-527.
Douglas, M. *Purity and danger.* New York: Praeger, 1966.
Douglas, M. *Implicit meanings: Essays in anthropology.* London: Routledge & Kegan Paul, 1975.
Dover, K. J. *Greek homosexuality.* Cambridge, MA: Harvard University Press, 1978.
Eliade, M. *From primitives to Zen.* New York: Harper & Row, 1967.
Evans-Pritchard, E. E. Sexual inversion among the Azande. *American Anthropologist,* 1970, *78*, 1428-1439.
Firth, R. *We, the Tikopia.* Boston: Beacon Press, 1957.
Ford, C. S., & Beach, F. A. *Patterns of sexual behavior.* New York: Harper & Row, 1970. (Originally published, 1951.).
Fortune, R. F. *Manus religion.* Lincoln: University of Nebraska, 1934.
Friedl, E. *Women and man: An anthropologist's view.* New York: Holt, Rinehart & Winston, 1975.
Herdt, G. H. *Guardians of the flutes: Idioms of masculinity.* New York: McGraw-Hill, 1981.
Hoffman, R. Some cultural aspects of Greek male homosexuality. *Journal of Homosexuality,* 1980, *5*, 217-226.
Kaufmann, Y. *The religion of Israel from its beginnings to the Babylonian exile.* (M. Greenberg, trans.) New York: Schocken Books: 1960.
Krader, L. Buryet religion and society. In J. Middleton (Ed.), *Gods and ritual.* New York: Natural History Press, 1967.
Leach, E. *Genesis as myth and other essays.* London: Jonathan Cape, 1969.
Meigs, A. S. Male pregnancy and the reduction of sexual opposition in a New Guinea highlands society. *Ethnology,* 1976, *15*, 393-407.

Norbeck, E. African rituals of conflict. In J. Middleton (Ed.), *Gods and ritual.* New York: Natural History Press, 1967.

Nottingham, E. K. *Religion and society.* New York: Random House, 1954.

Ochshorn, J. *The female experience and the nature of the divine.* Bloomington: Indiana University Press, 1973.

O'Flaherty, W. D. *Asceticism and eroticism in the mythology of Siva.* London: Oxford University Press, 1973.

Ortner, S. B. Gender and sexuality in hierarchical societies: The case of Polynesia and some comparative implications. In S. B. Ortner & H. Whitehead (Eds.), *Sexual meanings: The cultural construction of gender and sexuality.* Cambridge: Cambridge University Press, 1981.

Pitt-Rivers, J. *The fate of Shechem, or the politics of sex.* Cambridge: Cambridge University Press, 1977.

Poole, F. J. P. Transforming "natural" woman: Female ritual leaders and gender ideology among Bimin-Kuskusmin. In S. B. Ortner & H. Whitehead (Eds.), *Sexual meanings: The cultural construction of gender and sexuality.* Cambridge: Cambridge University Press, 1981.

Rigby, P. Some Gogo rituals of "purification": An essay on social and moral categories. In E. Leach (Ed.), *Cambridge Papers in Social Anthropology,* 1968, *5,* 153-178.

Selby, H. A. *Zapotec deviance: The convergence of folk and modern sociology.* Austin: University of Texas Press, 1974.

Thayer, J. S. The berdache of the Northern Plains: A socioreligious perspective. *Journal of Anthropological Research,* 1980, *36,* 287-293.

The Torah: The five books of Moses. Philadelphia: The Jewish Publication Society of America, 1962.

Whitehead, H. The bow and the burden strap: A new look at institutionalized homosexuality in native North America. In S. B. Ortner & H. Whitehead (Eds.), *Sexual meanings: The cultural construction of gender and sexuality.* Cambridge University Press, 1981.

The Bisexual Identity:
An Idea Without Social Recognition

Jay P. Paul, PhD (cand.)

University of California, Berkeley

ABSTRACT. Theories of sexuality reflect popular notions by treating
sexual identity as a simple dichotomy. There is research evidence for the
coexistence of homosexual and heterosexual interest and behavior in a significant portion of the population. This paper examines how various con-
ceptualizatons of human sexuality have failed to adequately deal with
bisexuality. The lack of acknowledgement by both the larger heterosexual
society and the emerging lesbian/gay community, and its impact on the individual bisexual is examined by using the sociological concept of
marginality. Some of the differences in self-labeling by women and men
are noted in the light of social sex-roles. Finally, the implications of society's acceptance of bisexuality for evolving forms of relationships are suggested.

In American culture sexual orientation is usually conceptualized as a
simple dichotomy: One is either heterosexual or homosexual. Yet the
truth of human sexuality is that the gender of one's sexual object is not
necessarily fixed and invariant over time, nor do people necessarily eroti-
cize only the members of one sex at any one point in time. The fact that
homoeroticism and homosexual activity are parts of the lives of many
who are not exclusively homosexual is generally avoided in most discussions of sexuality. Bisexuality can be defined as the sexual, emotional,
and social attraction to individuals of both biological sexes. It is often
treated as a myth (Bieber, Dain, Dince, Drellich, Grand, Gundlach,
Kremer, Rifkin, Wilber & Bieber, 1962), as a developmental phase that
has no meaning in and of itself, or as a pathology—either a neurotic in-
ability to choose between a heterosexual or homosexual orientation or a
sign of an incapacity to make any serious emotional commitment. References to bisexuals in professional journals have grouped them with individuals suffering from some physiological defect with regard to sexual

The author is currently a PhD candidate in clinical psychology at The University of California,
Berkeley, and serving as Board member and Secretary of The Bisexual Center of San Francisco.
Reprint requests should be sent to the author c/o The Bisexual Center, 1757 Hayes Street, San Francisco, CA 94117, or c/o The Department of Psychology, University of California, Berkeley, CA
94720. This work was partially supported by NIMH training grant MH 05036.

45

differentiation (Austin, 1978). Alternatively, bisexuality is subsumed under a discussion of homosexuality. MacDonald (1981) reports on numerous studies that purport to focus on issues affecting homosexual subjects but which are in fact confounded by the inclusion of sizable numbers of subjects who might more appropriately be termed bisexual.

An "either-or" system of defining sexual orientation is pleasingly simple and therefore attractive, but this dichotomous classification not only hampers our understanding of the full range of human sexuality, it exacts its toll on many who find their sense of self invalidated by society's suppositions about sex. Klein (1978) describes the self-doubt and distress of those whose awareness of their bisexual orientation has left them in a position where their own sense of reality is contradicted by the powerful cultural message that one must choose between heterosexuality or homosexuality.

Given the diversity of human sexual responsiveness, it may be as artificial to use a three-category system to describe individuals as it is to employ a two-category system. Nevertheless, it is important to recognize the bisexual option as an identity because sexual orientation (with the myths that surround it) is a powerful determinant of social roles and social stigmatization. For this reason, too, it is time we reexamine our culture's myths and theories of sexuality in light of existing evidence.

RELIGIOUS, LEGAL, AND SCIENTIFIC THEORIES OF BISEXUALITY

Western Religion

The sexual norms and mores of Western society, as well as the laws governing sexual behavior, are heavily influenced by the Bible. Both the Old and New Testaments contain passages condemning homosexual behavior (in particular, Leviticus 18:22, 20:13; Judges 11:22-30; I Kings 22:46; Romans 1:27; I Corinthians 6:4; and Timothy 1:10). It was predominantly male homosexuality that was explicitly forbidden, perhaps because women were accorded a relatively inconsequential role in society and because their sexuality was scarcely recognized. Legal statutes of Western countries continue to treat homosexuality differently in men than in women (Gagnon, 1977; Kinsey, Pomeroy, Martin, & Gebhard, 1953; Szasz, 1970).

The early church, which placed a premium on asceticism and celibacy, condemned all sexual behavior not directly connected to procreation. Homosexuality was an obvious case of sex solely for pleasure and, hence, a sin. The notion that Sodom and Gomorrah were destroyed by a God angered by the presence there of homosexuality provided further "evidence'' for antihomosexual zealots. In the Middle Ages, the dominant ideology was theological, and any deviation socially isolated the individual. The church went so far as to equate sodomy with heresy: Heretics were assumed to engage in prohibited sexual practices; sodomites were all supposed to be heretical. Indeed, the English word *buggery* denoted both ''heresy'' and ''sodomy'' (Szasz, 1970). Today the power of religious institutions is considerably diminished, but their values continue subtly to influence much scientific thought on sexuality.

19th Century Thought

The 19th century saw the ascendance of biological determinism. Sexual deviance was transformed from a vice to an illness, from a behavior to a condition; an interest in labeling sexual *deviance* was abandoned for labeling sexual *deviants*. Heterosexual behavior was viewed not only as the norm within society but as normal in terms of biological functioning. The physiological explanations for homosexual behavior were varied, but all betrayed their founders' belief in the direct biological bases for socially conventional behavior. Ulrichs (1868) proposed that homosexuality was akin to hermaphroditism. For example, he described male homosexuality as a congenital variation in which a female soul inhabits a male body. Psychiatry embraced this simplistic condensation of biological sex, sex role, and sexual orientation, and regarded all three as dependent on the same biological factors. Thus, homosexuality was termed an ''inversion,'' a reversal of the appropriate sex-role identity. Bisexuality (described as psychosexual hermaphroditism) was studied as an imperfection in the physical process of sexual differentiation. Much time was spent trying to isolate the characteristics of the ''third sex,'' ''intersexes,'' or ''sexual intermediates.''

Krafft-Ebing (1906/1935) at first viewed inversion as a sign of physiological and psychological degeneration, probably inherited. He later developed a complex classification of several forms of ''acquired'' as well as congenital homosexuality (the acquired forms were often those in which heterosexual response was a significant part of the individual's sexual history), but his emphasis remained on congenital types. Krafft-Ebing eventually regarded inversion simply as an anomaly of nature. Other psychiatrists continued the congenital/acquired debate, arguing that homosexual behavior had to be biologically based, even if it coexisted with heterosexual interests and activity (which were consequently seen as the ''acquired'' behaviors). In a sense, this indicated a bias still current today, that homosexuality is more determinative of an individual's sexual identity than is coexistent heterosexuality.

Ellis, another strong advocate of the congenital theory, also came to view homosexuality as a nonpathology; that is, as simply a ''biological variation." He reinforced the fundamental heterosexual/homosexual dichotomy and elaborated upon a broad range of other "physical and psychic characteristics" (beyond sexual behavior) that he saw as congruent with such labels (Ellis, 1915).

Freud

Freud's rejection of the concept that people are innately and immutably homosexual appears to have ended the dominance of this paradigm. However, he expected scientific research eventually to provide firm biological explanations for his own probings, and he relied on biological suppositions in offering his own theories, but he challenged the prevailing assumptions of his contemporaries when he stated:

> [T]he exclusive sexual interest felt by men for women is also a problem that needs elucidating and is not a self-evident fact based upon an attraction that is ultimately of a chemical nature. A person's final sexual attitude is not decided until after puberty and is the result of a number of factors . . . It seems probable that the sexual instinct is in its first instance independent of its object; nor is its origin likely to be due to its object's attractions. (1905, pp. 146–148)

Freud's schema of psychosexual development sees homosexual urges as something everyone has to deal with in the normal course of maturation. The variations in object choice that he identified led him to the notion of a sexual continuum, but only for "homosexuals." He devised three main categories of inverts:

> They may be *absolute* inverts . . . their sexual objects are exclusively of their own sex . . . They may be *amphigenic* inverts . . . In that case their sexual objects may equally well be of their own or of the opposite sex . . . They may be *contingent* inverts. In that case, under certain external conditions . . . they are capable of taking as their sexual object someone of their own sex and of deriving satisfaction from sexual intercourse with him. (1905, pp. 136–137)

In these definitions, individuals who might be labeled "bisexual" are seen simply as variants of a larger homosexual group. Bisexuality is legitimized as a feature of normal sexual development preliminary to the stage at which an individual develops a specifically heterosexual or homosexual orientation. In the adult, bisexuality is pathologized, usually as a developmental failure.

Freud proposed the following set of causative factors for male homosexuality: fixation on, and identification with, the mother; inclination toward a narcissistic object-choice; overevaluation of the penis and consequent depreciation of or aversion to women, as they lack a penis; regard for or fear of the father, which leads to an avoidance of sexual rivalry with him; "the influence of the organic factor which favors the passive role in love" (1922, p. 231); homosexual object choice based upon a repression and reaction-formation to feelings of hostility, jealousy, and aggression toward same-sex rivals (usually older brothers). This last explanation was an attempt by Freud to explain homosexual attitudes that do not exclude heterosexuality and do not involve a fear of the opposite sex. Most of his other explanations regard a homosexual orientation as the consequence of a fear of or aversion to the opposite sex—implicitly pathological interpretations. Freud recognized that his list was not all-inclusive and remained perplexed by the fact that many individuals might share developmental histories similar to "inverts" without exhibiting any sign of homosexual interests. His conceptualization of female sexuality was generally sketchy.

Freud claimed to make no moral judgements about sexuality and was active in the movement to decriminalize homosexuality in Austria and Germany. Yet, his rigid notions of what constitutes mature sexual behavior (e.g., the primacy of the genitals in the service of reproduction), as opposed to sexual perversion, strongly echo his culture's sexual mores. His theories are still used in psychiatric and psychological circles to justify notions that nonconformity in sexual behavior is indicative of immaturity or perversion.

Stekel

Stekel, a disciple of Freud, emphasized what he regarded as the bisexual disposition of all individuals up until puberty, at which time the heterosexual theoretically represses her or his homosexuality and sublimates some of those homosexual cravings in friendship and social bonding.

Stekel was evidently ambivalent in his attitude toward bisexuality: though normalizing it as a basic part of human nature, he pathologized anyone who tried to express bisexuality through feelings and behavior. A choice was expected to be made between homosexual and heterosexual activity, and Stekel refused to recognize the possibility of a nonpathological exclusive homosexuality. The bisexual was expected to act as a heterosexual. Describing how to "cure" a male homosexual, he stated that "the proper therapeutic course would be to remove the inhibitions which stand between him and women, *to make him de facto again bisexual and heterosexual for all practical purposes*" (Stekel, 1922/1945, p. 244, emphasis added). The contradictions inherent in his theory seem to arise from twin beliefs: (1) that bisexuality may possibly be natural for the human species, but (2) that heterosexuality is normative for the individual within society. Stekel was explicit in his translation of social norms into standards of psychological health; his assumption was that the healthy individual will endeavor to conform as closely as possible to established values and mores.

Mead

Mead, a protegee of Boas' (which committed her early on to an emphasis on cultural determinism), is well known for her cross-cultural work in highlighting the variability of what is termed masculine and what is termed feminine. She used her work on sex-roles as a launching point for her discussion of sexual orientation. Mead's idea (1935/1968; 1949/1975) was not that homosexuals fear the opposite sex, but that they despair of being able to fulfill the demands of the socially determined standards of behavior and temperament appropriate to their own sex—and consequently adopt the sex-role of the opposite sex. She believed the society that has a rigid and extensive dichotomy of approved characteristics and behavior for females and males leaves a great number of children insecure with regard to their sex-role and, therefore, liable to become homosexual.

Mead failed to make a convincing argument for a sense of sex-role inadequacy being determinative of homosexuality, however. Her thesis depends upon a dichotomy of sexual orientation as rigid as that of biological sex. The chief blind spot in her observations is that people would seem to be labeled homosexual only if their general behavior indicated an inversion of sex role in addition to homosexual activity. She mentioned neither bisexuality nor the sexual orientation and sexual identity of seemingly "masculine" males who engage in sexual relations with "effeminate" males who may take on a special social role, as do the berdaches of the Plains Indians. Mead (1975) later concluded that bisexuality is a normal form of human behavior and validated the right of individuals to form affectional and sexual attachments with whomever they wish.

Kinsey

Kinsey and his associates (Kinsey, Pomeroy, & Martin, 1948; Kinsey, Pomeroy, Martin, & Gebhard, 1953) expressed concern that scientific judgements about homosexuality and sexual deviance seemed grounded more in popular prejudices than in hard data. One of the intentions, therefore, of their studies of sexual behavior in the U.S. was to provide objective information on patterns of homosexual activity as they related to patterns of heterosexual activity in the population as a whole. Kinsey pioneered in applying the concept of a continuum (i.e., his 7-point rating scale) to the full range of human sexuality in a descriptive, nonjudgemental fashion. He emphasized that if an individual's sexual orientation is assessed on the basis of behavior, it can be seen to change markedly in the course of a lifetime.

The Kinsey group rejected the view that erotic reactions between individuals of the same sex are rare and therefore abnormal, unnatural, or indicative or neurosis or psychosis. They based their judgement not only on the incidence and frequency of homosexual responses, but also "on its coexistence with heterosexual [response] in the lives of a considerable portion of the male population" (1948, p. 659). Fully 15% of the male sample could be termed bisexual on the basis of reported behavior, having had both "more than incidental homosexual experiences or reactions" and "more than incidental heterosexual experiences or reactions" (1948, pp. 650-651). This figure exceeds the 10% of the male population whom the Kinsey group found to have had more or less exclusively homosexual histories (1948, pp. 650-651). The findings for women show a similar ratio of "bisexuals" to "homosexuals," although the general incidence of any homosexual experiences or reactions is far lower than that in males.

Ford and Beach

In 1951, Ford and Beach published *Patterns of Sexual Behavior,* a study of variations in sexual behavior based on the written observations of numerous anthropologists (a compilation known as the Human Relations Area Files). Ford and Beach found that homosexual behavior of one sort or another was considered normal and socially acceptable for certain members of the community in 64% of the 76 societies for which data were available. They concluded:

> When it is realized that 100 percent of the males in certain societies engage in homosexual as well as heterosexual alliances, and when it is understood that many men and women in our society are equally capable or relations with partners of the same or opposite sex, and finally, when it is recognized that this same situation obtains in many species of subhuman primates, then it should be clear that one cannot classify homosexual tendencies and heterosexual tendencies as being mutually exclusive or even opposed to each other. (p. 236)

The Bieber Group

Bieber and his associates (1962) conducted what they referred to as a psychoanalytic study of homosexuality. Not only did the authors persistently fail to recognize the fundamental flaws in their research design and methods, they actually extolled the benefits of those errors:

> The questions asked were not the conventional "objective" ones,
> and they did not seek to eliminate the observer by pinpointing some
> specific bit of behavior . . . It must be recognized that the question-
> naires were not filled out by naive observers but by the patient's
> own psychoanalysts—well-trained psychiatrists with experience in
> making value judgments based on clinical impressions and interpre-
> tations. (p. 30)

Given the dubious value of generalizing from an analysand population,
generating a study group and a control group through no more exacting a
procedure than the personal choices of contributing psychoanalysts, and
presenting experimental data that have little grounding in concrete fact
(and are, rather, the biased impressions of observers), almost no researcher could see this study as lending proof to any hypothesis. The authors,
however, conclude: "The study provides convincing support for a fundamental contribution by Rado on the subject of male homosexuality: A
homosexual adaptation is the result of hidden but incapacitating fears of
the opposite sex" (p. 303).

The psychoanalytic formulations by Bieber et al. make clear distinctions between two exclusive categories, the heterosexual and the homosexual. Homosexuality is seen as an inherently pathological symptom
originating in disturbing family relations. The pathological quality of homosexuality is emphasized by the authors' assumption that heterosexuality has an innate bias that can be subverted only by a severe disturbance.
This goes beyond the theories of Freud and Stekel and ignores the concept
of bisexuality, which Bieber scoffs at, seeing it as a label assumed by
someone who is "really" homosexual.

Bell and Weinberg

Bell and Weinberg (1978) in conducting an extensive survey of homosexual sexual and social patterns, ended up tapping information on
bisexuality. Using Kinsey's rating scale first for behaviors and then again
for feelings, they found their sample clustered at the exclusively homosexual end of the continuum. A subsample, however, showed a significant degree of bisexuality:

> [O]n the basis of these several investigations it would not be
> unreasonable to suppose that a fairly strong heterosexual element is
> to be found in about one-third of those homosexual men most likely
> to participate in surveys of this kind. Even large numbers of com-
> parable homosexual women are apt to exhibit a "partial bisexual
> style" . . . Many homosexuals of both sexes have a history of sex-
> ual contact with persons of the opposite sex and, although they may

not presently engage in such contact, sometimes are aware of their continuing potential for heterosexual sexual response. (pp. 60-61)

Interestingly, their use of two Kinsey scales, one for behavior and another for feelings, revealed discrepancies between the two ratings for approximately one-third of each of the four "homosexual" groups under study (blacks and whites, males and females). Of those who saw their behavior rating as discrepant with their feelings rating, most saw their behavior as more exclusively homosexual than their feelings. It appears that patterns of sexual behavior are more readily constrained by the dichotomous notions of sexuality pervasive in our culture than are sexual feelings.

Ross and the APA Report

Other studies of homosexuality have noted that some subjects reported significant heterosexual experiences in their lives, but researchers have often either ignored or denied such differences. An example is a study by Ross (1971) that referred constantly to married "homosexual" men and made only one reference to a subject who "claimed" to be bisexual. A survey by the American Psychological Association's Board of Social and Ethical Responsibility for Psychology's Task Force on the Status of Lesbian and Gay Male Psychologists (1979) found that one-fifth of the women and one-third of the men who responded defined themselves as bisexual, though most of these respondents also described themselves as having a positive gay identity. The authors concluded that the bisexual subjects suffered from the same social pressures and stresses as did the lesbians and gay males, but the bisexuals lacked similar support systems and had had fewer positive experiences.

BISEXUALITY AND THE CONCEPT OF MARGINALITY

In trying to understand the dilemma of the bisexual—an individual without legitimate social status or social identity, and somehow outside the conventional sexual categories—it helps to consider the sociological concept of marginality. The notions of marginality and marginal personality were elaborated by Stonequist (1937/1961). Marginality refers to the set of circumstances faced by people who have not found, or cannot accept, a clear group-membership role. As they are not fully integrated into any one group, there is no group from which they are not to some extent deviant. Traditional applications of the concept of marginality have been to members of ethnic minorities (e.g., "half-breeds"), but it is also useful in addressing some of the special problems and experiences of the bisexual.

This situation has ramifications for both the individual and the larger social system. The individual must cope with or try to integrate what can be seen as two very different self-notions, sets of activities and social groups; this was presumed to lead to certain specific consequences for the person in question. The larger social system necessarily has to make certain accommodations or decisions when faced with the marginal individual. Stonequist describes this in the case of someone of mixed ethnicity, noting that such a person

> presents a special problem for the community: What is to be his place in the social organization? As he matures he too will become aware of his problematic and anomalous social position. He will become the target of whatever hostile sentiments exist between the parent races. Thus his problem of adjustment will be made more acute. (1937/1961, p. 10)

The Bisexual and the Gay/Lesbian Community

The 1970s saw the emergence of a tremendously vital gay/lesbian community, which has recently fought its battles for civil rights on the basis of being a disadvantaged "ethnic" minority. Yet the development of a lesbian/gay subculture (especially as it moves more toward separatism) does not solve the problem of the bisexual. Bisexuals, for example, who associate with the gay/lesbian community as well as with the heterosexual mainstream may find themselves shifting social identities; the attempt to bridge both worlds with a single identity can be a source of stress and discomfort in both social arenas.

Several researchers have reported that individuals' claims to being bisexual are commonly met with ambivalence and suspicion in the homosexual community (Altman, 1981; Austin, 1978; Blumstein & Schwartz, 1974, 1976a, 1977; Bode, 1976; Klein, 1978). This reaction can be especially strong toward self-labeled bisexuals who are judged to be lacking sufficient heterosexual experience to "qualify" as bisexual; these people are assumed to be trying to avoid the fuller stigma of being labeled homosexual. Furthermore, as increasing numbers of men and women who have been in heterosexual marriages come out as gay or lesbian, they may appear to be confirming the basic heterosexual/homosexual dichotomy. Given that many heterosexually married individuals may go through a stage of seeing themselves as bisexual before identifying as homosexual, it is easy to generalize that pattern for all who identify as bisexual, and to regard bisexuality as never anything more than a transitional phase.

The gay/lesbian community's unwillingness to acknowledge an individual's bisexual self-definition is also rooted in a concern that such an identity bespeaks a "holier-than-thou" attitude, an independence from or rejection of homosexuality. It is feared that the bisexual will invariably value heterosexuality over homosexuality.

In addition, bisexuality may be viewed as an unwillingness to make a serious emotional commitment to a homosexual partner. This may stem, in part, from our society's equation of commitment with a long-term, monogamous relationship, a value that is echoed by many gay males and lesbians who are actually involved in very different types of relationships themselves. Blair (1974) argues that counselors should discourage clients from seeing bisexuality as a viable option because "it is difficult enough in our society to manage a sexual relationship with one person, let alone to try to bring together two or more other people and other worlds in intersecting and interacting relationships" (p. 29). He fails to recognize the realities of relationships for those who define themselves as heterosexual or homosexual, in that monogamy is not implied by a single-sex sexual orientation. Nor does a bisexual identity exclude the possibility of sustaining a monogamous relationship.

Related to this is the political bitterness sometimes directed toward bisexuals, born of the belief that they can easily merge into the heterosexual community when the struggle against prejudice gets too intense, but are all too willing to enjoy the benefits of the battle to end antihomosexual discrimination and harassment.

Sexual Labels and Sexual Histories

In light of the ungenerous reception accorded bisexuals by the heterosexual and homosexual societies, it is hardly surprising that many researchers have observed that the correspondence between their subjects' sexual biographies and sexual self-identifications often proves to be surprisingly imperfect (Blumstein & Schwartz, 1977). Similar rationalizations are used by both the self-identified homosexual for heterosexual activity and the self-identified heterosexual for homosexual activity (Blumstein & Schwarz, 1976a, 1976b). Tripp (1975) describes a series of rationalizations that an individual may use in order to "engage in homosexuality while continuing to define himself as a regular member of society, one who in no essential way is set apart from it" (p. 131). These include viewing same-sex sexual contacts as homosexual only for the partner whose gender-role is seemingly inverted; letting oneself be "seduced" so that one can see oneself as reacting to another's homosexual desires rather than acting on one's own; viewing a relationship as a unique "special friendship" that transcends sexual labels; and defining the homosexual activity and interest as situational, transitory, displaced from the "true" opposite-sex sexual object, and thus unrelated to one's "true sexuality."

The meaning of sexual labels—one's summing up of one's sexual and affectional experiences and interests—is a personal process and also a declaration to the social organization of one's standing within it. Therefore, if the individual can arrive at a personally satisfying self-labeling, the issue of marginality would be greatest when and if the individual's sexual identity is directly challenged by socially significant others. If the identified sexual orientation is at variance with at least some aspect of one's sexual behavior, that behavior—potentially disruptive to one's social position and relationships—is likely to be carried out in a more secretive manner. There was a time when this was predominantly an issue for self-identified heterosexuals engaging in homosexual behavior; with the new strength of the gay/lesbian community and its current separatist position, this has become more of an issue for the self-defined homosexual who is actively heterosexual as well. The need to hide significant parts of oneself or one's behavior must inevitably create distance between oneself and others. This exacts a psychological toll and probably feeds an underlying sense of marginality.

As a consequence of either being confronted on the issue of one's sexual identity or attempting to maintain two independent social lives and identities (that is, in heterosexual society and in the gay/lesbian community), the bisexual is vulnerable to the confusion arising from a dual sense of self:

> We develop an idea of ourselves through imagining how we appear to other persons, and imagining their judgment of that appearance. Thence arises a self-feeling ranging from pride to mortification. In the case of the marginal man, it is as if he were placed simultaneously between two looking-glasses, each presenting a sharply different image of himself. The clash in the images gives rise to a mental conflict as well as to a dual self-consciousness and identification. (Stonequist, 1937/1961, pp. 145–146)

Whether or not one chooses to self-label as a bisexual, the acknowledgement of one's bisexuality can still spark conflicts around one's identity. To an adolescent struggling with such a question, it may appear that he or she is facing the foreclosure of future options; to someone older, it may seem that there is danger of losing much of the life known and valued so far, the familiar people and patterns of behavior. One's experience of bisexuality is apt to be different based upon whether one's bisexuality is *sequential* (varying from a solely homosexual to a solely heterosexual pattern, and back again) or *contemporaneous* (having male and female partners during the same period).

In addition, it appears that the meanings and consequences of sexual orientation are different for men and women. Blumstein and Schwartz (1976a) noted:

Males were much more likely to maintain an uninterrupted bisexual self-definition once the label was adopted than were female bisexuals. This probably reflects the women's greater commitment to norms of sexual monogamy. It was not uncommon for women to express the irrelevance of the label "bisexual" except when unattached, but [to use the label] heterosexual when they were involved with a man and homosexual when with a woman. Males on the other hand, seemed to be keeping their prospects open, even when monogamously involved, and reported being erotically attuned to both men and women even when not in active pursuit. (pp. 351-352)

These differences in labeling by men and women are apt to reflect much more than the differing patterns of sexuality and relationships suggested as normative for males and females; there is also a difference in terms of the social costs of these labels for men and women.

BIOLOGICAL SEX, SOCIAL SEX-ROLE, AND THE BISEXUAL ORIENTATION

Our society grants superior prestige and power to males; in addition, it tends to value "masculine" over "feminine" behavior, making masculinity the basis for our norms of healthy functioning. Thus, the equation of homosexual activity with a reversal of sex-roles results in differing consequences for men and women. The male is seen as relinquishing a more powerful set of prerogatives by his sexual choice than is the female; in women, the reversal in sex-role can be taken as a confirmation of the greater worth of the male role.

Freud proposed a psychosexual developmental theory in which sex-role identity and sexual orientation are interconnected. The normative resolution of the Oedipal crisis supposedly leads to an internalization of societal values and mores (and the formation of the superego), a same-sex parental identification, repression of the "opposite-sex disposition," and an opposite-sex object choice. To his credit, Freud recognized the difficulty created by relying on vaguely defined sex-linked dispositional factors in his theory, given the inadequate understanding by science of masculinity and femininity:

But psychoanalysis cannot elucidate the intrinsic nature of what in conventional or in biological phraseology is termed "masculine" and "feminine," it simply takes over the concepts and makes them the foundation of its work. When we attempt to reduce them further, we find masculinity vanishing into activity and femininity into passivity, and that does not tell us enough. (1920/1953, p. 171)

Mead's linking of sexual orientation and social sex-role has been outlined earlier. Another interpretation of her observations might be that societal rules about what is feminine and masculine help determine the patterns of same-sex relationships in a culture but do not cause a homosexual orientation. When social sex-roles are rigidly defined in a society, there may be less social approval for an individual to vary between female and male sex-typed behaviors than to adopt a single sex-role—even if that role is at odds with the individual's actual biological sex. Thus a society can demand that a deviant "outgroup" conform in certain respects to the values of the dominant group.

Altman (1982) suggests that "under modern conditions greater freedom for women and a breakdown in the rigidity of sex roles (the two are closely connected) has repercussions in allowing a greater freedom for homosexuals, both women and men" (p. 92). Fasteau (1975) has argued that the depolarization of sex roles and the development of a more androgynous society would lead to a higher incidence of homosexual activity but to less exclusive homosexuality—in other words, a higher incidence of bisexuality. By challenging traditional assumptions about relationships between women and men, social acknowledgement of bisexuality would necessarily be part of a larger social change.

The differences in the stigma currently attached to female and male homosexual behavior manifest themselves at a number of levels. Homosexuality has generally been viewed as a grave offense for males and has either been denied in females or viewed as less serious. This may spring from males in our society generally having more power that can be forfeited. Furthermore, homosexuality in males has been the subject of more pathologizing theories than homosexuality in females. Aversion and disgust toward males who enjoy homosexual relationships tends to be most strongly expressed by males; males' negative attitudes toward lesbianism are less pronounced. Heterosexual responsiveness or interest is not automatically assumed to be impaired in women who engage in homosexual activity; Blumstein and Schwartz (1976b) found that, for some of their female interviewees, the initial sexual experience with another woman had been orchestrated by male partners, who had arranged a "three-way."

In addition, masculinity seems to be a more fragile attainment for a male than femininity is for a female. In many ways, masculinity is defined as the absence of femininity rather than as the presence of particular characteristics of its own.

Both Chodorow (1974) and Fasteau (1975) have described the male identity as more dependent upon the activities males engage in—and thus more readily threatened by action defined as more appropriate to the opposite sex—than is women's sense of being female. So not only is the male possibly in greater peril vis-a-vis loss of superior social status by engaging in homosexual behavior, his own sense of masculinity and male identity may be at risk in the process. Blumstein and Schwartz (1977) echo this in their findings:

> Women found initial [homosexual] experiences much less traumatic than men, and they were less likely to allow a single experience or a few experiences to lead them to an exclusive homosexual orientation. Women often felt that such activities were a natural extension of female affectionate behavior and did not have implications for their sexuality. Men, on the other hand, were much more preoccupied with what the experience meant for their masculinity, sometimes fearing that they might never again be able to respond erotically to a woman. (p. 43)

> Males reported much more difficulty coping with homosexual behavior and developing a homosexual identification than women. We attribute this to the stigma attached to homosexuality among American men (more than among women). Masculinity is a major element in men's sense of self-worth, and homosexuality, in the popular imagination, implies impaired masculinity. (p. 44)

This is not to say that in our society acknowledging one's homosexuality is a problem only for males; Rubenstein (1982) found that, although self-esteem ratings were generally high in her bisexual sample, they were lower for those who had previously identified as homosexual (as opposed to heterosexual). But for a male, the sexual label (as bisexual, heterosexual, or homosexual) may be more highly charged in terms of perceived social consequences than for a female. A woman, as in Blumstein and Schwartz's study, may find it less disruptive than a man to move from seeing herself as homosexual when in one relationship to seeing herself as heterosexual when in another.

Gender and Developing Patterns of Sexuality and Relationships

Adult males exploring homosexual relationships are also likely to find little ideological support such as women may find in feminist thought. Likewise, whereas women gain a great deal of emotional support from friendships with other women, friendships among men often seem to be emotionally limited, despite American society's celebration of the male bond. Differences in patterns of sexual development and the establishment of interpersonal bonds might be expected to influence how males and females would come to terms both with their own bisexuality and with society's failure to acknowledge bisexuality. Weinberg (1973) suggests that differences between the sexes with regard to self-acceptance of homosexuality may be a consequence of the different ways in which men and women discover their sexuality.

> [W]omen are more apt to make the discovery in adulthood, and fre-
> quently a woman makes it when she is already in love with another
> woman. When this happens, she is in many cases so buoyed by the
> relationship that the concept of herself as homosexual may seem
> empty and unimportant. Only when the relationship ends, if it does,
> may she feel guilty in some degree . . . In contrast, great numbers
> of teenage boys recognize they are homosexual long before they
> have even met another homosexual . . . Many lived for years with
> the sense that they were emotionally misshapen and doomed. (pp.
> 89-90)

If females do not explore their homosexuality until after adolescence, this
may put them at a lower risk for experiencing feelings of alienation and
deviance than males, whose first homosexual experimentation is often as
teenagers. This distinction may be important in determining how sexual
orientation is integrated in the larger process of identity formation.

In distinguishing between initial male and female homosexual exploration, Weinberg (1973) suggests that such experimentation by a bisexual
female is less likely to be considered an isolated and irrelevant part of her
life (that is, something to be insulated against by various rationalizations)
than would be the case for a bisexual male. Weinberg found that once
homosexual activity had begun, it was seen as a meaningful part of the
women's experiences. This accords with Klein's (1978) findings that the
women in his study of participants at the Bisexual Forum in New York
City were able to develop a bisexual identity at roughly the same age as
the males surveyed (the mean ages for both groups were about 24 years),
though this was only a little over a year after the mean age at which the
women reported their first homosexual experience—compared with six
years after the mean age of the males' first homosexual experience. These
differing schedules of significant events in the formation of a sexual identity suggest differences in the dynamics of bisexual identity formation for
females and males.

Rubenstein (1976) discovered the male bisexual's sense of self as
bisexual was usually facilitated by their friends, whereas female bisexuals' friends seemed to hinder as much as aid the women's developing
awareness of being bisexual. Similarly, there were mixed reports from
female bisexuals concerning the value of therapy for working on issues of
sexual identity, whereas lesbians and males (both bisexual and homosexual) valued therapy much more highly. It may be that achieving a bisexual
identity, which implies a process of individuation from the lesbian/gay
community as well as from the heterosexual community, requires greater
physical separation for women than it does for men, given that women are
more communion-oriented.[1]

An explanation may rest in the fact that, in our culture, socialization promotes a division of social sex-roles that leaves males less able to provide each other with emotional support, and so makes them rely on intimate relationships with females for that support. Rubenstein's (1982) findings that both the females and the males in her bisexual sample were more emotionally satisfied with their relationships with women could be taken as evidence for this argument. Bisexual males, therefore, can easily use the gay male community solely as a sexual marketplace without developing social supports within that community. In the absence of support from community or friends, the bisexual male may maintain an exclusively heterosexual label and isolate his homosexual interests from the rest of his life, leaving him open to the experience of marginality described by Stonequist (1937/1961).

BISEXUALITY: A CONTRIBUTION TO SOCIAL CHANGE

There is potential for positive social change to emerge from the current difficult position of bisexuals in our society. To resolve the experience of being affiliated with two opposing "camps," the heterosexual and homosexual, while being an outsider in relation to both, requires the bisexual individual to reject the common frame of reference and adopt a broader, better integrated perspective on human sexuality and social relationships.

Altman (1982) describes how the "new gay culture"—with its thrust toward a freer sexuality, its nourishing of alternatives to the family as a system of social organization, and its record of increased social flexibility—has had an impact on mainstream American culture. At the same time, he acknowledges that homosexuals "have largely taken for granted the model offered by heterosexual marriage" (p. 185), and that the writings of gay men have emphasized the monogamous ideal (though paradoxically teamed with the theme of sexual adventure in gay male fiction). It was primarily in lesbian writings that Altman found a concern for the development of other relational forms (p. 188). It appears that despite the different coupling arrangements common to the gay and lesbian communities, homosexuals continue to measure their experiences against an idealized norm of monogamy. This tendency may in part account for the greater dissatisfaction reported by those in homosexual relationships that diverged most from the ideal of exclusivity, as noted by Bell and Weinberg (1978).

The bisexual, on the other hand, must immediately confront the issue of monogamy when considering the possibility of having relationships with both men and women. The bisexual, therefore, may be more apt not only to seek new types of relationships but to question the values placed by mainstream American culture on such relationships. Furthermore, the bisexual who has social and affectionate relationships with both men and women has an opportunity to compare these experiences and so to learn of the subtle constraints that sex-roles impose on intimate interactions— and to exchange such patterns for freer forms in which biological sex is not a central concern in choosing partners.

In the bisexual's social world there are not necessarily clear distinctions between individuals to whom one relates affectionately and those to whom one relates sexually. What begins as a nonsexual friendship may easily move to a sexual level (Bode, 1976) and vice versa. Ties to friends, therefore, may have as much emotional meaning over the years as the bonds of family or of romantic love. From these experiences the bisexual may be able to construct new forms of intimacy and to place new values on such constructions. The society that recognizes the bisexual is also likely to enjoy this broader range of lifestyles available for all its members—bisexual, heterosexual, or homosexual.

NOTE

1. Communion is a female-related concept that suggests merging of the self with the field. At an interpersonal level, it involves subjectivity, closeness, affiliation, cooperation, and acceptance (Carlson, 1971).

REFERENCES

Altman, D. *The homosexualization of America, the Americanization of the homosexual.* New York: St. Martin's Press, 1982.

American Psychological Association. *Removing the stigma.* Final Report of the Board of Social and Ethical Responsibility for Psychology's Task Force on the Status of Lesbian and Gay Male Psychologists, September 1979.

Austin, C. R. Bisexuality and the problems of its social acceptance. *Journal of Medical Ethics,* 1978, *4,* 132-137.

Bell, A. P., & Weinberg, M. S. *Homosexualities: A study of diversity among men and women.* New York: Simon & Schuster, 1978.

Bieber, I., Dain, H. J., Dince, P. R., Drellich, M. G., Grand, H. G., Gundlach, R. H., Kremer, M. W., Rifkin, A. H., Wilber, C. B., & Bieber, T. B. *Homosexuality: A psychoanalytic study.* New York: Basic Books, 1962.

Blair, R. Counseling concerns and bisexual behavior. *The Homosexual Counseling Journal,* 1974, *1*(2), 26-30.

Blumstein, P. W., & Schwartz, P. Lesbianism and bisexuality. In E. Goode & R. Troiden (Eds.), *Sexual deviance and sexual deviants.* New York: William Morrow, 1974.

Blumstein, P. W., & Schwartz, P. Bisexuality in men. *Urban Life,* 1976, *5,* 339-358.

Blumstein, P. W., & Schwartz, P. Bisexuality in women. *Archives of Sexual Behavior,* 1976, *5,* 171-181. (b)

Blumstein, P. W., & Schwartz, P. Bisexuality: Some social psychological issues. *Journal of Social Issues,* 1977, *33*(2), 30-45.

Bode, J. *View from another closet: Exploring bisexuality in women.* New York: Hawthorn Books, 1976.

Carlson, R. Sex differences in ego functioning: Exploratory studies of agency and communion. *Journal of Consulting and Clinical Psychology,* 1971, *37,* 267-277.

Chodorow, N. Family structure and feminine personality. In M. Z. Rosaldo & L. Lamphere (Eds.), *Women, culture, and society.* Stanford: Stanford University Press, 1974.

Ellis, H. *Sexual inversion*. New York: F. A. Davis, 1915.

Fasteau, M. F. *The male machine*. New York: Delta Books, 1975.

Ford, C. S., & Beach, F. A. *Patterns of sexual behavior*. New York: Harper & Row, 1951.

Freud, S. [Three essays on the theory of sexuality]. *Standard edition of the complete psychological works of Sigmund Freud* (Vol. 7). London: Hogarth Press, 1953. (Originally published, 1905.)

Freud, S. [Psychogenesis of a case of homosexuality in a woman]. *Standard edition of the complete psychological works of Sigmund Freud* (Vol. 18). London: Hogarth Press, 1953. (Originally published, 1920.)

Freud, S. [Some neurotic mechanisms in jealousy, paranoia and homosexuality]. *Standard edition of the complete psychological works of Sigmund Freud* (Vol. 18). London: Hogarth Press, 1953. (Originally published, 1922.)

Gagnon, J. H. *Human sexualities*. Glenview, IL: Scott, Foresman, 1977.

Kinsey, A. C., Pomeroy, W. B., & Martin, C. E. *Sexual behavior in the human male*. Philadelphia: W. B. Saunders, 1948.

Kinsey, A. C., Pomeroy, W. B., Martin, C. E., & Gebhard, P. E. *Sexual behavior in the human female*. Philadelphia: W. B. Saunders, 1953.

Klein, F. *The bisexual option*. New York: Berkley Books, 1978.

Krafft-Ebing, R. von. *Psychopathia sexualis*. F. J. Rebman, (Transl.) New York: Physicians & Surgeons Book Co., 1935. (12th German edition, 1906).

MacDonald, A. P. Bisexuality: Some comments on research and theory. *Journal of Homosexuality*, 1981, 6(3), 21-33.

Mead, M. *Sex and temperament in three primitive societies*. New York: Dell, 1968. (Originally published, 1935.)

Mead, M. *Male and female: A study of the sexes in a changing world*. New York: William Morrow, 1975. (Originally published, 1949.)

Mead, M. Bisexuality: What's it all about? *Redbook*, January 1975, 29-31.

Ross, H. L. Modes of adjustment of married homosexuals. *Social Problems*, 1971, 18(3), 385-393.

Rubenstein, M. *Bisexuality and androgyny: An investigative study*. Unpublished masters thesis, Lone Mountain College, CA, 1976.

Rubenstein, M. *An in-depth study of bisexuality and its relationship to self-esteem*. Unpublished doctoral dissertation, Institute for Advanced Study of Human Sexuality, San Francisco, CA, 1982.

Stekel, W. *Bi-sexual love*. New York: Emerson Books, 1945. (Originally published, 1922.)

Stonequist, E. B. *The marginal man: A study in personality and culture conflict*. New York: Russell & Russell, 1961. (Originally published, 1937.)

Szasz, T. *The manufacture of madness*. New York: Harper Colophon Books, 1977. (Originally published, 1970.)

Tripp, C. A. *The homosexual matrix*. New York: Signet Books, 1975.

Ulrichs, K. H., Memnon. *Die geschlechtsnatur des mannliebenden urnings*. Leipzig: Max Spohr, 1868.

Weinberg, G. *Society and the healthy homosexual*. New York: Anchor Books, 1973.

Freud Reconsidered:
Bisexuality, Homosexuality,
and Moral Judgement

Timothy F. Murphy, PhD
Boston College

ABSTRACT. This article examines methodological problems and unacknowledged moral judgements in Freud's theory of homosexuality. Freud raises the issue of bisexuality in connection with the origins of homosexuality. When critically examined, the theory of bisexuality reduces to a theory of the capacity to be attracted to either females or males, and in that sense explains little about the origin of exclusive homosexual orientation. Freud's further investigations into the origin of homosexuality, strictly speaking, do not provide a clear explanation of sexual exclusivity. Finally, it is argued that Freud's moral assumptions color the nature of his conclusions. At the very least, without morally justifying his procedure, he transforms the course of psychosexual development as determined by psychoanalysis into a moral imperative against which homosexuality is judged a fixated and immature state.

In Freud's later works he gradually turned his attention from the psychical constitution of the mind per se to the reflection of that constitution in social institutions and practices as well as in historical progress. In his polemic on religion, *The Future of an Illusion,* Freud remarks on the irreconcilable antagonism that exists between an individual's happiness and the demands of civilization: "The decisive question is whether and to what extent it is possible to lessen the burden of the instinctual sacrifices imposed on men, to reconcile men to those which must necessarily re-

Timothy Murphy received his PhD in philosophy from Boston College and is the author of the forthcoming *Nietzsche as Educator* (University Press of America). He has written for the *Journal of Medicine and Philosophy* and *The New Scholasticism,* and is currently working on the place of values in the natural science and therapeutic traditions of psychiatry and psychology. Reprint requests may be addressed to him at Boston College, Department of Philosophy, Chestnut Hill, MA 02167.

main and to provide a compensation for them'' (Freud, 1927/1961, p. 7). He advocates eliminating any surplus repressions that impede human happiness.

In light of Freud's view of sexual liberation, this essay will examine both his methodological approach and his moral judgements on the subject of homosexuality in order to assess the legitimacy of his analysis and his contribution to the understanding of homosexuality. This essay proceeds by (1) examining Freud's theory of bisexuality, (2) sketching his analysis of the origin of homosexuality, and (3) looking at the moral judgements that he makes about homosexuality as a sexual orientation.

FREUD'S CONCEPT OF BISEXUALITY

One of the most interesting, yet least examined, notions of Freud is the idea of bisexuality, a concept found scattered throughout the entire corpus.[1] The idea of bisexuality is most often used in explaining the origins of homosexuality. However, it also arises in conjunction with several other topics: (1) the causes of symptoms associated with hysteria; (2) the explanation of some traits uncovered in dream analysis (Freud, 1916–17/1953, p. 237); (3) the ambivalence of the child toward the father in the Oedipal situation (Freud, 1928/1961, pp. 183–185; cf. Freud, 1931/1961, p. 220); (4) the theory of paranoia; (5) the discussions of female and male anatomical distinctions and personality and behavior; and, most importantly, (6) the choice of females or males as love-objects. About bisexuality, Freud states: "I have regarded it as the decisive factor and without taking bisexuality into account I think it would scarcely be possible to arrive at an understanding of the sexual manifestations that are to be observed in men and women" (Freud, 1905/1953, p. 220). Unfortunately, Freud does not always use the term in clear and unequivocal ways.

It is probably best to begin the explication of his concept of bisexuality with some remarks on his general view of sexuality. In *An Autobiographical Study* (1925/1959), Freud summarizes the conception of sexuality employed in *Three Essays:*

> In the first place sexuality is divorced from its too close connection with the genitals and is regarded as a more comprehensive bodily function, having pleasure as its goal and only secondarily coming to serve the ends of reproduction. In the second place the sexual impulses are regarded as including all of those merely affectionate and friendly impulses to which usage applies the exceedingly ambiguous word "love." (p. 38; cf. Freud, 1905/1959, p. 134 and Freud, 1920b/1957, pp. 222–223)

"Sexuality," in this framework, is generally synonymous with "pleasure." Bisexuality, then, would seem to mean that the individual is able to take pleasure in both female and male objects. Indeed, Freud often uses the term in this fashion.

However, Freud also seems to differentiate sexuality into *components*, thus speaking about the *bisexual nature* of human beings rather than a human sexual nature that is manifestly diverse. For example, in *Civilization and Its Discontents*, Freud speaks of female and male wishes as constituting human desire generally (Freud, 1930/1961, p. 105, n. 3). Freud borrowed this differentiation of sexuality into "female" and "male" components from Wilhelm Fliess, using it to explain certain facets of behavior. The origin of such sexual differentiation is highly problematic, however, as Freud himself recognized. Additionally, there seems to be a physical or anatomical component to the notion of bisexuality. In *Three Essays*, Freud notes the presence of male anatomy in females and female anatomy in males. This physical aspect of bisexuality, however, is only of marginal concern to Freud. What is important is the psychical expression of bisexuality since, as Freud notes, libidinal expression does not depend on physical traits.

Freud's notion of bisexuality, therefore, means *both* the ability to distribute one's libido "either in a manifest or latent fashion, over objects of both sexes" (Freud, 1937/1961, p. 243) *and* the differentiation of sexual desire into masculine and feminine components.

Although the notion of bisexuality is raised by Freud with regard to several aspects of sexuality, he treats the issue systematically only in the case of sexual inversion.[2] He begins the discussion of inversion with a few remarks on physical hermaphroditism: "These long familiar facts of anatomy lead us to suppose that an originally bisexual disposition has, in the course of evolution, become modified into a unisexual one, leaving behind only a few traces of the sex that has become atrophied" (Freud, 1905/1953, p. 141). Although he repudiates a direct link between inversion and somatic hermaphroditism, he insists that bisexuality is involved in inversion "though we do not know in what that disposition consists, beyond anatomical structure" (Freud, 1905/1953, p. 144). As used here, the notion of bisexuality has little explanatory power. The presumption of bisexuality precludes the need for an inquiry into the origin of homosexuality, because bisexuality means "characterized by homosexual desire."

Freud also used the idea of bisexuality to explain the origin of female homosexuality. In the "Psychogenesis of a Case of Homosexuality in a Woman," Freud remarks that the question of whether the patient's inversion was inherited or acquired is shown by the entire case to be "fruitless and inappropriate (Freud, 1920/1961. p. 154). His analysis of this case reveals that several elements were operative in the woman's homosexual orientation: distress at her mother being the father's love object, a psychological retirement in favor of her mother whom she did love in spite of everything, an early preference for members of her own sex, revenge against her father, and the presumed bisexuality of all human beings. Despite his own stated reluctance to characterize homosexuality as either acquired or innate, Freud finally states that "a consideration of the material compels us to conclude that it is rather a case of congenital homosexuality which, as usual, became fixed and unmistakably manifest only in the period following puberty" (Freud, 1920/1961, pp. 169-170). He bases his conclusion—that her homosexuality was congenital—on the belief that most women seem to survive the psychical slights of their family situation without becoming homosexual. This woman's basic genital organization must have been such that the main current of her libido was apparently always homosexual (Freud, 1920/1961, p. 168). In drawing this conclusion, Freud relies on the characterization of humans as bisexual which, in this case, means a female's capacity to pursue female objects, e.g., as the result of a dominance of a masculine sex drive. Although it might appear that Freud is holding to a theory of innate object choice (a position rejected in *Three Essays*), he goes on to state that the homosexual orientation of her libido "was probably a direct and unchanged continuation of an infantile fixation on her mother" (Freud, 1920/1961, p. 168). However, it seems inappropriate to call this a case of congenital homosexuality if, in fact, sexual orientation has followed from physical attachment, however early.

THE ORIGIN OF HOMOSEXUALITY

Freud conceived the origin of the exclusive homosexual orientation generally as a blend of constitutional (i.e., biological) and psychical factors. He opposed any explanation that required a strict distinction between constitutional and acquired characteristics since "we see in practice a continual mingling and blending of what we should try to separate into a pair of opposites—namely, inherited and acquired features" (Freud, 1920/1961, p. 169). His biographer, Ernest Jones, calls attention to Freud's belief in the etiological complexity of homosexuality. Jones reports that central to Freud's understanding of homosexuality were the pronounced libidinal fixation of the child to the parent of the opposite sex and the assumption, acquired from Fliess, of the natural bisexuality of human beings (Jones, 1955, pp. 280-281).

In explaining the origin of homosexuality, Freud considered several additional factors: surrender to the mother or father in the Oedipal complex out of fear or deference; fear of castration (Freud, 1923b/1961, p. 144); an organic factor favoring passivity; a regression to a primary auto-erotic stage; obstacles in the path of ordinary sexual satisfaction (Freud,

1908b/1959, pp. 200–201); love of men following and replacing the hatred of father or a sibling (Freud, 1923a/1961, p. 37; cf. pp. 43–44); a fixation on the notion of the woman having a penis (Freud, 1908c/1959, p. 216); inversion of the subject versus inversion of the object (Freud, 1905/1953, p. 145, n. 1); the universality of homosexual libidinal attachments; a psychical stage of phallic primacy (Freud, 1925/1959, p. 37); resentment; and narcissism. Furthermore, it was necessary to distinguish among manifest, latent, aim-inhibited, and sublimated homosexuality. All these issues bear on Freud's consideration of the origin of homosexuality and make grasping the overall theory quite difficult even before trying to assess the validity of each separate claim.

Freud's first extended discussion of homosexuality occurs in the *Three Essays* (1905), under the heading "Aberrations," where it is defined as a deviation "in respect of the sexual object" (p. 136). First of all, it is important to realize that Freud is using behavior, in this case sexual attraction to members of the same sex, as a symptom of deviance. Deviance and aberration, of course, are terms that imply a pre-established norm. Thomas Szasz maintains that Freud would use such terms (including perversion) to indicate his moral disapproval (Mass, 1981, p. 38). Although the term "deviance" can imply disapproval, it is not clear that Freud intended, with his nomenclature, to make a moral pronouncement. What is clear is that, if the norm by which Freud determined that homosexuals are deviants is a moral dictum, then he has transgressed the value-free character he ascribes to psychoanalysis.[3] If, on the other hand, Freud means that the norm against which homosexuals are judged as deviant is statistical, then a statistical norm is useless, *eo ipso,* as a basis for moral judgement.

Freud recounts a "poetic fable" about how the original human beings were cut into halves, man and woman, and that sexual longing and love are the result of desire to return to this unified state. Thus, he remarks, it "comes as a great surprise" to learn that other objects of sexual desire "exist apart from this norm" (Freud, 1905/1953, p. 136). However, to the reader of Plato's *Symposium,* the original source of this fable, it comes as no surprise at all, since Plato clearly states that the gods (in their ire) had created *three* kinds of human beings: those with heterosexual desire and those with either female or male homosexual desires (Plato, pp. 542–544).

In a later essay, Freud does argue that homosexuality is not a form of degeneracy (cf. Freud, 1916–17/1953, p. 307). Inversion and degeneracy are not necessarily causally linked because (a) inversion is found in intellectually and ethically developed persons and (b) it is found in ancient civilizations at their height, sometimes as a veritable social institution. But even if homosexuality is not a form of degeneracy (see the often lurid case histories in Krafft-Ebing), one must still account for its origin.

Freud considers three explanations: either homosexuality is innate, it is acquired, or it is innate and acquired. He rejects strictly innate and strictly acquired etiologies. No evidence seemed strong enough to justify an innate sexual object preference, "the crude explanation that everyone is born with his sexual instinct attached to a particular sexual object" (Freud, 1905/1953, pp. 140-141). He believes, however, that it is difficult to explain how accidental features of a person's experience could alone explain the acquisition of inversion. Consequently, he states: "We are therefore forced to a suspicion, that the choice between "innate" and "acquired" is not an exclusive one or that it does not cover all the issues involved in inversion" (Freud, 1905/1953, p. 140). Freud does not claim to discover the cause of homosexuality; neither does he claim there is a single cause. But he does believe that psychoanalysis "has discovered the psychical mechanism of its development, and has made essential contributions to the statement of the problems involved" (Freud, 1905/1953, pp. 144-145, n. 1, added 1910). Freud dismisses the claim of some contemporary homosexual theorists that they are a "third sex," created as such by nature. (Karl Heinrich Ulrichs was a chief spokesman for this position. See Kennedy, 1981.) Freud disputes the third sex theory in his *Three Essays,* his book on Leonardo da Vinci, and in his *Introductory Lectures on Psychoanalysis* (1916-17/1953, pp. 304; 307-308): The third sex theory, he thinks, simply cannot adequately explain the phenomena of sexual life.

Freud's summary remarks on the origin of inversion are phrased largely in the negative: Neither a theory of innate predisposition nor a theory of strictly acquired inversion is satisfactory. By opposing theories of innateness, Freud is opposing widespread, traditional degeneracy theories as well as those advanced by Ulrichs (namely, that homosexual males have a feminine mind in a masculine body). Freud is to be commended for his even-handed treatment of homosexuality in *Three Essays.* Yet, it is evident that psychoanalysis cannot alone dispose of innate theories of homosexuality since, presumably, that can be accomplished only through empirical, biological studies on the nature and physiology of sexual desire.

If the theorist of sexual orientation accepts the premise of human bisexuality, it is not necessary to explain the presence of heterosexual or homosexual desire. It is important to show how one or the other form comes to dominate psychical life, a task Freud turned to in his book on Leonardo da Vinci. Freud summed up the specific stages in Leonardo's sexual development in several steps: (1) the child has a very intense erotic attachment to his mother; (2) this attachment awakes a precocious sexual desire in the child; (3) this attachment is reinforced by a distant father; (4) "After this preliminary stage a transformation sets in whose mechanism is known to us but whose motive forces we do not yet understand"

(Freud, 1910a/1957, pp. 99–100), i.e., the child's love for the mother cannot continue and succumbs to repression; (5) the child puts himself in the mother's place, identifies himself with her; (6) the child takes his own likeness as a model for his objects of love; and (7) "In this way he has become a homosexual. What he has in fact done is to slip back to autoeroticism, for the boys whom he knows and loves as he grows up are after all only substitutive figures and revivals of himself in child-hood—boys whom he loves in the way in which his mother loved him when he was a child" (Freud, 1910a/1957, p. 100).

The crucial point in Freud's theory of homosexuality is the identifica-tion of the child with the mother. It seems that an early and intense attach-ment to the mother, coupled with the lack of paternal presence, generates an identification with the mother when a later repression forces the son to withdraw from his libidinal attachment to his mother. Freud intended this as an explanation, but important questions find no answers here: why an identification with the mother takes the form of pursuing male objects, why children with identical family dynamics do not follow this pattern of sexual development, and why the later repression does not suffice to abrogate the attachment to the mother rather than figure in homosexuality.

Moreover, in "The Dissolution of the Oedipus Complex," Freud makes reference to phylogenetic concerns that contribute to the abandon-ment of Oedipal attachments (Freud, 1924/1961, p. 174). How does it happen that these are suspended or overridden in the development of a homosexual? In some ways the steps Freud outlined are not so much a description of the mechanism of homosexuality as an exclusive sexual orientation as they are the conclusions of that mechanism.

In a 1919 footnote to his treatise on da Vinci, Freud asserted "two facts" he believed were established by psychoanalysis on the etiology of homosexuality: (a) the fixation of the erotic needs on the mother and (b) "that even the most normal of persons is capable of making a homosexual object-choice, and had done so at some time in his life, and either still adheres to it in his unconscious or else protects himself against it by vigorous counter-attitudes" (Freud, 1910a/1957, p. 99, n. 2). These facts do little to elucidate the origin of homosexuality. In the first place, the Oedipus complex means that the son's erotic needs are focused on the mother. Freud has not explained why the Oedipus complex and its subse-quent repression are resolved differently for homosexuals than for heterosexuals. Secondly, the theory of bisexuality implies homosexual object choice. In one sense the presumption of constitutional bisexuality eliminates the need for any psychical theory of the origin of homosexual-ity. The physiological basis of sexual desire adequately explains its presence. If sexuality is physically constituted, then no psychical explana-tion is required; bisexuality is coeval with human existence.

In Freud's view, the apparently innate capacity for homosexual object choice becomes reinforced by a series of psychical events into a more or less exclusive psychosexual orientation. This use of the concept of bisexuality depends on the notion of *capacity*, i.e., to be attracted to females or males; it does not require having the sex of love-objects be innately predetermined. Freud's theory of inversion depends primarily on the ability of the individual to cathect objects of either biological sex (as the sexes are differentiated through anatomical and social traits), with one sex moving to the forefront of attention. It does not need recourse to a belief in the presence of masculine and feminine drives, soldered together, as Freud sometimes depicted sexual desire (cf. Freud, 1930/1961, p. 105, n. 3).

The idea of bisexuality applies further to the origin of inversion in Freud's contention that a child theorizes that his mother has a penis. In this image of the mother, the child blends characteristics of both sexes. The child suffers psychical shock when he discovers that the mother and other females do not have penises. Freud thought that the male child interpreted this discovery as evidence for the reality of castration. The shock was enough to transform some boys into homosexuals who, as adults, required a penis in their potential love objects. Nevertheless, the original attraction to feminine features persisted. Freud thought that homosexual men looked for feminine traits in order to satisfy their original cathexis, the image of the mother with a penis (Freud, 1905/1953, p. 144; Freud, 1908c/1959, p. 216). It is hard to see, then, how he could legitimately call male homosexuality a perpetual flight from women (Freud, 1905/1953, p. 145, n. 1; Freud, 1910a/1957, p. 100).[4] On the contrary, homosexuality would seem to be a continual flight to the original image of woman!

This theory about the original image of the mother-with-a-penis precludes the possibility of making a distinction between the heterosexual and homosexual orientations on the basis of anatomy and the secondary sex traits of the object. The originally cathected object does not admit of this distinction in any equivocal manner; that is, the child does not originally designate the maternal object as either male or female and desire her as such. Only later does he learn what is anatomically and socially designated as male or female.

Inversion is possible, then, because human beings have the capacity to be attracted to objects of the same sex under certain psychical or social circumstances. Object choice can be unconscious and temporary or conscious and abiding. For all the importance he attached to it, Freud's notion of bisexuality has limited explanatory power since it suggests little more than the capacity to cathect a certain kind of object. Bisexuality, then, is not so much a theory of instincts as Freud thought it was, as a theory of love-objects. Furthermore, the important question is not how to account for homosexual desire (once one admits the notion of bisexuality) but how to account for exclusive homosexual orientation, even if the explanation does not fall within the domain of psychoanalysis.

MORAL ASSESSMENT IN FREUD

There is no doubt that Freud earns our admiration for his dispassionate assessment of homosexuality. He attempts to explain homosexuality in terms of family dynamics, and in so doing he breaks with degeneracy theories (see Krafft-Ebing, 1886/1978). His letter to an American mother is often cited as an example of his benevolence toward homosexuals (Freud, 1960, pp. 423–424; cf. Ruse, 1981, pp. 377–378). Although Freud does not sketch out any implications of his sexual theories vis-à-vis social and legal practices, as Krafft-Ebing did, he generally shows tolerance for homosexuals. Nevertheless, there are aspects of the conceptual architecture of his thought that show moral evaluations at the expense of homosexuals. Certain features of psychoanalysis reflect Freud's often unarticulated but presupposed moral judgements about the proper conduct of human life, including his conception of homosexuality as a psychically fixated state, and as a state properly the object of conversion therapy.

Freud does not explicitly condemn homosexuals. Indeed he says such things as: "The most important of these perversions, homosexuality, scarcely deserves the name" (Freud, 1925/1959, p. 38). Or again: "Homosexuality is assuredly no advantage, but it is nothing to be ashamed of, no vice, no degradation; it cannot be classified as an illness; we consider it to be a variation of the sexual function, produced by a certain arrest of sexual development" (Freud, 1960, p. 423). Yet neither does he consider homosexual exclusivity as representing mature human sexual development. Even if human beings are constitutionally bisexual, even if sexuality is not primarily tied to procreation, Freud still considered heterosexuality as normal, the mark of full psychical maturity. Homosexuality remains a fixation along the expected route of psychical development. This is evident from any number of remarks Freud makes in the very same works in which he sketches his theory of the origin of homosexuality. I mention only three:

> [About the relationship of da Vinci with his mother, Freud says:] So, like all unsatisfied mothers, she took her little son in place of her husband, and by the too early maturing of his eroticism robbed him of a part of his masculinity. (Freud, 1910a/1957, p. 117)

> One of the tasks implicit in object choice is that it should find its way to the opposite sex. (Freud, 1905/1953, p. 229)

Indeed, it almost seems as though the presence of a strong father would ensure that the son made the correct decision in his choice of object, namely someone of the opposite sex. (Freud, 1910a/1957, p. 99; cf. pp. 101, 132, 133; Freud, 1905/1953, p. 137; Freud, 1920/1961, pp. 135, 148; Freud, 1925/1959, pp. 35–36)

Freud's basic model for understanding homosexuality rests on the process of repressing Oedipal desires. Fixation occurs, tying sexual gratification to the level at which the repression occurred. It is evident that Freud thought that genital sexuality ought to be heterosexual in development. However, the reason for this is not evident. There is no apparent grounding within psychoanalysis for primary genital heterosexual exclusivity as the resolution of the Oedipal complex. Thus, any view about a "normal" course of development implies moral judgements and is, properly speaking, a philosophical question. The answer requires grounded value judgements, those that cannot be made by appeal to empirical data alone. Though it is true that Freud does not treat the question of "normal" sexual development in a genuinely philosophical manner, he rests his claims about ultimate sexual development on moral assumptions.

If humans are bisexual—namely, predisposed to seek objects of both sexes—plotting a heterosexual course for normal development requires the demarcation and justification of moral criteria. To make the "normal" course appear to be the consequence of psychical research is philosophically and scientifically objectionable. It may well be that some moral system does exist that, for whatever reasons, justifies heterosexuality as the only morally appropriate sexual orientation. Freud, however, is never explicit about any such moral foundation for his sexual theories. Freud's attitude about "treating" homosexuality also implies that he morally disapproved of homosexuality insofar as he envisioned it as a psychical problem subject to remedy. On the heels of speaking about the cause of inversion, Freud discusses a cure for it. A cure would consist of a universally applicable method of converting a homosexual into a heterosexual. He does say: "Thus it would be premature, or a harmful exaggeration, if at this stage we were to indulge in hopes of a 'therapy' of inversion that could be generally used" (Freud, 1920/1961, p. 171). Yet, while Freud disclaims having such a therapy, his language implies that it is merely too early to look for one, not that it is objectionable *in se*.

One should also note the persons who initiated contact with Freud about possible treatment. In the case recorded in "Psychogenesis," it was the young woman's father, not the woman herself, who wanted to "stifle her unnatural tendencies" (Freud, 1920/1961, p. 171). In the famous letter to an American mother, Freud is willing, even though he is pessimistic about its outcome, to undertake psychoanalysis of the son at the mother's behest. What is evident in both instances is that it is a person other than the homosexual who seeks treatment for homosexuality. Freud's willingness to attempt a therapy of homosexuals (however problematic it might be), shows that he is viewing homosexuals as psychosexual failures.

The moral foundations of Freud's position on homosexuality are manifestly evident in the following discussion of conversion therapy:

> One must remember that normal sexuality also depends upon a restriction in the choice of object; in general, to undertake to convert a fully developed homosexual into a heterosexual is not much more promising than to do the reverse, only that for good practical reasons the latter is never attempted. (Freud, 1920/1961, p. 137)

Actually, the reasons are not so much practical as they are moral. There would seem to be no reason to convert heterosexuals to homosexuality since heterosexuality is the professed sexual ethic in Western civilization. Even though Freud did not believe that all homosexuals should require conversion, he actively analyzed homosexuals and, by implication, lent moral credibility to conversion therapy.

Freud does mention his humanitarian interest in homosexuals (Freud, 1910a/1957, pp. 98–99) and states that homosexuality scarcely deserves the name of perversion. He notes the achievements of homosexuals (Freud, 1905/1953, pp. 138–139). However, such statements do not mean that he sees exclusive homosexuals as fully developed human beings. His psychoanalytic investigations reveal then to be, though not strictly neurotic, psychosexually incapacitated, even if they are less incapacitated than other groups of neurotics. A guiding image of man and what he should be—a set of moral assumptions, in other words—pervades Freud's understanding of homosexuality.

It should be noted in passing that toleration can be a form of oppression. Toleration implies that, although a group of persons is engaging in some objectionable practice, it is ethically reprehensible to persecute them actively. This does not mean that the tolerated group is genuinely freed from all objection. Freud does advocate tolerance of homosexuals in his psychoanalytic writings; by itself, however, psychoanalysis cannot serve as a basis for moral philosophy.

CONCLUSION

There is no doubt that Freud saw through the eyes of his own age as he explored the labyrinth of the human psyche. Many criticisms of his work point to its cultural bias, which temporal distance permits us to discern clearly. In this paper I have shown that there are several places in Freud's writing on homosexuality that do not possess the certainty or explanatory power that Freud sought to give them. In the first place, Freud consistently noted the importance of bisexuality in the psychical order of things. Yet, if we examine the meaning of bisexuality, it appears only to signify that a human being can be attracted to a person of either sex. Freud's principal use of this notion is in the explanation of inversion. Yet, in the end, his explanation is little more than an analytic assertion. The really significant question becomes one of explaining sexual exclusivity in emotional life, a question not entirely answered by psychoanalysis. When compared to the "normal" resolution of the Oedipal situation, it seems that Freud has identified only the consequences of various repressions rather than the mechanisms of homosexual exclusivity.

Moral judgements are characterized principally by the language of *should* or *ought*. While Freud attempted a dispassionate account of homosexuality, there are many indications that he thought that human beings ought to act as exclusive heterosexuals. They ought not actively seek immature, psychically fixated, and regressive forms of sexual gratification. Conversion therapy remains a justifiable possibility no matter how difficult, despite the fact that many homosexuals are eminent and ethical persons. Freud's position depends on moral presuppositions, and these presuppositions intrude on the scientific legitimacy of his claims, particularly as he transforms the "normal" course of human development, as described by psychoanalysis, into a moral imperative.

NOTES

1. Philosophical commentators altogether bypass this notion which, because it concerns the very nature of human desire, has a pivotal status in a theory of the psyche (cf. Fromm, 1979/1980; Marcuse, 1955; Ricoeur, 1970; Roazen, 1968). With respect to empirical testing, Fisher and Greenberg (1977) have a chapter on "The Origins of Homosexuality." The authors note that Freud consistently highlighted the importance of bisexuality as the basis for the origin of homosexuality—that psychical factors work within the context of an innate, bisexual predisposition. However, they do not make further use of this notion and limit their review of the literature to family dynamics, castration anxiety, and anal fixation. In a subsequent volume, Fisher and Greenberg (1978) reprint studies on the origin of homosexuality, which altogether bypass the notion of bisexuality.

2. Sometimes one sees that Freud did not work out the implications of bisexuality even when he specifically raises the issue. For example, in "Hysterical Phantasies and their Relation to Bisexuality," he uses the concept in order to explain the masculine and feminine character of hysterical symptoms. Yet in that very same essay he says that a man's daydreams show "that all his heroic exploits are carried out and all his successes achieved only in order to please a woman and to be preferred by her to all other men" (Freud, 1908a/1959, p. 159). Such a remark hardly seems compatible with the possibility afforded by an innate disposition that favors both sexes.

3. In *The Future of an Illusion*, Freud says: "In point of fact psycho-analysis is a method of research, an impartial instrument, like the infinitesimal calculus, as it were" (Freud, 1927/1961, p. 36). Such a statement clearly puts psychoanalysis beyond the realm of subjective interpretation.

4. Though Freud was fond of repeating this point, he seemed to give evidence to the contrary. In *Three Essays*, he remarks on how inverts can retain an amount of masculine mental quality that expresses itself in attraction to feminine tastes in objects, women's clothing and behavior, and so on. This example shows Freud's conceptualization of sexual desire in terms of masculine and feminine desires soldered together to form a bisexual disposition.

REFERENCES

Fisher, S., & Greenberg, R. P. *The scientific credibility of Freud's theories and therapies.* New York: Basic Books, 1977.

Fisher, S., & Greenberg, R. P. *The scientific evaluation of Freud's theories and therapies.* New York: Basic Books, 1978.

Freud, S. [Three essays on the theory of sexuality]. (J. Strachey, Ed. and trans.). *The standard edition of the complete psychological works of Sigmund Freud* (Vol. 7). London: The Hogarth Press, 1953. (Originally published, 1905.)

Freud, S. [The sexual enlightenment of children]. *S.E., 9,* 1959. (Originally published, 1905.)

Freud, S. [Hysterical phantasies and their relation to bisexuality]. *S.E., 9,* 1959. (Originally published, 1908.) (a)

Freud, S. ["Civilized" sexual morality and modern nervous illness]. *S.E., 9,* 1959. (Originally published, 1908.) (b)

Freud, S. [On the sexual theories of children]. *S.E., 9,* 1959. (Originally published, 1908.) (c)

Freud, S. [Leonardo da Vinci and a memory of his childhood]. *S.E., 11,* 1957. (Originally published, 1910.) (a)

Freud, S. ["Wild" psycho-analysis]. *S.E., 11,* 1957. (Originally published, 1910.) (b)

Freud, S. [Introductory lectures on psycho-analysis]. *S.E., 16,* 1953. (Originally published, 1916-17.)

Freud, S. [The psychogenesis of a case of homosexuality in a woman]. *S.E., 18,* 1961. (Originally published, 1920.)

Freud, S. [The ego and the id]. *S.E., 19,* 1961. (Originally published, 1923.) (a)

Freud, S. [The infantile genital organization]. *S.E., 19,* 1961. (Originally published, 1923.) (b)

Freud, S. [The dissolution of the Oedipus complex]. *S.E., 19,* 1961. (Originally published, 1924.)

Freud, S. [Autobiographical study]. *S.E., 20,* 1959. (Originally published, 1925.)

Freud, S. [The future of an illusion]. *S.E., 21,* 1961. (Originally published, 1927.)

Freud, S. [Dostoevsky and parricide]. *S.E., 21,* 1961. (Originally published, 1928.)

Freud, S. [Civilization and its discontents]. *S.E., 21,* 1961. (Originally published, 1930.)

Freud, S. [Libidinal types]. *S.E., 21,* 1961. (Originally published, 1931.)

Freud, S. [Analysis terminable and interminable]. *S.E., 21,* 1961. (Originally published, 1937.)

Freud, S. *Letters of Sigmund Freud.* (E. L. Freud, Ed.; T. Stern & J. Stern, trans.). New York: Basic Books, 1960.

Fromm, E. *Greatness and limitations of Freud's thought.* New York: Harper & Row, 1980. (Originally published, 1979.)

Jones, E. *The life and work of Sigmund Freud* (Vol. 2). New York: Basic Books, 1955.

Kennedy, H. The "third sex" theory of Karl Heinrich Ulrichs. *Journal of Homosexuality,* 1981, 6, 103-111.

Krafft-Ebing, R. von *Psychopathia sexualis.* (F. S. Kraf, trans.). New York: Stein & Day, 1978. (Originally published, 1886.)

Marcuse, H. *Eros and civilization.* Boston: Beacon Press, 1955.

Mass, L. An interview with Thomas Szasz. *Christopher Street,* March/April 1981, 32-39.

Plato. *Symposium.* In E. Hamilton & H. Cairns (Eds.), *The collected dialogues of Plato.* Princeton, NJ: Princeton University Press, 1961.

Ricoeur, P. *Freud and philosophy: An essay on interpretation.* New Haven: Yale University Press, 1970.

Roazen, P. *Freud: Political and social thought.* New York: Knopf, 1968.

Ruse, M. Medicine as social science. *Journal of Medicine and Philosophy,* 1981, 6, 361-386.

The Dilemma of Essentiality in Homosexual Theory

Diane Richardson, PhD
University of Sheffield

ABSTRACT. A close examination of the literature on homosexuality reveals a long history of definitional crises in which the central consideration has been the maintenance of a belief in homosexuality as a state of being. This paper asks what, if anything, can be considered *essential* to the homosexual category. To answer this question, various approaches to homosexuality in the literature have been examined: as a general state of being (the person), as a state of desire (sexual orientation), as a form of behavior (sexual acts), and, more recently, as a personal identification (sexual identity). In addition, the interrelationships of these categorizations are explored.

The literature on homosexuality represents, in the main, a continuing search for answers to two questions: "Who is a homosexual?" and "What makes a person homosexual?" In searching for causal explanations, theoreticians have tacitly adopted certain assumptions about the nature of homosexuality. They assume that there exist, and probably always have existed, two groups of people: those who are homosexual and those who are not. In such assumptions the term *homosexual* is used to refer to a core and enduring aspect of being of a group of individuals.

In recent years, however, studies of homosexuality by sociologists and social historians have suggested that the view that individuals are sexually either one essence or another is specific to history and culture (e.g., Foucault, 1979; McIntosh, 1968; Plummer, 1975, 1981a, 1981b; Weeks, 1981, 1982). There is some disagreement among these writers as to precisely when the idea of the homosexual person emerged. Their general belief, however, is that, in Europe at least, the use of the term homosexual to designate a certain type of person is a relatively recent one.

Diane Richardson lectures in the Department of Sociological Studies at the University of Sheffield, Sheffield S10 2TN, South Yorkshire, England (Reprint requests may be addressed to her there.) She is joint author and editor with John Hart of *The Theory and Practice of Homosexuality*, and is currently conducting research into the development of sexual identity.

79

This paper is mainly devoted to discussion of the roles that medicine, psychiatry, and psychology have played in the development of the idea of the homosexual. I shall begin, therefore, by examining the ways in which homosexuality has traditionally been conceptualized within the scientific literature, as a *state of sexual being.*

HOMOSEXUALITY AS A STATE OF BEING: THE HOMOSEXUAL PERSON

The medical and psychiatric discourse on sexuality has been extremely important in the establishment of the homosexual category. The objectification of homosexuality has created a concern for explaining the homosexual "condition." Foucault (1979) recognizes this in underlining the emergence of a "scientific" interest in sex during the late eighteenth and early nineteenth centuries, the crucially important period for the development of categorizations associated with the intrinsic sexuality of *individuals* rather than with particular sexual *acts.* Previously, the legal and moral discourse on sex, he argues, focussed on homosexual *practice* (i.e., sodomy) rather than on the homosexual *condition* of the individual. Apart from its role in the establishment of a homosexual category, the medical and psychiatric discourse on sexuality has also been particularly important in the elaboration of specific criteria for the application of such categories to individuals.

At least initially, it would seem that it was not so much the concept of sexual orientation but of gender inversion that dominated medical and psychiatric theorizing about homosexuality. Attempts to "explain" homosexuality emphasized congenital anomalies in biological sex rather than anomalies in the nature and direction of sexual desire. This was a reflection of the centrality of biological sex in defining sexual identity. During the nineteenth and early twentieth centuries, no clear distinctions were made among biological sex, femininity and masculinity, and sexual orientation (Marshall, 1981). Theoreticians did, however, differ in the meaning they gave to the term *inversion,* particularly in considering male homosexuals to be "essentially" female and female homosexuals to be "essentially" male. Although it has been argued that the clinical categories of transvestism and transsexuality were not clearly differentiated until the 1950s (King, 1981), some writers had earlier distinguished between: (1) inversion as a preference for the social sex-role of the opposite sex, whether it consisted only of cross-dressing (transvestism) or a fundamental identification with the opposite sex (transsexualism); and (2) inversion of the direction of the sexual "impulse" or "drive" toward an individual of the same sex. Ellis (e.g., 1897/1915, 1928) and Hirschfeld (e.g., 1938) made this distinction by pointing out that a preference for homosexual relationships did not necessarily imply a preference for the social sex-role of the opposite sex, or vice versa.

The scientific literature of the early twentieth century also distinguished between inversion and perversion. This distinction was between homosexuality as a congenital condition involving a permanent inversion of the sexual impulse, and homosexuality as an immoral and perverse sexual act. This distinction between homosexuality as a state of being (i.e., inversion) and homosexuality as a form of behavior (i.e., perversion) was complicated, however, by the effort within the medical and psychiatric literature to conceptualize homosexuality more specifically as a *state of sexual desire,* that is, in terms of sexual orientation and sexual object choice.

HOMOSEXUALITY AS A STATE OF SEXUAL BEING: DESIRE AND BEHAVIOR

A number of developments within psychology and medicine contributed to the redefinition of the homosexual category, increasingly associating it with sexual desire and behavior. At the turn of the century, Freud (1905/1953) theorized an innate, unconscious sexual capacity to be attracted to females and males. Freud, following in the footsteps of writers such as Krafft-Ebing, endorsed the view that the human infant is congenitally bisexual. The concept of bisexuality was based on evidence that embryological remnants of the anatomical characteristics of the opposite sex, however rudimentary, are present in all individuals. Freud applied this to the individual's mental life, suggesting that remnants of psychological characteristics of the opposite sex also remained in the adult individual. Freud's theory of psychosexual development, of course, embraces an essentialist vision of biological sex and assumes as well that heterosexuality is the normal outcome of libidinal development. Within the theoretical framework of bisexuality, Freud was able to propose that sexual attraction to both sexes was present in every individual throughout the life span. He asserted that, in the case of heterosexuals, attraction to an individual of the same sex was a dormant and unconscious force that could nevertheless influence social behavior. The term used to describe this was latent homosexuality.

The putative existence of homosexual attraction in every individual, whether conscious or unconscious, was explained by Freud in terms of his assumption that there exists in all human beings dormant and unconscious psychological characteristics of the opposite sex. In one sense, then, while he averred the existence of the bisexual nature of human beings, Freud's formulation of homosexual attraction incorporated the concept of sexual inversion by suggesting that homosexual tendencies in men reflect an inherently "feminine," and in women an inherently "masculine," aspect of their personalities.

Throughout the psychoanalytic discourse, homosexuality was discussed in terms of libidinal development. It was associated with sexual attraction to individuals as sexual (love) objects (e.g., Deutsch, 1932; Freud, 1931/1961, 1933/1964) and with actual erotic acts (e.g., Klein, 1932).

Behaviorism provided a contrasting theoretical approach to the idea of the homosexual. Indeed, during the 1930s and 1940s, behaviorism was the dominant theoretical perspective within English and American psychology. As a conceptual framework its emphasis was on the categorization of behavior rather than particular states of mind. Increasingly, then, the idea of the homosexual became associated with certain forms of overt sexual behavior.

In addition to these developments, there occurred a shift in emphasis away from the view of sexual desire as an undifferentiated instinctual force. This gave rise to the belief that sexual desire was organized as a relatively fixed orientation to either males or females. It was this organization of desire as a particular sexual orientation that identified an individual as either a homosexual or a heterosexual. Individual differences in the type and frequency of sexual behavior could be accounted for not only in terms of differences in sexual drive or instinct but, more importantly, in terms of fundamental differences between individuals in the *direction and aim* of desire.

The Kinsey studies of male and female sexuality (Kinsey, Pomeroy, & Martin, 1948; Kinsey, Pomeroy, Martin, & Gebhard, 1953) showed a widespread occurrence of homosexual feelings and activity. They also showed that, in some individuals, sexual preferences could and did change over the life span. Such evidence posed a serious challenge to the view that individuals could be categorized as homosexuals or heterosexuals, a view that Kinsey rejected. Here, then, is the first in a series of *definitional crises* in the scientific discourse on homosexuality.

The conceptualization of homosexuality as a pathological condition affecting only a small percentage of people, and the evidence that homosexual interests are common to many people, poses a paradox where homosexual feelings and behavior are associated with a discrete homosexual category.[1] A variety of theoretical constructs were invoked in attempting to deal with this paradox and thus to preserve the notion of homosexuality and heterosexuality as distinct states of being. For example, while psychoanalytic explanations appealed to the idea of the inherent bisexuality of all human beings, other theories employed a variety of contrasting concepts in describing homosexuality: real vs. pseudo, incidental vs. exclusive, acquired vs. congenital, genuine vs. situational, chosen vs. determined, and temporary vs. permanent. There were also inverts vs. normals. Such contrasts, especially the concept of real vs. apparent homosexuality, make it theoretically possible to account for the widespread occurrence of homosexual behavior while preserving a belief in homosexuality as an essential state of being.

The distinction between homosexual behavior and homosexual persons—between doing and being—also made it possible for theoreticians to "diagnose" as homosexual individuals who had no overt homosexual experience. Such individuals were typically described as repressing their homosexual desires either consciously, for fear of stigmatization or punishment, or unconsciously. In the latter case they were called "latent" homosexuals.

Latent homosexuality, as a concept, implies that certain individuals may be unaware of their homosexual desires and only come to recognize that they are homosexual after prolonged psychoanalysis. The category of latent homosexuality, therefore, can include persons who have experienced neither homosexual activity nor fantasies and who do not consider themselves to be homosexual. The addition of this category constitutes a second definitional crisis in the scientific literature on homosexuality. It leads to the consideration of research studies that have emphasized the individual's *self-categorization* as homosexual (rather than medical or behavioral assessments) as the essential feature of homosexuality.

HOMOSEXUALITY AS A STATE OF PERSONAL IDENTIFICATION

Particularly important in the development of theoretical conceptualizations of homosexuality was the concern in the 1960s and 1970s with the idea of sexual identity. This idea took shape as part of the growing sociological literature on (primarily male) homosexuality and the social effects of labeling individuals as homosexuals (e.g., Schofield, 1965). It also reflected social and political changes that were occurring in Europe and America during this period, in particular, the emergence of the feminist and gay liberation movements. It was a period of significant change in attitudes toward homosexuality by homosexual men and women. Their emphasis on sexual identity was expressed in their concern with coming out, that is, with openly declaring oneself to be "gay."

The process of self-labeling as bisexual, heterosexual or homosexual reflects a concern with "being" rather than "doing." It is, however, a different form of "being" than previously conceived, where the fundamental question was what caused a person to develop into a homosexual. The new question is: How does the state of being a person who *self-identifies as homosexual* come about?

These questions appear similar but are distinct. The former question stems from an approach to homosexuality that Plummer (1981a) calls the "sexual orientation model." Research based on this approach tries to isolate specific etiological factors that supposedly cause a person to become homosexual. It does not examine the process of identity formation. Homosexuality is defined in terms of sexual orientation, which is assumed to be a relatively enduring psychological characteristic of the individual, largely determined in early life. (For a critical review of theories of causation, see Richardson, 1981a.)

The concept of sexual identity receives little attention in theories that adopt the sexual orientation approach to homosexuality. In that approach it is assumed that sexual self-awareness inevitably emerges through a process of maturation. The individual's sexual identity is merely a cognitive "realization" of the "true" sexual nature of the self. Sexual identity, then, bears a close relationship to sexual desire. It is assumed that, as a homosexual, one will experience erotic attraction to the same sex and will thereby come to identify as "a homosexual."

The question of how a person comes to make this identification stems from an approach to understanding homosexuality that Plummer (1981a) calls the "identity construct model." Here the aim of research is not to produce causal explanations of sexual orientation, but rather to investigate the developmental processes wherein individuals construct and maintain a particular sexual identity as bisexual, heterosexual, or homosexual. Contrary to the sexual orientation model, in the construct model sexual identity is not *assumed to be* a core and enduring characteristic of the individual that is fixed in early childhood. Rather, it is considered to be constructed and maintained through the process of social interaction.

The constructionist approach acknowledges the need to distinguish between feelings of desire for homosexual experiences, whether acted upon or not, and the process whereby individuals take on a particular identity as a homosexual. Therefore, the homosexual identity is the result of the social and personal categorization of sexual feelings and experiences as indicative of being a certain type of person (Richardson, 1981b). Within such a framework it is important to examine the social and historical context in which homosexual acts occur and homosexual identities develop.

Of specific relevance to this paper is the way in which the idea of the homosexual, as embodied in the scientific literature, may influence the process of identity formation in the individual. The increasing association of the homosexual category with feelings of sexual desire for and sexual activity with a partner of the same sex means that each experience could be interpreted by individuals as indicating that they are homosexual. Yet, although there would seem, on the basis of the Kinsey statistics alone, to be an enormous potential for such interpretations, most individuals who experience homosexual attraction do not take on a homosexual identity. If definitions of homosexuality as sexual acts and feelings can be seen as increasing the possibility of a homosexual identification, then the lack of precision resulting from these definitions paradoxically enables individuals to avoid self-categorization as homosexuals.

Attention has been paid to the meanings individuals associate with their sexual behavior in an attempt to understand the development and maintenance of a sexual identity. This approach has provided a challenge to the view that homosexuals constitute a homogeneous category of persons subject to identical motivations. Researchers such as Dank (1971), Plummer (1975), Ponse (1978), Richardson and Hart (1981), and Weinberg (1978) have described the diversity that exists within the female and male homosexual populations in the meanings and significance attributed to a homosexual identity.

There are studies that stress the similarities between homosexual and heterosexual groups. For instance, Gagnon and Simon (1973; Simon, 1967) believe that both heterosexual and homosexual women are subject to a common socialization as women, and that their learning of the female role is more significant than sexual orientation in their sexual relationships. More recently, Masters and Johnson (1979) have described the similarity of sexual response in heterosexual and homosexual groups.

The emergence of the view that homosexuality is socially constructed as a stable and central identity (instead of being a product of nature) which has diverse meanings, and the acknowledgement of the similarity between heterosexuals and homosexuals, have challenged the belief that there are two discrete categories of individuals. We are faced with a new definitional crisis to which theoreticians of homosexuality must respond.

THE HOMOSEXUAL CATEGORY: DESIRING, DOING, AND BEING

We have now reached a point where, theoretically at least, it is possible to consider homosexual desire, homosexual behavior, and homosexual identity as separate categories. The previous theoretical distinction between homosexual *persons* and homosexual *acts* is confusing because it is based on a definition of homosexuality as sexual preference. Sexual fantasy and practice, however, is inevitably the major, if not the sole, criterion by which sexual orientation might be inferred. The constructionist approach to sexual identity, on the other hand, has made possible a clear conceptual distinction between the state of being homosexual (defined in terms of self-identification) and homosexual behavior. This distinction has been supported by several studies (e.g., Bell & Weinberg, 1978; Ponse, 1978; Weinberg, 1978) that have indicated that there is no necessary relationship between a particular pattern of sexual behavior and the taking on of a particular sexual identity. In the constructionist approach what is crucial is the meaning that individuals ascribe to their sexual feelings, activity, and relationships.

The distinction between sexual identity and sexual behavior is another form of the doing/being distinction that pervades the literature on homosexuality. It does not immediately weaken the assumption that there are different types of sexual beings. A stronger challenge to that assumption is the putative relationship between sexual identity and sexual desire. Central to scientific and popular explanations of homosexuality has been the belief that homosexual identity develops naturally from a permanent and underlying homosexual orientation.

The alternative theoretical perspective, that sexual identities are socially constructed and maintained and thus potentially open to change, acknowledges the possibility that a person may identify as homosexual at any stage of the life cycle (Richardson & Hart, 1981). The likelihood of this identification occurring depends, according to this view, on the social and personal significance a homosexual identity would have for the individual. It would not depend on anything fundamental to the organization of sexual desire.

The view of homosexual identity as socially constructed would seem to pose a fundamental challenge to the belief that persons are essentially heterosexual or homosexual. If, however, sexual identity and sexual orientation were to be considered independent factors, it should be theoretically possible for individuals to change their sexual identity while retaining an underlying sexual orientation. Labeling theory, in making a distinction between primary and secondary deviance, encompasses the idea that there may be fundamental differences between individuals in sexual preference (primary deviance) and the idea of social labeling of such preferences in the creation of lifestyles and identities (secondary deviance).

More specifically, Plummer (1981a), using a symbolic interactionist perspective, has suggested that there may be "a very real separation" between the development of a sexual orientation and the development of a sexual identity. In his view, orientations are probably established in childhood even though individuals may remain completely unaware of what their orientation is. In such cases, their sexual identity as "essentially" bisexual, heterosexual or homosexual would be "out of harmony" with their underlying orientation (cf., the concept of latent homosexuality).

Plummer acknowledges that individuals may differ in the degree to which an underlying sexual orientation may be "restricted and rigid" or "open and flexible." Still, his view lends support to the essentiality of sexual orientation, if not of sexual identity. Also, Plummer's view retains the idea that different types of sexual beings can be identified by differences in the organization of sexual desire. However, his suggestion that people may never become aware of their underlying sexual and emotional proclivities poses important theoretical and methodological difficulties. How is it possible to ascertain an unconscious orientation? If it is not possible, the usefulness of his conceptualization for a more precise understanding of how sexual desire, sexual behavior, and sexual identity are interrelated is questionable.

An alternative to Plummer's view is one that raises the question of how sexual orientation may develop alongside the development of identity. We need to recognize, of course, that one or more redefinitions of sexual identity may occur over the life span. This does not, however, preclude the possibility that cognitive "realizations" may act as organizing influences on both sexual desire and sexual behavior. This alternative view does not ignore or deny the possibility that, prior to the process of sexual self-awareness, the child or adolescent may experience feelings of sexual and emotional attraction or may engage in such acts, which for certain individuals may have later significance for sexual identity formation. Rather, this view suggests that such feelings and acts are selected and organized as a "unity"—as a particular sexual orientation—through the cognitive process of sexual identification as bisexual, heterosexual, homosexual, or asexual.

Such an analysis can account for those individuals who identify themselves as homosexuals but recall no prior existence of homosexual attraction or desire. For example, in a sexually polarized world individuals may assume that because they do not have a "relationship" with a person of the opposite sex, they are not attractive to the opposite sex. They further may assume that this means they must be attracted to individuals of the same sex, and therefore are homosexual. In this case, homosexual feelings of attraction and homosexual acts may be evoked as a *consequence* of a homosexual self-evaluation (Richardson & Hart, 1981).

We have now reached an important stage in theorizing about homosexuality. After a series of definitional crises in which the central consideration has been the belief in homosexuality as a permanent and universal state of being, we must confront the question of what is *essential* to the idea of the homosexual. There are indications in the research that the individual's sexual identity may undergo redefinition during the life span (e.g, Ponse, 1978; Troiden, 1980). Similarly, patterns of sexual behavior do not necessarily remain habitual and unchanged. Kinsey et al. (1948; 1953) suggested that it is perfectly possibly for an exclusively heterosexual pattern of behavior to be exchanged for an exclusively homosexual one. In the face of evidence of developmental variability, we must re-examine the belief that we are essentially heterosexual or homosexual. But even this questioning may not pose too fundamental a challenge to an essentialist view of sexuality.

Although Kinsey documented the diverse nature of human sexual experience and rejected the notion that there were basically two types of sexual beings, he did assume the existence of a basic sexual drive that required release through particular sexual outlets. Other writers have more recently questioned not only the relevance of assuming the "natural" existence of heterosexuals and homosexuals, but also the assumption that sexual desire, and its expression in sexual activity, is a transhistorical and transcultural phenomenon (e.g., Gagnon & Simon, 1973; Foucault, 1979; Lacan, 1977). Rather than merely assuming that the motivation to be sexual exists in us all as part of a biological endowment, they raise this question: Is sexual desire a universal experience?

Weeks (1981, 1982) believes that this challenge to sexual essentiality comes from three theoretical approaches: the interactionist, the psychoanalytic, and the discursive. He notes that, within an interactionist framework, the work of Gagnon and Simon (1973; Gagnon, 1973) has been particularly significant. Basically, in abandoning a "naturalistic" view of a compelling instinctual drive, they have suggested that not only is the meaning and object of sexual desire socially constructed, but also the experience of desire itself. Because the body has a repertoire of gratifications, including a biological capacity for orgasm, Gagnon and Simon believe that the reason an individual repeatedly seeks out one of these bodily potentialities for pleasure (i.e., comes to *desire* that particular experience) will depend upon the relative importance and meaning the individual ascribes to these potentialities. These meanings derive from the particular social, cultural, and historical context in which the individual develops. Thus, as Gagnon (1973) points out, although the human infant demonstrates a capacity for orgasm, it is unclear whether this experience has a specifically sexual meaning for the infant, or whether, by virtue of orgasmic capacity alone, the infant would seek orgasmic gratification. Simon and Gagnon imply that the body's repertoire of gratifications, including the sexual, have no governing laws but are selected and organized as a sexual unity through sexual scripts. These scripts, borrowing from the culture, provide plans and goals which motivate, shape, and coordinate sexual conduct.[2]

The discursive challenge to essentiality is characterized by the writings of Michel Foucault (e.g., Foucault, 1979; Sheridan, 1980). Foucault, however, rejects both the notion of sexual desire as a biological given with its own laws and constraints and the idea that this "essential reality" has been concealed or repressed by the discourse on sexuality as shaped by religion, law, medicine, and psychiatry. Foucault argues that the discourse on sexuality, taking the "sexual" as its object of knowledge and commentary, has produced an artificial unity derived from the body and its pleasures, a compilation of bodily sensations, feelings, experiences, and actions brought together under the unifying principle of sexual desire. Moreover, Foucault states that this fictional unity has been allowed to function as a causal principle, as the motive to be sexual.

Foucault locates the rise of this unified notion of sexuality in the eighteenth century. He believes that over the last two hundred years, and particularly since the emergence of "scientific" discourse on sexuality, sex has come to be seen not as one potential (and harmless) source of pleasure, nor as a function to be carried out in order to maintain the species, but as a fundamental and inherent aspect of both the structure of society and of the individual psyche.

CONCLUSION

The history of homosexuality as a concept has been dominated by the medical and psychiatric discourse on sex, in which homosexuality has been defined as an inherent aspect of both the structure of society and of individual personality. A close examination of this discourse reveals a history of definitional crises that have posed a threat to the idea of essentiality. The crises have arisen in deciding what is essential to the homosexual category: Is it a particular pattern of sexual behavior? Is it a particular sexual identity? Is it an underlying orientation? The belief that we are "essentially" heterosexual or homosexual has nevertheless remained an extremely powerful one.

I have tried to demonstrate that we have now reached a stage in theorizing about homosexuality where we can no longer continue to dismiss the theoretical difficulties that a view of an essential sexuality poses. A fundamental reappraisal of theoretical beliefs about homosexuality is required. Recent discussions within various theoretical frameworks, as adumbrated in this paper, question the assumption that we are "essentially" heterosexual or homosexual as well as the basic concept of sexual desire. As theoreticians, our most immediate task is to explore the implications of these questions in order to understand and investigate more fully the complexities of human sexual experience.

NOTES

1. Previously, this inconsistency was avoided by defining homosexuality in terms of biological sex rather than as sexual orientation and by employing the distinction between inversion and perversion.

2. The psychoanalytic school of thought, as expressed in the work of Jacques Lacan and his followers, has posed a similar challenge to traditional beliefs about sexuality (e.g., Lacan, 1977; Mitchell, 1974). Lacan implies that desire is not a natural energy that is repressed; it is desire for a symbolic and powerful position that is instigated by the "law of the father," castration anxiety, and the entry of the child into the sphere of language and symbolic meaning.

REFERENCES

Bell, A. P., & Weinberg, M. S. *Homosexualities: A study of diversity among men and women.* London: Mitchell-Beazley, 1978.

Dank, B. Coming out in the gay world. *Psychiatry,* 1971, *34,* 180-197.

Deutsch, H. On female homosexuality. *Psychoanalytic Quarterly,* 1932, *1,* 484-510.

Ellis, H. *Sexual inversion* (3rd ed.). In *Studies in the psychology of sex* (Vol. 2). Philadelphia: F. A. Davis, 1915. (Originally published, 1897,)

Ellis, H. *Eonism and other supplementary studies.* In *Studies in the psychology of sex* (Vol. 7). Philadelphia: F. A. Davis, 1928.

Foucault, M. *The history of sexuality* (Vol. 1). London: Allen Lane, 1979.

Freud, S. [Three essays on the theory of sexuality.] *S.E.*, 7, London: Hogarth Press, 1953. (Originally published, 1905.)

Freud, S. [Female sexuality.] *S.E.*, 21, 1961. (Originally published, 1931.)

Freud, S. [Femininity.] *S.E.*, 22, 1964. (Originally published, 1933.)

Gagnon, J. H. Scripts and the coordination of sexual conduct. In J. K. Cole & R. Dienstbier (Eds.), *Nebraska Symposium on Motivation,* (Vol. 21). Lincoln: University of Nebraska Press, 1973.

Gagnon, J. H., & Simon, W. *Sexual conduct: The social sources of human sexuality.* London: Hutchinson, 1973.

Hirschfeld, M. *Sexual anomalies and perversions.* London: Encyclopaedic Press, 1938.

King, D. Gender confusions; psychological and psychiatric conceptions of transvestism and transsexualism. In K. Plummer (Ed.), *The making of the modern homosexual.* London: Hutchinson, 1981.

Kinsey, A. C., Pomeroy, W. B., & Martin, C. E. *Sexual behavior in the human male.* Philadelphia & London: W. B. Saunders & Co., 1948.

Kinsey, A. C., Pomeroy, W. B., Martin, C. E., & Gebhard, P. H. *Sexual behavior in the human female.* Philadelphia & London: W. B. Saunders, 1953.

Klein, M. *The psychoanalysis of children.* London: Hogarth Press, 1932.

Lacan, J. *The four fundamental concepts of psychoanalysis.* London: Hogarth Press, 1977.

McIntosh, M. The homosexual role. *Social Problems,* 1968, *16,* 182-192.

Marshall, J. Pansies, perverts and macho men: Changing conceptions of male homosexuality. In K. Plummer (Ed.), *The making of the modern homosexual.* London: Hutchinson, 1981.

Masters, W. M., & Johnson, V. E. *Homosexuality in perspective.* Boston: Little, Brown, 1979.

Mitchell, J. *Psychoanalysis and feminism.* London: Allen Lane, 1974.

Plummer, K. *Sexual stigma: An interactionist account.* London: Routledge & Kegan Paul, 1975.

Plummer, K. Homosexual categories: Some research problems in the labelling perspective of homosexuality. In K. Plummer (Ed.), *The making of the modern homosexual.* London: Hutchinson, 1981. (a)

Plummer, K. Going gay: Identities, life cycles and lifestyles in the male gay world. In J. Hart & D. Richardson (Eds.), *The theory and practice of homosexuality.* London: Routledge & Kegan Paul, 1981. (b)

Ponse, B. *Identities in the lesbian world: The social construction of self.* Westport, CT: Greenwood Press, 1978.

Richardson, D. Theoretical perspectives on homosexuality. In J. Hart & D. Richardson, *The theory and practice of homosexuality.* London: Routledge & Kegan Paul, 1981. (a)

Richardson, D. Lesbian identities. In J. Hart & D. Richardson, *The theory and practice of homosexuality.* London: Routledge & Kegan Paul, 1981. (b)

Richardson, D., & Hart, J. The development and maintenance of a homosexual identity. In J. Hart & D. Richardson, *The theory and practice of homosexuality.* London: Routledge & Kegan Paul, 1981.

Schofield, M. *Sociological aspects of homosexuality.* London: Longman, 1965.

Sheridan, A. *Michel Foucault: The will to truth.* London: Tavistock, 1980.

Simon, W. The lesbians: A preliminary overview. In J. H. Gagnon & W. Simon (Eds.), *Sexual deviance.* New York: Harper & Row, 1967.

Troiden, R. R. Variables related to the acquisition of a gay identity. *Journal of Homosexuality,* 1980, 4, 383-392.

Weeks, J. Discourse, desire and sexual deviance: Some problems in a history of homosexuality. In K. Plummer, (Ed.), *The making of the modern homosexual.* London: Hutchinson, 1981.

Weeks, J. *Sex, politics and society.* London: Longman, 1982.

Weinberg, T. S. On "doing" and "being" gay: Sexual behavior and homosexual male self-identity." *Journal of Homosexuality,* 1978, 4, 143-156.

Homosexual Identity Formation as a Developmental Process

Henry L. Minton, PhD
Gary J. McDonald, MA, PhD (cand.)
University of Windsor

ABSTRACT. Homosexual identity is conceptualized as a life-spanning developmental process that eventually leads to personal acceptance of a positive gay self-image and a coherent personal identity. Habermas' theory of ego development is utilized to provide a synthesis and understanding of the literature on the construction and maintenance of the homosexual identity. It is concluded that the homosexual identity generally emerges in a three-stage process in which the person progresses from: (1) an egocentric interpretation of homoerotic feelings to (2) an internalization of the normative, conventional assumptions about homosexuality to (3) a post-conventional phase in which societal norms are critically evaluated and the positive gay identity is achieved and managed. Developmental tasks associated with each stage are outlined in terms of their ego-integrative functions. Although the stages in the process of homosexual identity formation are theoretically the same for females and males, because of the paucity of research on the homosexual identity in females, this paper deals chiefly with males.

Personal identity encompasses the ascribed, achieved, and adopted roles characteristically enacted by the individual (de Levita, 1965). Sexual orientation is one of the roles that comprise personal identity. Other role-specific identities are associated with gender, parenthood, occupation, ethnicity, and social class. In the context of this paper, homosexual identity formation is conceptualized as a life-span, developmental process that is part of the general maturational process of achieving a coherent sense of personal identity.

As conceived in the present analysis, two developmental tasks can be delineated in the formation of the homosexual identity. First, there is the

Henry L. Minton is Professor of Psychology, University of Windsor, Windsor, Ontario. Gary J. McDonald is a doctoral student in the Department of Psychology at the same University. Earlier versions of this paper were presented by the senior author at the annual meetings of the Canadian Psychological Association, Calgary, June 1980; and of the American Psychological Association, Los Angeles, August 1981. Reprint requests should be addressed to Henry L. Minton, Department of Psychology, University of Windsor, Windsor, Ontario, N9B 3P4.

process of forming a homosexual self-image—one that reaches completion with the individual's acceptance of a positive gay identity. Once a gay identity has been attained, the second task is that of identity management. Identity management refers to the extent to which the person chooses to be identified as gay by self or others in interpersonal or public situations. Both tasks are interrelated and require the person to integrate all aspects of personal identity. Successful completion of the tasks leads to an identity synthesis; conversely, failure will leave personal identity fragmented.

For the purposes of the present analysis, it is important to differentiate homosexual identity from homosexual behavior. Richardson and Hart (1981) have made this distinction: "[M]any people engage in same-sex acts without necessarily indentifying as homosexual. Alternatively, a person may not have actually engaged in same-sex sexual acts, although they would define themselves as homosexual" (p. 73).

Consistent with the symbolic interactionist perspective, as explicated by Plummer (1975), and with the position of Richardson and Hart (1981), our focus in this paper is on how the person interprets his or her acts and feelings and how such interpretations eventually contribute to a crystallized and stable adult homosexual orientation. We endorse the symbolic interactionist position that the individual, immersed in a particular social context, actively selects and ascribes meanings to personal experience. These eventually contribute to the development and maintenance of an integrated and positive self-image. The conceptual framework provided by symbolic interactionism illuminates the existence of all sexual orientations.

THE CONCEPT OF PERSONAL IDENTITY

The notion of personal identity refers to the unity, consistency, and continuity of the individual's self-perception (Breger, 1974; de Levita, 1965; Erikson, 1959). Identity, as a concept, is akin to the idea of self— that is, the way in which the individual perceives, knows, and feels about the self. After the individual attains an integrated sense of self he or she feels a sense of unity—an awareness of personal identity. Identity emerges from the various selves the individual has achieved along a developmental continuum: the bodily self of infancy, the "good boy" or "good girl" of childhood, and the idealistic self of adolescence (Breger, 1974).

The ability to attain an integrated sense of self emerges during adolescence. In the pre-adolescent period the child lacks wholeness (Breger, 1974). To experience a sense of who one is, who one was, and who one will be requires the ability for introspection.

Erikson (1950, 1959, 1968) stated that the process of identity formation involves an interaction between the personality dynamics of the individual and the individual's context. Thus, on the one hand, a person's consistency over time is shaped by the way he or she goes about satisfying needs and developing preferences; on the other hand, a person's identity is dependent on the acknowledgement provided by significant others and by society. As Erikson (1959) states: "[T]he term identity expresses . . . a mutual relation in that it connotes both a persistent sameness within oneself . . . and a persistent sharing of some kind of essential character with others" (p. 102).

The concept of identity is part of various theoretical traditions: analytic ego psychology (Erikson), cognitive developmental psychology (Piaget, Kohlberg), and symbolic interaction theory (Mead, Parsons). Habermas (1979) has developed a theory of ego development that borrows from these three traditions. According to Habermas, identity formation depends on the development of the individual's ego functions, including cognitive, linguistic, affective, motivational, and social interactive processes. He identified four stages of ego development: symbiotic, egocentric, sociocentric-objectivistic, and universalistic. Habermas does not believe that these stages follow a strict linear progression because regression can occur during the transition from one stage to the next.

Habermas' conception of ego development assumes a reciprocal interaction between the individual and societal beliefs and values. After first incorporating and then critically evaluating societal beliefs and values, the individual eventually achieves an integrated personal identity. Habermas' model also assumes that a theory (in this case, a theory of personal identity) should serve to articulate the ideological basis of knowledge and, in so doing, "emancipate" people from oppressive ideologies (see Habermas, 1971; Minton, Note 1, Note 2). To foster the process of personal identity formation, it is necessary to understand how it is related to social and political ideology.

In this paper, Habermas' model of ego development is applied to the process of homosexual identity formation and management over the life span. This model, we believe, provides a framework for interpreting and unifying the apparently disparate theories of homosexual identity development.

HABERMAS' MODEL AND HOMOSEXUAL IDENTITY DEVELOPMENT

Over the past decade there have been a number of theoretical analyses and empirical studies of homosexual identity formation (e.g., Cass, 1979; Coleman, 1981/82; Dank, 1971; de Monteflores & Schultz, 1978; Hencken & O'Dowd, 1977; Lee, 1977; McDonald, 1982; Plummer, 1975;

Schafer, 1976; Troiden, 1979; Kooden, Morin, Riddle, Rogers, Sang, & Strassburger, Note 3). Among these, Cass, Coleman, Dank, Hencken and O'Dowd, Lee, Plummer, and Troiden have proposed models that include sequential stages of development. What these models have in common is the conceptualization of a three-stage process: (1) the egocentric interpretation of homosexual feelings, (2) the internalization of the normative assumptions about homosexuality, and (3) the achievement of a positive gay identity. This tripartite conception of homosexual identity formation is consistent with the Habermas (1979) model of ego development. The way in which the various theories of homosexual identity development can be incorporated into Habermas' model is shown in Table 1.

The Symbiotic and Egocentric Stages

Habermas' (1979) first stage of ego development, the symbiotic stage, occurs in the first year of life. At this level, the child does not develop any consistent sense of bodily self and therefore has no sense of the self apart from the social and physical environment. At the second, or egocentric stage, the child is able to differentiate between self and environment. The demarcation of self and environment, however, is not decentered; that is, "[T]he child cannot perceive, understand, and judge situations independently of its own standpoint—it thinks and acts from a body-bound perspective" (Habermas, 1979, p. 101). The child has attained a "natural" identity or sense of separation from its surroundings that is based on the capacity of its body to produce environmental effects. During this period the child acquires a sense of his or her own uniqueness as a person. It is possible that the primitive awakening of homoerotic sentiment occurs at this stage.

The egocentric stage, as it relates to the formation of the homosexual identity, appears in both Plummer's (1975) and Troiden's (1979) concept of "sensitization."[1] Plummer defines sensitization as "those first conscious and semi-conscious moments in which an individual comes to perceive of himself potentially as a homosexual" (p. 135). This belief in the initial awareness of a homosexual identity does not assume that the person understands the label, "homosexual." As Troiden implies, it is at the egocentric stage that the individual has experiences that, in the future, may serve as the bases for labeling the self homosexual.

According to Plummer, there are several experiences that could occur during the sensitization period and lead to a homosexual identification. These include a person engaging in genital sex (such as masturbation), forming a strong emotional attachment, or daydreaming about erotic encounters with a member of the same sex. The individual's perception of the self as inadequately feminine or masculine may also serve as a

Table 1. Theoretical stages of homosexual identity formation as compared with Habermas' stages of ego development

Habermas' Stages of Ego Development	Stages of Homosexual Identity						
	Plummer	Troiden	Lee	Hencken & O'Dowd	Dank	Coleman	Cass
1. Symbiotic (lack of identity)							
2. Egocentric (natural identity)	Sensitization	Sensitization				Pre-coming out	
3. Sociocentric-Objectivistic (role identity)	Signification	Dissociation and signification	Signification	Awareness	Identification	Coming-out (acknowledgment)	Identity confusion / Identity comparison
4. Universalistic (ego identity)	"Coming Out"	"Coming Out"	"Coming Out"	Behavioral acceptance	Self-acceptance	Exploration	Identity tolerance / Identity acceptance
	Stabilization	Commitment				First relationships	Identity pride
			Going public	Public identification		Identity integration	Identity synthesis

"homosexual" cue. In essence, the first phase of homosexual identity formation involves experiences of an erotic, emotional, or social nature that serve as bases for viewing the self as possibly homosexual. This stage is egocentric because the individual labels the self as homosexual on the basis of personal experience rather than a normative understanding of homosexuality.

Based on interviews with a sample of 150 homosexual males, Troiden (1979) divided the sensitization phase into childhood (prior to age 13) and adolescent (age 13–17) periods. Characterizing both periods "is a sense of apartness from more conventional peers" (p. 363). During the early period, the child had a sense of being different, which was experienced as general alienation, a gender inadequacy, and warmth and excitement in the presence of other males. Troiden asserts that the presence of these feelings does not necessarily imply that there exists an innate homosexual predisposition. Boys who become heterosexuals as adults may also recall childhood feelings of estrangement. Troiden concludes:

> What *is* suggested here is that homosexual and heterosexual males may differ in terms of the *meanings* they later come to attribute to a childhood sense of apartness. The same childhood feelings which the adolescent heterosexual may come to redefine as the initial signs of, for instance, artistic sensitivity may be reinterpreted by the teenaged male who later becomes homosexual as the first stirrings of homosexual interest. (p. 364)

Troiden reports that all but one of the males in his sample reported feeling sexually different during the adolescent period of sensitization. For example, they had less interest in females and more interest in males than did other males, engaged in sexual activity with other males, and felt inadequate as males. Nearly two-thirds had their first orgasmic homosexual experience during adolescence.

Further evidence of childhood and adolescent manifestations of homosexual feelings, in females as well as males, was reported by Bell, Weinberg, and Hammersmith (1981) in their study of 979 homosexuals and 477 heterosexuals. They concluded that adult homosexuality stems from homosexual feelings experienced during childhood and adolescence. As in Troiden's findings, they reported that it was during adolescence that homosexual feelings were expressed in sexual activity—for men between the ages of 15 and 17, and for women between 18 and 20.

Bell and associates also proposed that a relationship existed between the development of the homosexual identity and gender nonconformity. They found, however, that not all their homosexual informants reported atypical gender traits or interests in childhood. Nearly half of the homosexual men seemed to have been typically "masculine," while almost a quarter of the heterosexual males were not. Additional evidence of an association between gender nonconformity in childhood years and adult homosexuality is reported by Green (1980). He asserted, however, that not all adults with a homosexual preference recall childhood gender nonconformity.

In conclusion, the initial phase of homosexual identity formation appears to emerge in childhood and adolescence as a sense of being different from one's peers. This feeling of separateness may be manifested in a variety of ways, such as emotional and sexual arousal in the presence of same-sex peers, gender nonconformity, and feelings of alienation. During adolescence the earlier childhood feelings of isolation combine with a specific sense of sexual difference to sensitize the teenager to the possibility of his or her homosexuality. Whether homosexuality can be traced to early social learning or biological predisposition, the evidence now available suggests that, at least for some individuals, childhood and adolescent experiences may serve as the basis for the adult homosexual identity.

The Sociocentric Stage

During the sociocentric-objectivistic stage of ego development, the individual forms a subjective perspective of the world that is demarcated from the social and physical environment. Social norms are internalized. A personal identity, formerly based on bodily capacity, is transformed into an identity based on role performance. Social norms begin to affect the process of personal identity formation about the seventh year, the time when the child has acquired the cognitive ability to move beyond subjective, egocentric interpretations. The impact of sexual norms, however, is unlikely to be experienced until puberty. In homosexual identity formation, sociocentricity emerges when the individual has a heightened awareness of possibly possessing the homosexual identity and a corresponding awareness of the societal attitudes about the homosexual role. Plummer (1975) and Lee (1977) refer to this phase of development as "signification." According to Plummer, signification

> entails all those processes which lead to a heightened homosexual identity: subjectively, from the nagging inner feeling that one may be "different" through to a developed homosexual identity, and objectively, from minor homosexual involvements through to the stage known as "coming out." For some these changes are passed quickly; for others they groan through the life span. (p. 141)

Heightened awareness provides relief for some individuals; for others it involves anxiety and confusion. It is likely, as Plummer notes, that the societal rejection of homosexuality will lead to secrecy, guilt, and isolation. The homosexual experience becomes significant for the individual because society's negative view of homosexuality renders it so.

Troiden (1979) also uses the idea of signification to characterize the second developmental phase. However, he believes that the heightened awareness of homosexual tendencies results from the process of "dissociation." Dissociation "consists of the partitioning in consciousness of sexual feelings and/or activity from sexual identity" (pp. 364–365). Rather than reducing the growing awareness of possible homosexual feelings, dissociation has the unintended and ironic effect of "signifying" those feelings. Thus, individuals who resort to dissociation to avoid homosexual self-labeling cannot escape facing the possibility that their homosexual activity or interests stem from a homosexual orientation. Malyon (1981), in discussing the evolution of homosexual awareness during adolescence, also refers to a defensive process involving the compartmentalization of sexual desire and sexual identity. Compartmentalization juxtaposes the individual's homosexual desire and the rejection of a homosexual identity. Rejection of the homosexual identity, Malyon believes, is the result of the individual's internalized homophobia.

Evidence of both heightened awareness of homosexuality (signification) and separation of identity from activity or feelings (dissociation) is provided in Troiden's (1979) study. The average age at which informants started to question their heterosexuality was 17. Doubts about their heterosexuality arose from experiences that they viewed as more explicitly homosexual than those which, in the earlier sensitization stage, had led them to believe they were merely sexually different. The most frequently reported events leading to heightened awareness were becoming sexually aroused by another male and engaging in physically enjoyable homosexual acts or fantasies. Nevertheless, not all informants defined even these experiences as unequivocally homosexual, assuming that their homosexual attractions were only a passing phase. They also believed they had little or nothing in common with homosexuals as a group.

A number of models of homosexual identity development refer to the discrepancy that may exist between homosexual feelings, thoughts, or behavior and the homosexual identity (Cass, 1979; Coleman, 1981/82; Dank, 1971; Hencken & O'Dowd, 1977; Lee, 1977; Plummer, 1975). According to Cass, this discrepancy is experienced by the individual as "identity confusion." The person becomes preoccupied with the question, "If my behavior may be called homosexual, does this mean that I am a homosexual?" (p. 223). Cass suggests that identity confusion can be resolved in various ways. The individual can perceive homosexual behavior as correct and acceptable and proceed to reducing confusion by obtaining information about homosexuality (e.g., reading books, listening to discussions about homosexuality, and seeking professional counseling).

Reducing confusion leads to a second phase, one Cass labels "identity comparison." It is characterized by a tentative commitment to a homosexual self-definition. At this point the person is still at the sociocentric stage of development since concern about the social denigration of homosexuality prevents the complete acceptance of homosexuality as an aspect of personal identity.

Cass identifies two additional ways of resolving identity confusion: (1) inhibition of any behavior that is perceived as homosexual and avoidance of further information about homosexuality; and (2) the continued participation in homosexual activity while denying that such experiences are homosexual. Both strategies, with their mechanisms of avoidance and denial, bind large amounts of psychic energy that could be channeled into productive and rewarding activities. The latter strategy, although temporarily resolving identity confusion, precludes the possibility of achieving an integrated personal identity. The individual's identity and behavior remain dichotomous, opposing entities.

What appears to characterize the sociocentric phase is an increased awareness of homoerotic desires that are accompanied by a marked feeling of identity confusion. Various strategies are employed to resolve this confusion. For some individuals the culmination is a stronger, though still tentative, commitment to the homosexual self (i.e., Cass's concept of identity comparison). For others, defense mechanisms delay or completely foreclose further progress toward acceptance of the homosexual identity.

It is not fully understood why some individuals progress to the level of identity comparison while others remain fixated at a previous stage of development. Cass (1979) indicates that progression beyond identity comparison is associated with the extent to which an individual can tolerate being different from others as well as resist the pressure of social norms. When the strength and willingness to resist outside pressures is present, the individual is ready to enter into the post-normative, universalistic stage of identity development.

The Universalistic Stage

In the universalistic stage, which is the last level of ego development, the individual realizes that societal norms can be critically evaluated. If the universalistic stage is successfully achieved, the individual will be able to separate particular norms from general principles upon which all norms are based. Furthermore, the identity of the individual will be transformed from role identity to ego identity. The person can then present the self "credibly in any situation as someone who can satisfy the requirements of consistency even in the face of incompatible role expectations and in the passage through a sequence of contradictory periods of life" (Habermas, 1979, pp. 85-86). Thus, at the universalistic stage, the individual has attained the unity, consistency, and continuity that characterize personal identity.

The universalistic stage of the homosexual identity process is characterized by the acceptance of a positive gay identity and commitment to that identity even in the face of its social condemnation. Three phases of the universalistic stage can be delineated: (1) homosexual identity acceptance, (2) commitment to a homosexual identity, and (3) identity integration. The first two phases complete the process of homosexual identity formation; the last phase represents a process of homosexual identity management. In all aspects of the universalistic stage the individual is engaged in a critical evaluation of social attitudes toward homosexuality.

Acceptance and Commitment to a Homosexual Identity

The term that is often used to refer to this phase of emerging self-acceptance as gay or lesbian is "coming out."[2] Plummer (1975), Lee (1977), and Coleman (1981/82) characterize this period as the first major exploration of the homosexual community. It provides the opportunity to interact with other homosexuals, legitimates the homosexual experience, and thereby enables the individual to develop an acceptance of a gay or lesbian identity.

Cass (1979) conceives of the process of seeking contacts with other homosexuals as initially leading to "identity tolerance" and then to "identity acceptance." It is likely that, once a person has decided to interact with other homosexuals, it will take time for that individual to feel comfortable with them. Coleman (1981/82) points out that, during the phase of exploration, there are several developmental tasks to be mastered. Interpersonal skills are needed to socialize with others who have homosexual interests. Some individuals may also need to develop a sense of personal attractiveness and sexual competence; others may have to overcome the feeling that self-esteem is tied to sexual conquest. Since individuals with homosexual preferences usually have only limited opportunity during adolescence to explore and act on their homosexual feelings, they appear to be developmentally delayed as adults (Coleman, 1981/82; Grace, Note 4). If the individual is able to increase contact with the gay community, progress from identity tolerance ("I probably am a homosexual") to identity acceptance ("I am a homosexual") will occur (Cass, 1979).

From the available evidence it would appear that the acceptance of a positive homosexual self-image is closely linked to the opportunity one has to interact with other homosexuals and to learn more about homosexuality (Humphreys, 1972, 1979; Humphreys & Miller, 1980). After the individual has attained self-acceptance of the homosexual identity there are further tasks on the road to achieving an integrated ego identity. Plummer (1975), Troiden (1979), and Cass (1979) describe a post-acceptance stage in which the individual takes pride in possessing a homosexual identity and, at the same time, rejects heterosexual values. The feeling of pride may be related to the realization that the heterosexual identity is not superior to the homosexual identity. In fact, the heterosexual identity and lifestyle may be viewed as distinctly distasteful, particularly as embodied in marriage. Troiden (1979), who refers to this phase as "commitment," points out that, in contrast to acceptance, "commitment presupposes a reluctance to abandon the [homosexual] identity even if given the opportunity to do so" (p. 371). Cass (1979) suggests that pride about and commitment to being gay are likely to be accompanied by feelings of anger over heterosexual values and institutions. Consequently, the individual is energized "into action against the established institutions . . .by feelings of this stage" (p. 233). As a by-product of this stage the individual is likely to abandon efforts to conceal the homosexual identity and even to disclose it to friends, family members, and fellow workers.

Having a love relationship appears to deepen the commitment to the homosexual identity (Coleman, 1981/82; Troiden, 1979; Warren, 1974). For gay men, the evidence indicates that being involved in the first love relationship usually follows identity acceptance by a few years (McDonald, 1982; Troiden, 1979; Kooden et al., Note 3). Several investigators have pointed out that once sexual exploration has been experienced there is a greater need for intimacy and commitment to a stable love relationship (Coleman, 1981/82; Gagnon & Simon, 1973; Troiden, 1979).

To achieve fully the homosexual identity, it must be integrated with all other aspects of self. According to Cass (1979) the final phase of homosexual identity formation, which she labels "identity synthesis," is reached when a person's homosexual identity is no longer viewed as the only identity, but instead is "given the status of being merely one aspect of self" (p. 235). To attain identity synthesis, the individual's personal and public sexual identities have to be integrated into a single self-image. This self-image must have the support of the person's interpersonal environment. Lee (1977) and Hencken and O'Dowd (1977) cite a special case of synthesizing one's personal and public identities—the decision to disclose the homosexual identity in the public media. Lee notes how difficult such public identification sometimes is: "Self-disclosure can become 'overdisclosure' with its own problems" (p. 75). For some individuals identity synthesis may not be possible given the powerful and overriding effects of social discrimination. In a general sense, the question arises as to whether identity synthesis can ever be achieved for all but a few as long as prejudice and discrimination prevail.

Homosexual Identity Management

In the last phase of the homosexual identity process lies the task of integrating personal and public identities. It involves disclosing the gay self-image to significant others, such as family members, friends, and co-workers. The disclosure of sexual orientation is a lifelong process, comprising decisions of whether or not to disclose, how and when to disclose, and how to face the consequences of disclosure. Self-disclosure, therefore, can be facilitative when interpersonal support is available or detrimental when it is lacking. In either case, the person's perception of self will be altered (Cass, 1979; de Monteflores & Schultz, 1978).

Revealing the homosexual identity may be an "all or none" phenomenon for some, but most will "fluctuate back and forth in degrees of openness, depending on a variety of personal, social and professional factors" (de Monteflores & Schultz, 1978, p. 62).

The decision to conceal the homosexual identity from significant others may be detrimental to psychological well-being. Is it possible to achieve an integrated personal identity or have authentic relationships while concealing fundamental aspects of the self? Recent studies suggest that closeted homosexual men have negative attitudes toward homosexuality, anticipate discrimination, and experience barriers to self-acceptance (Ross, 1978; Weinberg & Williams, 1974; McDonald, Note 5). In choosing to hide an essential part of the self, individuals are left with a gnawing feeling that they are really valued for what others expect them to be rather than for who they really are.

To be uncloseted also has its costs. No longer invisible, the individual becomes a target for discrimination. Everyday interactions may suddenly become apprehensive and uncomfortable. Social acceptance can never be guaranteed since each new situation holds the possibility of rejection. An individual's proclamation of a gay identity can be met with physical harassment and verbal abuse. More often, a person's civil liberties may be jeopardized, and rights to employment and housing may be abridged. In conveying these harsh realities, it is not our intention to alarm. Rather, we wish to emphasize that "to be openly gay in such a society says a clear 'no more' to this oppression and both confirms the individual gay person and challenges society's norms (de Monteflores & Schultz, 1978, p. 66).

NOTES

1. Coleman (1981/82) also refers to a comparable stage—"pre-coming out." However, he provides only a general discussion of childhood origins and manifestations of homosexual feelings rather than an elaborated account of an initial stage of homosexual identity.

2. Dank (1971) and Hencken and O'Dowd (1977) use the term "coming out" in a broader sense that includes the initial signification or awareness of a homosexual identity (the sociocentric level) as

well as the subsequent phase of acceptance. In the case of Hencken and O'Dowd, the still later phase of public identification is included. Coleman (1981/82) uses the term to refer specifically to the period of initial awareness.

REFERENCE NOTES

1. Minton, H. L. *Emancipatory social psychology as a paradigm for the study of homosexuality.* Paper presented at the annual meeting of the Canadian Psychological Association, Toronto, June 1981.
2. Minton, H. L. *Emancipatory social psychology as a paradigm for the study of minority groups.* Paper presented at the annual meeting of the Western Association of Sociology and Anthropology, Saskatoon, February 1982.
3. Kooden, J. D., Morin, S. F., Riddle, D. I., Rogers, M. Sang, B. E., & Strassburger, F. *Removing the stigma: Final report, Task Force on the Status of Lesbian and Gay Male Psychologists.* Washington, D.C.: American Psychological Association, 1979.
4. Grace, J. *Gay despair and the loss of adolescence: A new perspective on same sex preference and self esteem.* Paper presented at the Fifth Biennial Professional Symposium of the National Association of Social Workers, San Diego, November 1977.
5. McDonald, G. J. *In and out of the closet: Similarities and differences for gay men.* Paper presented at the annual meeting of the American Psychological Association, Washington, D.C., August 1982.

REFERENCES

Bell, A. P., Weinberg, M. S., & Hammersmith, S. K. *Sexual preference: Its development in men and women.* Bloomington: Indiana University Press, 1981.
Breger, L. *From instinct to identity: The development of personality.* Englewood Cliffs, NJ: Prentice-Hall, 1974.
Cass, V. C. Homosexual identity formation: A theoretical model. *Journal of Homosexuality,* 1979, *4,* 219-235.
Coleman, E. Developmental stages of the coming out process. *Journal of Homosexuality,* 1981/82, 7(2/3), 31-43.
Dank, B. M. Coming out in the gay world. *Psychiatry,* 1971, *34,* 180-197.
de Levita, D. J. *The concept of identity.* The Hague: Mouton, 1965.
de Monteflores, C., & Schultz, S. J. Coming out: Similarities and differences for lesbians and gay men. *Journal of Social Issues,* 1978, *34*(3), 59-72.
Erikson, E. H. *Childhood and society.* New York: Norton, 1950.
Erikson, E. H. Identity and the life-cycle. *Psychological Issues,* 1959, *1(1),* 1-171.
Erikson, E. H. *Identity, youth and crisis.* New York: Norton, 1968.
Gagnon, J. H., & Simon, W. *Sexual conduct: The social sources of human sexuality.* Chicago: Aldine, 1973.
Green, R. Patterns of sexual identity in childhood: Relationship to subsequent sexual partner preference. In J. Marmor (Ed.), *Homosexual behavior: A modern reappraisal.* New York: Basic Books, 1980.
Habermas, J. *Knowledge and human interests.* Boston: Beacon Press, 1971.
Habermas, J. *Communication and the evolution of society.* Boston: Beacon Press, 1979.
Hencken, J. D., & O'Dowd, W. T. Coming out as an aspect of identity formation. *Gai Saber,* 1977, *1*(1), 18-22.
Humphreys, L. *Out of the closets: The sociology of homosexual liberation.* Englewood Cliffs, NJ: Prentice-Hall, 1972.
Humphreys, L. Exodus and identity: The emerging gay culture. In M. P. Levine (Ed.), *Gay men: The sociology of male homosexuality.* New York: Harper & Row, 1979.
Humphreys, L., & Miller, B. Identities in the emerging gay culture. In J. Marmor (Ed.), *Homosexual behavior: A modern reappraisal.* New York: Basic Books, 1980.

Lee, J. A. Going public: A study in the sociology of homosexual liberation. *Journal of Homosexuality*, 1977, *3*, 49–78.

Malyon, A. K. The homosexual adolescent: Developmental issues and social bias. *Child Welfare*, 1981, *60*, 321–330.

McDonald, G. J. Individual differences in the coming out process for gay men: Implications for theoretical models. *Journal of Homosexuality*, 1982, *8*, 47–60.

Plummer, K. *Sexual stigma: An interactionist account*. London: Routledge & Kegan Paul, 1975.

Richardson, D., & Hart, J. The development and maintenance of a homosexual identity. In J. Hart & D. Richardson (Eds.), *The theory and practice of homosexuality*. London: Routledge & Kegan Paul, 1981.

Ross, M. The relationship of perceived societal hostility, conformity, and psychological adjustment in homosexual males. *Journal of Homosexuality*, 1978, *4*, 157–168.

Schafer, S. Sexual and social problems of lesbians. *Journal of Sex Research*, 1976, *12*, 50–69.

Troiden, R. R. Becoming homosexual: A model for gay identity acquisition. *Psychiatry*, 1979, *42*, 362–373.

Warren, C. A. B. *Identity and community in the gay world*. New York: Wiley, 1974.

Weinberg, M. S., & Williams, C. J. *Male homosexuals: Their problems and adaptations*. New York: Oxford University Press, 1974.

Homosexual Identity:
A Concept in Need of Definition

Vivienne C. Cass, PhD (cand.)
Murdoch University

ABSTRACT. Despite the fact that the concept *homosexual identity* has been used extensively in the literature on homosexuality since the late 1960s, investigators have shown little concern for defining or discussing the manner in which it is used. As a result, the study of homosexual identity has been characterized by confusion, disarray, and ambiguity. A multiplicity of terminologies makes comparisons between studies difficult. There has been little attempt to place theoretical proposals or data within the framework of existing psychological literature on identity.

A number of assumptions critical to an understanding of homosexual identity are commonly made, and several of these are discussed: The synonymity of homosexual identity and self-concept; homosexual identity as childhood identity; homosexual identity as sexual identity; and homosexuality as distinct essence. This review also considers the following issues: The distinction between identity and behavior; the utility of an identity construct as applied to the study of homosexuals; the definition of identity in developmental theories of homosexual identity; and homosexual group identity.

Use of the concept *homosexual identity* to refer to an aspect of homosexual functioning spans little more than a decade. The proliferation of articles on homosexual identity since the early 1970s stands as testimony to the importance the concept has been given by both popular and scientific writers. Indeed, a perusal of the pages and indices of early bibliographies (e.g., Parker, 1971; Weinberg & Bell, 1972) clearly shows the lack of reference to, and interest in, the construct prior to that time.

One could postulate a number of factors that might account for the development of widespread interest: (1) the change in perspective, ap-

Vivienne Cass is a clinical psychologist who has been conducting research into homosexual identity formation for her doctorate at Murdoch University, where she also lectures. In 1974 she established the Homosexual Counselling and Information Service in Western Australia, which she also directed until 1981. In 1979 she was the recipient of the Theory Development Award of the national Gay Academic Union in the United States. This paper is drawn from a longer manuscript the author is presently completing. Reprint requests should be addressed to the author at the Department of Social Inquiry, Psychology Section, Murdoch University, Murdoch, Western Australia 6015.

parent since the 19th century, from *homosexual-as-object* to *homosexual-as-person;* (2) the gradual abandonment, during the 1960s of the notion of collectivity and its replacement with the ideology of the individual, which emphasized the rights of individuals, free expression, self-fulfillment, and social tolerance; (3) the increasing emphasis in social psychology and sociology on the humanistic approach to the individual. In sum, the climate of the 1970s was ripe for the homosexual to be defined into "personhood" against a backdrop of an oppressed minority group. Consequently, the concept of homosexual identity was adopted as an integral part of the language of the gay subculture, as well as that of the psychological and sociological professions.

With the literature of the 1980s already showing signs of a new emphasis on consolidation and scientific rigor, it is appropriate to review and assess the recent literature on homosexual identity. It is my contention that this literature can best be described as an overgrown garden, badly in need of pruning if its contents are to be given any life. While the existing literature on homosexual identity should be viewed as a pioneering rather than a definitive effort, nevertheless, it seems time for the study of homosexual identity to move into a more scientific mode. Otherwise it is in danger of lapsing into a static notion, adopted in a popular sense by the gay subculture and shunned by the scientific community.

The purpose of this paper is to examine critically the use of the construct *homosexual identity* in the psychological and sociological literature, to point out areas that require clarification, and to suggest guidelines for future research programs.

USES OF THE TERM IDENTITY IN RESEARCH ON HOMOSEXUALITY

There is considerable variation in the way the term *identity* is used in the homosexual context. Some authors refer to the phrase *homosexual identity* (e.g., Bell, 1973; Blumstein & Schwartz, 1977; Cronin, 1974; Dank, 1971, 1972, 1974; Goode, 1978; Goode & Haber, 1977; Hayes, 1981; Humphreys, 1979; Johnston, 1980; Latham & White, 1978; Lyman & Scott, 1970; Murphy, 1974; Plummer, 1973; Roesler & Deisher, 1972; Sagarin, 1976; Weeks, 1977, 1980/81; Whitam, 1981; Dank, Note 1. Others prefer *gay identity* (e.g., Adam, 1978; De Cecco, 1981; Hanckel & Cunningham, 1979; Hayes, 1976; Ponse, 1977, 1980; Warren, 1980; De Cecco, Note 2; DuBay, Note 3; Robertson, Note 4). At times "gay identity" and "homosexual identity" are used interchangeably (e.g., Goode & Troiden, 1979; Ponse, 1978; Troiden, 1979); at other times the meanings of the two phrases are distinguished from each other (e.g., Harry & DeVall, 1978; Morin & Schultz, 1978; Taylor,

1977; Troiden, 1979; Warren, 1974; Morin & Miller, Note 5; Somers, Note 6). *Lesbian identity* is a phrase that is adopted either exclusively (e.g., Ferguson, 1981; McLellan, Note 7) or in conjunction with the previously mentioned terminology (e.g., Cronin, 1974; Ponse, 1978, 1980). Dank (Note 1), Crites (1976), Goode and Troiden (1974), Miller (1978), Richardson and Hart (1981), and Weinberg (1978) mention homosexual *self-identity,* while a number of authors refer to identity in a homosexual context without further elaborations (e.g., Babuscio, 1979; Clinard, 1968; Cory, 1975; Freedman, 1975; Hencken & O'Dowd, 1977; Humphreys & Miller, 1980; Kimmel, 1978; Moses, 1978; Pattison, 1974; Simon & Gagnon, 1967a). Some authors make reference to a *gay self* (e.g., Cronin, 1974; Ponse, 1978, 1980), or *lesbian self* (e.g., Jay, 1975). *Sexual identity* is another commonly used term that plays a significant part in the literature (e.g., Hoffman, 1968; Horowitz, 1964; Miller, 1978; Robertson, Note 4). Finally, *deviant identity* (e.g., Goode, 1978; Williams & Weinberg, 1971) was a once popular expression that is currently losing favor.

Authors show little concern for justifying the particular terminology used, or recognizing that others may adopt quite different meanings for the same terms. The assumption appears to be that all terms mean roughly the same thing. One answer to the problem of multiple terms, would be to develop a more uniform set of words or phrases, which implies, of course, that researchers could agree on what is and is not acceptable. Another solution is for authors to include clear definitions of the particular terms adopted so that others can know the precise meanings referred to. Ideally, we need a terminology that is generally agreed upon, or at least understood, by most researchers with some allowances made for idiosyncratic augmentations.

DEFINING HOMOSEXUAL IDENTITY

The most noticeable feature of the literature on homosexual identity is an almost universal lack of definition of the term "identity" as it relates to the homosexual. There are literally hundreds of scientific articles that refer to homosexual identity without explaining what is meant by the concept (e.g., Bell, 1973; Cory, 1975; De Cecco, 1981; Freedman, 1975; Goode & Haber, 1977; Goode & Troiden, 1979, Hammersmith & Weinberg, 1973; Harry & DeVall, 1978; Hayes, 1976; Hencken & O'Dowd, 1977; Humphreys, 1979; Johnston, 1980; Kimmel, 1978; Lehman, 1978; Lyman & Scott, 1970; Morin & Schultz, 1978; Murphy, 1974; Plummer, 1973; Ponse, 1977, 1978, 1980; Sagarin, 1976; Simon & Gagnon, 1967b; Steffensmeier & Steffensmeier, 1974; Troiden, 1979; Weinberg & Williams, 1973; DuBay, Note 3; Robertson, Note 4; Morin & Miller,

Note 5). In these articles it is possible to infer diverse meanings such as (1) defining oneself as gay, (2) a sense of self as gay, (3) image of self as homosexual, (4) the way a homosexual person *is*, and (5) consistent behavior in relation to homosexual-related activity. Sometimes it can be inferred that identity is intrapersonal; at other times, that it is outside the individual; and still at others, that it is both within and outside the person. In addition, "sexual identity" and "self-identity" are sometimes used as explanations of homosexual identity, even though these terms also remain undefined. In several instances, the notion of self (e.g., "self-definition," "self-concepts," or "self-image") is intricately bound to the idea of identity (e.g., Cronin, 1974; Dank, 1971, 1972; Horowitz, 1964; Latham & White, 1978; Loewenstein, 1980; Simon & Gagnon, 1967b; Weeks, 1980/81; Dank, Note 1). The reader, however, will only be frustrated in any attempt to determine whether these concepts are inter-related, synonymous, or distinct.

Some authors (e.g., Goode & Troiden, 1974; Jandt & Darsey, 1981) do attempt to explain their perception of homosexual identity in terms of self, but then fail to define self [e.g., Jandt & Darsey's "considering self homosexual" (p. 19)]. Defining one broad and nebulous concept in terms of another is hardly calculated to illuminate the reader.

Other simplistic definitions of homosexual identity include Levine's (1979) "the knowledge that one is homosexual" (p. 4), Goode and Troiden's (1974) notion of homosexual self-identity as "how a person defines her gender preference" (p. 231), and Stoller's (1980) a "statement about a person's totality, his identity" (p. 20). Adam (1978) adds a further dimension with his reference to homosexual identity as equivalent to ethnic identity or minority identity, although once again the meanings of such terms are not explicated. In general, most authors subscribe to the idea that identity is "the answer to the questions Who am I? and Where do I belong?" (Warren, 1974, p. 145).

GENERAL CONCEPTIONS OF IDENTITY

A significant and unfortunate feature of the literature on homosexual identity is its isolation from established theory and data on the general concept of identity. Only a handful of researchers (e.g., Humphreys, 1979; Moses, 1978; Grzelkowski, Note 8) have made serious attempts to draw from this literature. Although the parent literature itself lacks coherence and clarity, it should not be ignored since it provides the broad framework and foundation which research on homosexual identity badly needs. Collating the existent identity literature may be difficult and time-consuming, but I firmly believe that the study of homosexual identity is impoverished by this neglect of general theory and research on identity.

When homosexual identity is considered from this perspective of *human identity*, interesting questions emerge: can homosexual identity be presented as a construct similar to that described in the general literature as a person's overall identity? Is homosexual identity essentially similar to or different than ethnic, occupational, or status identities? Can we assume homosexual identity and heterosexual identity are structurally alike? To what degree is homosexual identity time and space specific? What effects do particular sociological, psychological, political, or economic conditions have upon the nature of homosexual identity?

Berger and Luckman (1966) have emphasized that "theories about identity are always embedded in the more comprehensive theories about reality" (p. 160). In the homosexual literature, theorists have given little attention to the assumptions that form the underlying base for their views on homosexual identity. As researchers it is imperative that we recognize the degree to which our work is based upon personal beliefs about self (Riebel, 1982; Wegner & Vallacher, 1977). Our understanding of reality reflects our past experiences, present social and psychological functioning, and future aspirations, all of which can be easily and subtly incorporated into our research. I suggest that those studying homosexual identity should first scrupulously examine and identify the assumptions upon which they rest their notions of identity. They should then compare their personal framework with theoretical perspectives that have been presented in the identity literature. If, for example, a particular researcher firmly believes "once a gay, always a gay," then it is imperative that this attitude be made known to the reader and its validity defended within the context of the general and homosexual literature on identity. The homosexual literature is unfortunately characterized by the unquestioning adoption of a number of assumptions. Some of these will be discussed in this paper.

THE RELATIONSHIP BETWEEN IDENTITY AND SELF-CONCEPT IN THE HOMOSEXUAL CONTEXT

The homosexual literature is notably vague in its description of the relationship between identity and self. In most cases it implicitly suggests that these concepts are synonymous. Examination of the general literature, however, indicates that some theoreticians advocate a clear distinction between the two terms (e.g., Ball, 1972; Davis, 1970; Stone, 1962); others believe the terms can be used interchangeably (e.g., Laing, Phillipson, & Lee, 1966; Miller, 1963; Shibutani, 1961; Zavalloni, 1973); while a third group uses "identity" to refer to a component of self (e.g., Abend, 1974; Schwartz & Stryker, 1970).

Maslow (1968) noted, with reference to "identity," (and his comments are applicable to "self"), "partly identity is whatever we say it is . . . It means something different for various therapists, for sociologists, for self-psychologists, for child psychologists, etc., even though for all these people there is also some similarity or overlap of meaning" (p. 103). Schafer (1973) believes that the only way of dealing with the diffuse, multi-purpose uses of the terms "self" and "identity" is to "decide on the basis of the situational and the verbal context in which the word self . . . (or identity) is being used at any moment, which aspect of a person is being pointed at" (p. 53). These approaches are far from satisfactory for research purposes. If the study of homosexual identity is to achieve empirical precision, then a clear conceptual basis must be provided.

Despite different perspectives, theorists of identity commonly refer to (1) a personal aspect of individual functioning conceived of as self-representations and self-perceptions. The personal aspect is variously called personal identity, self, self-concept, personal self, self-identity, and so forth. Theorists also refer to (2) a social aspect of identity that is the representation of the personal aspect to others in a relatively consistent way. The social aspect has been termed social identity, social self, meta-identity, public identity, and identity. Both aspects are construed as essentially cognitive elements of functioning that emerge out of the interplay between the individual's own perceptions and perceived perceptions of self by others.

A THEORETICAL FRAMEWORK FOR CONCEPTUALIZING HOMOSEXUAL IDENTITY

The theoretical framework I have used in the study of homosexual identity has evolved from a number of different approaches. Self-concept is, to quote Rosenberg (1979), "the totality of the individual's thoughts and feelings having reference to himself as an object" (p. 7). It is all those self-perceptions or self-attitudes that a person holds, and the affective component attached to each of these self-representations. Self-concept also includes self-perceptions of how the individual *wishes* to be.

Identity refers to organized sets of self-perceptions and attached feelings that an individual holds about self with regard to some social category. It represents the synthesis of own self-perceptions with views of the self perceived to be held by others. Where self-perceptions and imagined other's view of self are in accord, then identity may be said to have developed.

Homosexual identity, then, evolves out of a clustering of self-images which are linked together by the individual's idiosyncratic understanding of what characterizes someone as "a homosexual." This understanding develops out of an integration of the individual's unique interpretation of socially prescribed notions and self-developed formulations. Early stages of homosexual identity development usually involve cognitive processing of self-information against a symbolically held image of the "generalized other." Development of a fully integrated identity, however, requires more direct communication with others. Ultimately this includes the presentation of a homosexual self-image to both homosexual and heterosexual others. Where presentation is to one but not the other of these groups, homosexual identity cannot completely evolve.[1] Commonly, the homosexual self-image is withheld from non-homosexual people and a heterosexual role adopted.[2] A fully developed sense of self as "a homosexual" requires accord between self-perception and imagined views of self held by *all* others constituting the individual's social environment. This sense of identity becomes translated into relatively predictable behavioral patterns. Stability is created through the constancy experienced in interaction with others. The individual strives to maintain cognitive and behavioral consistency which, in turn, serves to reinforce the way others are believed to see the self.

Both self-concept and identity are considered significant to an adequate understanding of homosexual identity. For example, the statements "I am a guilt-ridden homosexual" and "I am a proud homosexual" both reflect some degree of identity development ("I am a homosexual"). The two self-attitudes, "guilt-ridden" and "proud," illustrate a qualitative difference and clearly show the importance of taking self-conceptions into account. In addition, the multidimensional nature of homosexual identity is emphasized. There is no such thing as a single homosexual identity. Rather, its nature may vary from person to person, from situation to situation, and from period to period.

It is also possible to differentiate between the self-image, "I am a person who relates sexually to others of the same sex," (self-conception) and "I am a homosexual" (identity), a distinction commonly reported in the popular literature. I do not believe there is anything to be gained by devising something called homosexual self-concept (Plummer, 1975; Richardson & Hart, 1981; Weinberg & Williams, 1974). In the present theoretical formulation the components of self-concept (self-images) are the units upon which identity is built. The two constructs differ significantly in that identity necessitates reference to a specific social category while self-concept does not.

In order to avoid the conceptual difficulties present in the general literature, the terms *presented identity* and *perceived identity* are adopted. Strictly speaking, identity, as discussed previously, might more accurately be called *self-identity*, to distinguish it from presented identity and perceived identity. Unless otherwise indicated, "identity" will be used in the sense of self-identity. Presented identity is that picture of self presented to others with regard to a specific socially defined category, that is, the identity that a person wants others to believe one holds about self. Presented identity is closely linked with ideal components of self-identity. Perceived identity refers to that image held by another about self with regard to a specific social category. Such an image will develop out of a synthesis of the meaning others put on our behavior (presented identity) together with perceptions already held about us.

Human beings can choose to present an image of themselves that is quite distinct from the way they actually perceive themselves. Further, others may hold an image of a person that is at odds with that person's own perception of self. In the homosexual literature these distinctions have been consistently noted (e.g., Blumstein & Schwartz, 1974; Goode, 1978; Levine, 1979; Miller, 1978; Reiss, 1961; Weeks, 1977). Frequently, however, these concepts have been referred to as simply "identity." This makes cross-study comparisons particularly difficult.

In the literature on homosexual identity, both the personal and social elements of identity are alluded to. However, the social has received considerably more attention, while the personal has been sorely neglected. Consideration of the social aspects of identity has led to a number of studies that have produced descriptions of various aspects of the gay subculture and mainstream society, and the way these influence gay identity (e.g., Cronin, 1974; Humphreys & Miller, 1980; Moses, 1978; Ponse, 1978; Warren, 1974; Weinberg & Williams, 1974; Williams & Weinberg, 1971; Robertson, Note 4). Particular emphasis has been given in many cases to the ways persons experience their homosexual identity in the world within which they live. Focus has also been given to the study of characteristics commonly perceived as making up presented identity.

Unfortunately little attention has been given to the personal, cognitive aspects of identity, and this is, indeed, a grave error. Identity is a cognitive construct, "classes of self-representations" to use Schafer's (1973) terminology. If one is going to study the social aspects of identity, then describing elements of social structure is valid, provided the analysis is then extended to the cognitive restructuring that might or does take place for the individual within such settings.[3] After all, it is the individual's own perceptions of the world, rather than the world itself which are critical to the identity issue.

HOMOSEXUAL IDENTITY AS CHILDHOOD OUTCOME

The medical and psychiatric fields have sponsored the commonly held idea that homosexual identity arises out of early childhood developmental processes. Proponents of this theory work within either an *ego identity* framework (e.g., Gundlach & Riess, 1968; Pattison, 1974; Weis & Dain,

1979; McLellan, Note 7) or *sexual identity* framework (e.g., Green, 1974; Hoffman, 1968; Whitam, 1977, 1981).

Ego identity theorists either imply or state explicitly that homosexual identity is equivalent to, or closely aligned with, the concept of ego identity. Such a perspective is, however, confused in several respects. First, ego psychology, from which the notion of ego identity arises, is itself a derivative of psychoanalytic theory. Erik Erikson, one of the best known ego psychologists, proposed the notion of *ego identity* to refer specifically to the psychosocial integration of the individual. This integration normally occurs during adolescence but may continue into early adulthood (Erikson, 1959, 1968). Basing his work on psychoanalytic theory, Erickson emphasized the important function of the ego as organizing and synthesizing the processes of development, transforming them into a unique sense of self, which he called ego identity. Erikson makes clear, however, that ego identity is quite distinct from what he calls self-identity, which he defined as the identity that emerges from the integration of the individual's self-images (self-representations) with role images (perceptions of the social positions held).

Unfortunately, this distinction has been absent in the homosexual identity literature, where the term ego identity is often used in the context of self-identity. Some theorists have adopted the term "ego identity" while, at the same time, rejecting the construct "ego" and its theoretical implications as untenable. This practice makes for theoretical nonsense. What we need to ask is whether homosexual identity *is* equivalent to ego identity? Is the ego identity construct the most suitable theoretical structure and framework within which to present homosexual identity? Does the presentation of homosexual identity as an adolescent outcome exhaust all there is to know and understand about gay identity?

Proponents of the *sexual identity* model perceive homosexual identity as equivalent to sexual identity, believed to be developed in early childhood. Green's (1974) model of gender identity forms the basis for most of these theorists. This has led to confusion over what is meant by "identity." Early childhood identity theories are invariably proposals about how sexual preference or sexual orientation is formed. "Identity" in this sense refers primarily to consistent behavior patterns as they relate to a particular sexual role, not to cognitive aspects. Not surprisingly, this has led to confusion between the behavioral and cognitive aspects of homosexuality. Although intricately bound up with each other, behavior and identity are separate entities. Concern for the consequences of such confusion has prompted a number of theorists (e.g., Altman, 1979; Goode, 1981a; Kirkham, 1971; McDonald, 1981; Omark, 1978; Richardson, 1981a; Stoller, 1980; Weeks, 1981; Weinberg, 1978) to argue most strongly for a clear distinction between behavioral terms and concepts (e.g., sexual preference, sexual orientation) and identity terms.

Is the Green model the most acceptable framework within which to place homosexual identity? Is the concept of homosexual identity necessary to a theoretical account of how sexual preference develops? In a fresh approach, Storms (1979, 1980, 1981) has largely steered clear of the Green model and proposed a theory of erotic orientation development. His research was intended to study the process of "self-attribution" or perceiving oneself as a homosexual, by examining the information from which such attributions derived. Erotic fantasies and sexual behavior were considered the primary sources of this information.

The assumption that homosexual identity is the logical outcome of early childhood and adolescent developmental processes is clearly in need of examination. Can the concept of adult identity development be ignored? Can we conceive of a homosexual identity that arises in adulthood, in much the same way as other adult identities are formulated (such as the identity of "Jew" or "Catholic" following religious conversion as an adult; or the identity of "disabled" following trauma occurring during adult years)? Is homosexual identity developed in childhood to be perceived as the same phenomenon as that developed in adulthood? Given what we know about childhood cognitive and self-development, what difficulties might we have in formulating a theory of early homosexual identity development?

Proponents of adult identity acquisition mostly refer to the development of a homosexual self-image which is consonant with perceived environmental expectations. This may occur at any point in an individual's life-time. Because symbolic interactionism is commonly used as a theoretical base by these theorists, the influence of social factors in determining identity is given greater emphasis.

Argument has long waged between proponents of childhood versus adult homosexual identity. Plummer (1981) has proposed a synthesis of both approaches. He notes that there is evidence for the importance of both childhood and adult experiences. While the basic idea of seeing human development as a continuum rather than two separate categories is to be commended, Plummer comes close to falling into the old trap of mixing behavioral and cognitive concepts. As noted previously, the term "sexual identity" does not necessarily, and most times does not, refer to a cognitive construct but rather a behavioral one.

I am not claiming that cognitive and behavioral elements cannot be incorporated into a single theoretical formulation, but rather that care must be taken (1) not to confuse the two strands of development and (2) to use the word "identity" only in a cognitive sense.

I believe we need to direct our attention to the cognitive development of homosexual identity in a way that allows for a synthesis of childhood and adulthood processes. We know that one of the primary tasks of the developing child is to develop a picture of self as distinct from others. As the child grows older these self-perceptions gradually regularize and consolidate allowing a relatively consistent picture of self to be presented to the world. Adolescence is a time when such consolidation is likely to occur. At this time, according to the developmental theorist, children are cognitively, morally, emotionally, and socially equipped to place themselves in the world as unique individuals. We also know, however, that some identities are formulated prior to adolescence (e.g., ethnic, racial, gender identities).

The question for theorists is how *homosexual* identity should be conceived in relation to these developmental processes? As a part of a society that includes the social category "homosexual," a child will learn the descriptors of such a category. Conceivably this cognitive template (Gergan, 1977) may be applied to self, initiating the process of cognitive restructuring that leads to identity development.

Equally possible, an individual may make no such cognitive comparison until adulthood. Which factors (social, personal, developmental, etc.) are associated with childhood as compared with adult development of a homosexual identity is a relatively unexplored research question. The debate of childhood versus adult gay identity acquisition is a futile one, ignoring the fact that human development is a complexly varied and continuous process. Self-conceptions and identities are constantly evolving aspects of individual functioning. New self-perceptions are built upon existing ones, so that eventually a new gestalt is formed. This in turn is experienced as new psychological activity. Out of this, changes in old identities and formation of new ones may occur. Identities are not static pictures of how the individual conceives of self. How might the content and structure of gay identity change over time as the individual moves from childhood to adulthood, or from one period of adult life to another? There is little information available to researchers as to which self-images are grouped together during either initial or later formulations of homosexual identity.

HOMOSEXUAL IDENTITY AS SEXUAL IDENTITY

A great number of writers make explicit or implicit reference to the synonymity of homosexual identity with sexual identity (e.g., Coleman, 1981/82; Dank, 1971, 1974; Hoffman, 1968; Horowitz, 1964; Miller, 1978; Miller & Fowlkes, 1980; Ponse, 1978; Richardson & Hart, 1981; Roesler & Deisher, 1972; Weinberg, 1978; Robertson, Note 4; Troiden, Note 9). The belief that homosexual identity is the same as sexual identity is so ingrained that the tenability of this deduction is never questioned. It is, indeed, another assumption that requires examination.

It is possible to trace historically how sexual identity and homosexual identity might have become linked. The nineteenth-century medical model saw homosexuals classified as sexual perverts (Boswell, 1980; Bullough, 1974; Foucault, 1978). Arising out of this model, psychoanalytical theory presented a theoretical conception of human development that linked identity development (the satisfactory integration of id, ego, and superego) with sexual identity. According to this formulation, the consistent presentation of homosexuality in puberty and adult years is considered a sign of fixation at the Oedipal stage of sexual identity development. Therefore, equating homosexuality and sexual identity was clearly established by this line of thinking. The fact that it is sexual activity that most often prompts the eventual creation of homosexual identity no doubt reinforced this link.

The central question is whether homosexual identity *is* simply a synonym for sexual identity. Are the components of a gay identity those of sexual identity? Is a person's homosexual identity entirely bound up in sexual elements? The equation, sexual activity equals sexual identity equals homosexual (Ponse, 1978), is a theoretical proposal that is no longer relevant to the experiences of modern day homosexuals. The notion of "homosexual identity" is expanding to include new elements (such as the political, collective). The psychosocial framework within which the homosexual of the 1980s is constructed is no longer solely a sexual one. Identity, by definition, is time-bound, and theories of homosexual identity must allow for this.

I contend that it is necessary to separate the concepts "sexual identity" and "homosexual identity" since the structure and contents of each may refer to different phenomena. Sexual identity thus becomes the individual's overall conception of self as a sexual being. It might, for example, include the perception "I am a sensuous person," which illustrates a general view of personal responsiveness and sensitivity, without specifically describing the person to whom it is directed. The contents of a person's homosexual identity, while they may include sexual self-images, may also refer to non-sexual areas. For example, "I am a member of a minority group" and "I am a person who socializes with gay people" are percepts that may be unrelated to sexual responsivity. It is expected that in the early stages of identity development, sexual components will be more prominent than at later stages. This reflects the significance sexual cues have been given in Western characterizations of homosexual identity.

The multidimensional continuum approach suggests that homosexual identity may vary on any number of dimensions. There are a myriad of meanings that individuals can include in their perceptions of themselves as "a homosexual." A sound theory of gay identity must be able to incorporate within its proposals the multi-faceted nature of identity. What is the content of the different aspects of homosexual identity? What is the relative importance of each component in different life situations and for different individuals? Which personal and social factors are influential in changing identity components during identity acquisition?

HOMOSEXUAL IDENTITIES: GAY VS HOMOSEXUAL DICHOTOMY

A number of researchers have warned of the need to examine non-sexual aspects of identity (e.g., Bell, 1973; Loewenstein, 1980). A recent theoretical development is that of distinguishing between "homosexual identity" and "gay identity" (e.g., Chesebro, 1981; Harry & DeVall, 1978; Humphreys & Miller, 1980; Kimmel, 1979; Morin, 1977; Morin & Schultz, 1978; Taylor, 1977; Warren, 1974; Weinberg, Note 10). A *homosexual identity* "describes one's sexual orientation" (Warren, 1974, p. 149) and "places its focus on an explicit sexual act and then on its coincidental behavior" (Chesebro, 1981, p. 186). A *gay identity* "implies affiliation with the gay community in a cultural and sociable sense" (Warren, 1974, p. 149) and "identifies those who have adopted a particular *world view* or perspective of reality which is *self-imposed* and a *self-defined* determinant of the attitudes, beliefs, actions, and even the vocabulary affecting human interactions" (Chesebro, 1981, p. 186).

The change in conception of homosexual identity away from a totally sexual meaning is being expressed quite firmly in the homosexual/gay identity distinction. It suggests that, at times, identity is bound up with sexual concepts and, at other times, it is not. The difficulty with presenting such a dichotomy, however, is that it proposes a rigid division that is unlikely to exist in reality, and that cannot be easily operationalized for research purposes. What, for example, are the qualifying factors for defining someone "gay" as opposed to "homosexual?" It appears (Cass, in press) that individuals have a range of self-perceptions that relate to a homosexual identity and do not employ a simple two-way categorization.

The dichotomy model appears, therefore, to reflect a political stance rather than the subjective reality of the individual. Proponents of the homosexual/gay dichotomy suggest that a gay identity is a more "advanced" identity since it reflects the individual's development of strategies for effectively dealing with a stigmatized status. However, the notion of "homosexual identity" as proposed by these theorists runs counter to the definition of identity presented in this paper. I am not questioning the developmental emphasis. This has been almost uniformly advanced by a number of writers (e.g., Cass, 1979; Coleman, 1981/82; Hencken & O'Dowd, 1977; Lee, 1977; Miller, 1978; Plummer, 1975; McLellan, Note 7; Troiden, Note 9; Weinberg, Note 10). I question whether a homosexual identity, as defined by the dichotomy theorists, can be fully developed at the stages they suggest. My own model (Cass, 1979) contains the idea that identity is not fully developed until the final (Identity Synthesis) stage. It is not until this time that the individual's sense of self as "homosexual" represents an integration of self-images with the view of self believed to be held by others in all areas of the individual's life.

HOMOSEXUAL IDENTITY AND ITS DEVELOPMENT

Although space does not permit a full discussion of theories of homosexual identity formation, it is obvious that the theoretical form "identity" takes will be paramount in understanding the developmental paths proposed. However, many theorists have presented "identity" as a given, offering little more than simplistic reifications such as "self-definition," "self-perception," or "self-labeling" as definitions of the core constructs in their work. As a result, there is often confusion between self-concept and identity, between identity as perceived by others and as perceived by the self, as well as between cognitive and behavioral aspects. Reference to the cognitive components of homosexual identity is virtually nonexistent. Using the term "identity," some theorists refer to childhood developmental processes, others to adult processes, and yet others to a combination of the two. Some call the process "coming out," while others use this phrase to include both behavioral and identity processes. .

A theory purporting to outline identity formation should (1) offer a clear definition of what "identity" means and of its relationship to self-concept, (2) outline the structural components of identity, (3) trace the changes that occur as identity develops, and (4) describe both internal and external factors influencing such changes. Conceptually, it is necessary to keep distinct the cognitive, behavioral, and emotional changes, and to trace each area through all stages of development.

HOMOSEXUAL IDENTITY AS GROUP IDENTITY

In the past decade, direct and indirect references has been increasingly made to the notion of *minority identity* in relation to homosexuals (e.g., Abbott & Love, 1973; Adam, 1978; Fein & Nuehring, 1981; Ferguson, 1981; Gagnon, 1977; Kameny, 1969; Seidenberg, 1973). Unfortunately, little consideration has been given to actually defining or describing the nature of homosexual identity in the group or subcultural context. A reading of the literature on ethnic identity suggests, however, that the concept of group identity provides an important perspective to the understanding of identity.

I choose to define group identity as the perception a person has about self as sharing certain attributes with a particular community of others. A positive affective component is attached to such a perception. A particular sense of "Me" emerges out of seeing oneself as a "We." Group identity most commonly emerges where the attributes in question are perceived negatively by a dominant group.

In the homosexual literature, attention has been given to "gay pride" from a sociological perspective. When translated into the context of *positive group identity*, it is possible to consider it from a psychological viewpoint. What is the content of homosexual group identity? What affective and cognitive changes take place as an individual moves from a heterosexual to a homosexual group identity? Cass (1979) has suggested and found support (Cass, in press) for the notion that development of positive gay group identity marks an important stage in the development of a fully integrated homosexual self-identity.

HOMOSEXUAL IDENTITY: FACT, FANTASY OR CONSTRUCT?

This paper would not be complete without mentioning those authors who decry the use of the concept "homosexual identity" (e.g., Cappon, 1965; Pattison, 1974; Sagarin, 1976, 1979; Weltge, 1969; DuBay, Note 3). They argue that there is really no such thing as "a homosexual." It is a figment of the theorist's imagination and, therefore, should not be studied as if it were an objective reality. The concept of homosexual identity is believed to be destructive because (1) it places the individual in a stigmatized category that is dehumanizing, and (2) it attributes permanence and rigidity to the individual. Locked into a set category, there is little avenue for change. This view is strengthened from two other sources: (1) growing opposition to the assumption of essentiality in the idea of the homosexual identity and (2) the focus of the 1970s on "self" as process.

The notion of identity as essence (Katz, 1975) portrays homosexual identity as a pervasive and unchangeable fact that is acknowledged by the person about the self or by others about that person (Plummer, 1981; Ponse, 1978; Richardson, 1981b; Warren, 1974; Weeks, 1980/81). For some authors, this "fact" is believed to have been established in early childhood (or at conception) as an essential and integral part of the child's functioning. According to this latency perspective, the task becomes one of gradually acknowledging and exhibiting this identity. Other theorists do not hold this view but, nevertheless, believe that once identity is established, it becomes an inherent quality of the person. Thus we have the notion of homosexual identity as being equivalent to one's "true" or "real" self (e.g., Berzon, 1979; Guth, 1978), a view commonly held by members of the gay subculture as well as by theorists. Given the restrictiveness of this view, it is understandable that some authors have resisted adopting the concept of "homosexual identity."

While a case can be made for the idea that a static quality is seen to characterize the homosexual individual, it does not necessarily follow that the identity construct should be abandoned: (1) Homosexuals do perceive themselves as having an identity that is a relatively stable part of themselves. Do we, therefore, attack what is in effect a reality for the individual (subjective and socially influenced though it may be) or might we not do better to examine our theoretical conceptions of that identity. (2) Identities can change, and instances of this are readily available in everyday life. What we need to realize is that it is the theories of identity governing our thinking, as Berger and Luckman (1966) point out, that dictate the rigid and permanent quality of homosexual identity:

> Identity is a phenomenon that emerges from the dialectic between individual and society. Identity *types*, on the other hand, are social products and *tout court*, relatively stable elements of objective social reality (the degree of stability being, of course, socially determined in its turn). (p. 160)

What we do need to examine is why a fixed essence perspective has been, and still is, promoted so strongly within and outside the gay subculture. Zita (1981) and Harry and DeVall (1978), for example, suggest that defining oneself as a lesbian or homosexual brings about certain social and political consequences that are necessary to the survival of a gay woman or man. De Cecco (1981) proposes that the importance of an essence concept lies in its promotion of the status of homosexuals as a minority group. Plummer (1981) notes that categorization brings "comfort, security and assuredness" (p. 29).

The concept of identity based on self-as-object is considered restrictive because it ignores the "experiencing aspect" and, therefore, the very nature of "who I am." It is true that consideration of the structure of homosexual identity has often precluded a view of identity as process. Nevertheless, this is not sufficient grounds for ignoring the fact that, for homosexuals at this specific point in history, the concept of an identity is

Those theorists diametrically opposed to the concept of homosexual identity tend to adhere to the need to focus on the individual as existential, self-as-experiencing. The self may be viewed as both object and process. The study of identity as a construct pertains to the former, since it considers the way an individual perceives the self. The self-as-process perspective involves consideration of the way a person actually experiences the self as "a homosexual." It is experiencing rather than perceiving that experience. An individual is seen to be in a state of continuous becoming (Maslow, 1968; Stein, 1977). Therefore identity can never be "what is," only "what is becoming."

built into their cultural milieu. While some may wish it were not, yet it is a part of the "psychologies" of our time.

So, is homosexual identity fact, construct, or simply fanciful illusion? The answer, it would seem, is all three! To the homosexual, perception of self as "a homosexual" is seen to be as valid an experience as that of "being homosexual." Yet homosexual identity can only arise in those societies where the homosexual categorization is acknowledged. In this sense, homosexual identity is hypothetical, constructed out of a need to control and restrict (Plummer, 1981) rather than a reflection of any actual concrete form. For the researcher wishing to understand the individual's experiential sense of "being a homosexual," the "homosexual identity" becomes a suitable research tool, an explanatory construct with hypothetical properties. An adequate understanding of homosexual identity requires serious consideration be given to all three perspectives.

CONCLUSIONS

Throughout this paper it has been my contention that there are three areas for concern: (1) the lack of definition of what is meant by "homosexual identity," (2) researchers' persistence in isolating their work from the theoretical literature on identity and self-concept, and (3) the inadvertent inclusion of theoretical assumptions that play a critical role in the conceptualization of homosexual identity. It is suggested that researchers should return to the most basic of questions, namely, "What exactly do we mean by the term 'identity' as it pertains to homosexuals?" I suggest that a multidisciplinary approach to the issue is necessary if all facets of homosexual identity are to be adequately examined. To date, the psychological profession has been notably absent from both the theoretical and empirical areas. Because identity is a cognitive construct, this absence has produced an understandably limited and one-sided approach. It is precisely because the study of identity points us to "the dialectic between individual and society" (Berger & Luckman, 1966) that it offers an exciting opportunity for a combined-discipline approach.

On another level, an understanding of homosexual identity must have implications that go beyond homosexuals. What, for example, might we learn about heterosexual identity? How might our knowledge of the homosexual situation aid our understanding of other minority identities? Ultimately, the study of homosexual identity should allow us to consider the whole question of *human identity*.

NOTES

1. Grzelkowski (Note 8) refers to degrees of identity. Perhaps a phrase such as "partially developed homosexual identity" may be appropriate here.

2. A role is a behavioral concept referring to the patterns of behavior expected from a social position and may be distinguished from identity, which is a cognitive construct. For a discussion of

homosexual role, and an example of the confusion between the concepts of "identity," "role," and "behavior," see the debate presented by Goode (1981a; 1981b), Omark (1978; 1981), and Whitam (1977; 1978; 1981).

3. Dank (1971) suggested this direction over a decade ago, yet little attention has been given to cognitive processes in identity formation or maintenance.

REFERENCE NOTES

1. Dank, B. M. *The development of a homosexual identity: Antecedents and consequents.* Unpublished manuscript, University of Wisconsin, 1973.

2. De Cecco, J. P. *The normalization of homosexuality: Research, policy and practice.* Paper presented at the meeting of the Canadian Psychological Association, Toronto, Canada, 4 June 1981.

3. DuBay, W. H. *Gay identity: Concept problems and alternatives.* Unpublished manuscript, 1979. (Available from author, 615 "H" #102, Anchorage, Alaska 99501.)

4. Robertson, D. M. *Coming out gay.* Paper presented at the Pacific Sociological Association Conference, San Francisco, April 1977.

5. Morin, S. F., & Miller, J. S. *On fostering positive identity in gay men: Some developmental issues.* Paper presented at the American Orthopsychiatric Association Convention, San Francisco, March 1978.

6. Somers, M. *The relationships between present social support networks and current levels of gay identity.* Unpublished manuscript, California School of Professional Psychology, 1982.

7. McLellan, E. A. *Lesbian identity: A theological and psychological inquiry into the developmental stages of identity in a lesbian.* Unpublished manuscript, School of Theology at Claremont, Michigan, 1977.

8. Grzelkowski, K. P. *Who am I to me? Homosexual self-identity in a world of role versatility.* Unpublished manuscript, Indiana University, 1976.

9. Troiden, R. R. *Becoming homosexual: Research on acquiring a gay identity.* Unpublished manuscript, State University of New York at Stony Brook, 1977.

10. Weinberg, T. S. *Becoming homosexual: Self-discovery, self-identity, and self-maintenance.* Unpublished manuscript, University of Connecticut, 1977.

REFERENCES

Abbott, S., & Love, B. *Sappho was a right-on woman: A liberated view of lesbianism.* New York: Stein & Day, 1973.

Abend, S. M. Problems of identity: Theoretical and clinical applications. *Psychoanalytic Quarterly,* 1974, *43,* 606-637.

Adam, B. D. *The survival of domination.* New York: Elsevier, 1978.

Altman, D. *Coming out in the seventies: Sexuality, politics and culture.* New York: Penguin Books, 1979.

Babuscio, J. *We speak for ourselves: Experiences in homosexual counselling.* London, SPCK, 1979.

Ball, D. W. Self and identity in the context of deviance: The case of criminal abortion. In R. A. Scott & J. D. Douglas (Eds.), *Theoretical perspectives on deviance.* New York: Basic Books, 1972.

Bell, A. Homosexualities: Their range and character. In J. Cole & D. Dienstbier (Eds.), *Nebraska Symposium on Motivation* (Vol. 21). Lincoln: University of Nebraska Press, 1973.

Berger, P. L., & Luckman, T. *The social construction of reality.* New York: Doubleday, 1966.

Berzon, B. Developing a positive gay identity. In B. Berzon & R. Leighton (Eds.), *Positively gay.* Millbrae, Celestial Arts, 1979.

Blumstein, P. W., & Schwartz, P. Lesbianism and bisexuality. In E. Goode & R. R. Troiden (Eds.), *Sexual deviance and sexual deviants.* New York: William Morrow, 1974.

Blumstein, P. W., & Schwartz, P. Bisexuality: Some social psychological issues. *Journal of Social Issues,* 1977, *33,* 30-45.

Boswell, J. *Christianity, social tolerance, and homosexuality.* Chicago: University of Chicago Press, 1980.

Bullough, V. L. Homosexuality and the medical model. *Journal of Homosexuality*, 1974, *1*, 99-110.
Cappon, D. *Toward an understanding of homosexuality*. Englewood Cliffs, NJ: Prentice-Hall, 1965.
Cass, V. C. Homosexual identity formation: A theoretical model. *Journal of Homosexuality*, 1979, *4*, 219-235.
Cass, V. C. Homosexual identity formation: Testing a theoretical model. *Journal of Sex Research*, in press.
Chesebro, J. W. Views of homosexuality among social scientists. In J. W. Chesebro (Ed.), *Gayspeak*. New York: The Pilgrim Press, 1981.
Clinard, M. B. *Sociology of deviant behavior* (3rd ed.), New York: Holt, Rinehart & Winston, 1968.
Coleman, E. Developmental stages of the coming out process. *Journal of Homosexuality*, 1981/82, *7*, 31-43.
Cory, D. W. *The homosexual in America: A subjective approach*. New York: Arno Press, 1975. (Originally published, 1951.)
Crites, T. R. Coming out gay. In J. P. Wiseman (Ed.), *The social psychology of sex*. New York: Harper & Row, 1976.
Cronin, D. M. Coming out among lesbians. In E. Goode & R. R. Troiden (Eds.), *Sexual deviance and sexual deviants*. New York: William Morrow, 1974.
Dank, B. M. Coming out in the gay world. *Psychiatry*, 1971, *34*, 180-197.
Dank, B..M. Why homosexuals marry. *Medical Aspects of Human Sexuality*, 1972, *6*, 14-23.
Dank, B. M. The homosexual. In E. Goode & R. R. Troiden (Eds.), *Sexual deviance and sexual deviants*. New York: William Morrow, 1974.
Davis, K. E. Identity, alienation and ways of life. In M. Werthheimer (Ed.), *Confrontation: Psychology and the problems of today*. Glenview, IL: Scott, Foresman, 1970.
De Cecco, J. P. Definition and meaning of sexual orientation. *Journal of Homosexuality*, 1981, *6*, 51-67.
Erikson, E. H. Identity and the life-cycle. *Psychological Issues*, 1959, *1*, 1-17.
Erikson, E. H. Identity and identity diffusion. In C. Gordon & K. J. Gergen (Eds.), *The self in social interaction*. New York: John Wiley, 1968.
Fein, S. B., & Nuehring, E. M. Intrapsychic effects of stigma: A process of breakdown and reconstruction of social reality. *Journal of Homosexuality*, 1981, *7*, 3-13.
Ferguson, A. Patriarchy, sexual identity and the sexual revolution. *Signs*, 1981, *7*, 153-172.
Foucault, M. *The history of sexuality* (Vol. 1). New York: Pantheon Books, 1978.
Freedman, M. Homosexuals may be healthier than straights. *Psychology Today*, March 1975, 28-32.
Gagnon, J. *Human sexualities*. Glenview, IL: Scott, Foresman, 1977.
Gergen, K. J. The social construction of self-knowledge. In T. Mischel (Ed.), *The self: Psychological and philosophical issues*. Totowa, NJ: Rowman & Littlefield, 1977.
Goode, E. *Deviant behavior: An interactionist approach*. Englewood Cliffs, NJ: Prentice-Hall, 1978.
Goode, E. Comments on the homosexual role. *Journal of Sex Research*, 1981, *17*, 54-65. (a)
Goode, E. The homosexual role: Rejoinder to Omark and Whitam. *Journal of Sex Research*, 1981, *17*, 76-83. (b)
Goode, E., & Haber, L. Sexual correlates of homosexual experience: An exploratory study of college women. *Journal of Sex Research*, 1977, *13*, 12-21.
Goode, E., & Troiden, R. R. (Eds.). *Sexual deviance and sexual deviants*. New York: William Morrow, 1974.
Goode, E., & Troiden, R. R. Heterosexual and homosexual activity among gay males. *Deviant Behavior*, 1979, *1*, 37-55.
Green, R. *Sexual identity conflict in children and adults*. New York: Basic Books, 1974.
Gundlach, R. H., & Riess, B. F. Self and sexual identity in the female: A study of female homosexuals. In B. F. Riess (Ed.), *New directions in mental health*. (Vol. 1). New York: Grune & Stratton, 1968.
Guth, J. T. Invisible women: Lesbians in America. *Journal of Sex Education and Therapy*, 1978, *4*, 3-6.
Hammersmith, S. K., & Weinberg, M. S. Homosexual identity: Commitment, adjustment and significant others. *Sociometry*, 1973, *36*, 56-79.
Hanckel, F., & Cunningham, J. *A way of love, a way of life: A young person's introduction to what it means to be gay*. New York: Lothrop, Lee & Shepard Books, 1979.
Harry, J., & DeVall, W. B. *The social organization of gay males*. New York: Praeger, 1978.
Hayes, J. J. Gayspeak. *Quarterly Journal of Speech*, 1976, *62*, 256-266.

Hayes, J. J. Lesbians, gay men, and their "languages." In J. W. Chesebro (Ed.), *Gayspeak.* New York: The Pilgrim Press, 1981.

Hencken, J. D., & O'Dowd, W. T. Coming out as an aspect of identity formation. *Gai Saber,* 1977, *1,* 18–22.

Hoffman, M. *The gay world: Male homosexuality and the social creation of evil.* New York: Basic Books, 1968.

Horowitz, M. J. The homosexual's image of himself. *Mental Hygiene,* 1964, *48,* 197–201.

Humphreys, S. L. Exodus and identity: The emerging gay culture. In M. Levine (Ed.), *Gay men: The sociology of male homosexuality.* New York: Harper & Row, 1979.

Humphreys, L., & Miller, B. Identities in the emerging gay culture. In J. Marmor (Ed.), *Homosexual behavior: A modern reappraisal.* New York: Basic Books, 1980.

Jandt, F. E., & Darsey, J. Coming out as a communicative process. In J. W. Chesebro (Ed.), *Gayspeak.* New York: The Pilgrim Press, 1981.

Jay, K. Introduction: Identity and lifestyles. In K. Jay & A. Young (Eds.), *After you're out: personal experiences of gay men and lesbian women.* New York: Links Books, 1975.

Johnston, G. Keys to the ghetto. *Christopher Street,* January 1980, 20–32.

Kameny, F. E. Gay is good. In R. W. Weltge (Ed.), *The same sex: An appraisal of homosexuality.* New York: The Pilgrim Press, 1969.

Katz, J. Essences as moral identities: Verifiability and responsibility in imputations of deviance and charisma. *American Journal of Sociology,* 1975, *80,* 1369–1390.

Kimmel, D. C. Adult development and aging: A gay perspective. *Journal of Social Issues,* 1978, *34,* 113–130.

Kimmel, D. C. Adjustment to aging among gay men. In B. Berzon & R. Leighton (Eds.), *Positively Gay.* Millbrae, CA: Celestial Arts, 1979.

Kirkham, G. L. Homosexuality in prison. In J. M. Henslin (Ed.), *Studies in the sociology of sex.* New York: Appleton-Century-Crofts, 1971.

Laing, R. D., Phillipson, H., & Lee, A. R. *Interpersonal perception: A theory and a method of research.* London: Tavistock, 1966.

Latham, J. D., & White, S. D. Coping with homosexual expression within heterosexual marriages: Five case studies. *Journal of Sex and Marital Therapy,* 1978, *4,* 198–212.

Lee, J. A. Going public: A study in the sociology of homosexual liberation. *Journal of Homosexuality,* 1977, *3,* 49–78.

Lehman, L. What it means to love another woman. In G. Vida (Ed.), *Our right to love: A lesbian resource book.* Englewood Cliffs, NJ: Prentice-Hall, 1978.

Levine, M. (Ed.). *Gay men: The sociology of male homosexuality.* New York: Harper & Row, 1979.

Loewenstein, S. Understanding lesbian women. *Social Casework,* 1980, *61,* 29–38.

Lyman, S. M., & Scott, M. B. *A sociology of the absurd.* New York: Appleton-Century-Crofts, 1970.

Maslow, A. H. *Toward a psychology of being.* New York: Van Nostrand Reinhold, 1968.

McDonald, G. Misrepresentation, liberalism and heterosexual bias in introductory psychology textbooks. *Journal of Homosexuality,* 1981, *6,* 45–60.

Miller, B. Adult sexual resocialization: Adjustments toward a stigmatized identity. *Alternative Lifestyles,* 1978, *1,* 207–234.

Miller, D. R. The study of social relationships: Situation, identity and social interaction. In S. Koch (Ed.), *Psychology: A study of science. Vol. 5: The process areas, the person, and some applied fields.* New York: McGraw-Hill, 1963.

Miller, P. Y., & Fowlkes, M. R. Social and behavioral constructions of female sexuality. *Signs,* 1980, *5,* 783–800.

Morin, S. F. Heterosexual bias in psychological research on lesbianism and male homosexuality. *American Psychologist,* 1977, *32,* 628–637.

Morin, S. F., & Schultz, S. J. The gay movement and the rights of children. *Journal of Social Issues,* 1978, *34,* 137–148.

Moses, A. E. *Identity management in lesbian women.* New York: Praeger, 1978.

Murphy, J. Gay lib. In C. McCaghy, J. Skipper, & M. Lefton (Eds.), *In their own behalf: Voices from the margin* (2nd ed.). New York: Appleton-Century-Crofts, 1974.

Omark, R. C. A comment on the homosexual role. *Journal of Sex Research,* 1978, *14,* 273–274.

Omark, R. C. Further comment on the homosexual role: A reply to Goode. *Journal of Sex Research,* 1981, *17,* 73–75.

Parker, W. *Homosexuality: Selected abstracts and bibliography.* San Francisco: Society for Individual Rights, 1971.

Pattison, E. M. Confusing concepts about the concept of homosexuality. *Psychiatry*, 1974, *37*, 340-349.

Plummer, K. Awareness of homosexuality. In R. Bailey & J. Young (Eds.), *Contemporary social problems in Britain*. London: Lexington Books, 1973.

Plummer, K. *Sexual stigma: An interactionist account*. London: Routledge & Kegan Paul, 1975.

Plummer, K. Homosexual categories: Some research problems in the labeling perspective of homosexuality. In K. Plummer (Ed.), *The making of the modern homosexual*. London: Hutchinson, 1981.

Ponse, B. Secrecy in the lesbian world. *Sage Contemporary Social Science Issues*, 1977, *35*, 53-78.

Ponse, B. *Identities in the lesbian world: The social construction of self*. Westport, CT: Greenwood Press, 1978.

Ponse, B. Lesbians and their worlds. In J. Marmor (Ed.), *Homosexual behavior: A modern reappraisal*. New York: Basic Books, 1980.

Reiss, A. J. The social integration of queers and peers. *Social Problems*, 1961, *9*, 102-120.

Richardson, D. Theoretical perspectives on homosexuality. In J. Hart & D. Richardson (Eds.), *The theory and practice of homosexuality*. London: Routledge & Kegan Paul, 1981 (a)

Richardson, D. Lesbian identities. In J. Hart & D. Richardson (Eds.), *The theory and practice of homosexuality*. London: Routledge & Kegan Paul, 1981. (b)

Richardson, D., & Hart, J. The development and maintenance of a homosexual identity. In J. Hart & D. Richardson (Eds.), *The theory and practice of homosexuality*. London: Routledge & Kegan Paul, 1981.

Riebel, L. Theory as self portrait, and the ideal of objectivity. *Journal of Humanistic Psychology*, 1982, *22*, 91-116.

Roesler, T., & Deisher, R. W. Youthful male homosexuality. *Journal of the American Medical Association*, 1972, *219*, 1018-1023.

Rosenberg, M. *Conceiving the self*. New York: Basic Books, 1979.

Sagarin, E. The high personal cost of wearing a label. *Psychology Today*, March 1976, 25-30.

Sagarin, E. Deviance without deviants: The temporal quality of patterned behavior. *Deviant Behavior*, 1979, *1*, 1-13.

Schafer, R. Concepts of self and identity and the experience of separation-individuation in adolescence. *Psychoanalytic Quarterly*, 1973, *42*, 42-59.

Schwartz, M., & Stryker, S. *Deviance, selves and others*. Washington, D.C.: American Sociological Association, Rose Monograph Series, 1970.

Seidenberg, R. The accursed race. In H. M. Ruitenbeek (Ed.), *Homosexuality: A changing picture*. London: Souvenir Press, 1973.

Shibutani, T. *Society and personality*. Englewood Cliffs, NJ: Prentice-Hall, 1961.

Simon, W., & Gagnon, J. H. Homosexuality: The formulation of a sociological perspective. *Journal of Health and Social Behavior*, 1967, *8*, 177-185. (a)

Simon, W., & Gagnon, J. H. The lesbians: A preliminary overview. In J. H. Gagnon & W. Simon (Eds.), *Sexual deviance*. New York: Harper & Row, 1967. (b).

Steffensmeier, D., & Steffensmeier, R. Sex differences in reactions to homosexuals: Research continuities and further development. *Journal of Sex Research*, 1974, *10*, 52-67.

Stein, H. F. Identity and transcendence. *School Review*, 1977, *85*, 349-375.

Stoller, R. J. Problems with the term "homosexuality." *Hillside Journal of Clinical Psychiatry*, 1980, *2*, 3-25.

Stone, G. P. Appearance and the self. In A. M. Rose (Ed.), *Human behavior and social processes*. Boston: Houghton Mifflin, 1962.

Storms, M. D. Sexual orientation and self-perception. In P. Pliner, K. Blankstein, & I. Spiger (Eds.), *Perception of emotion in self and others*. New York: Plenum Press, 1979.

Storms, M. D. Theories of sexual orientation. *Journal of Personality and Social Psychology*, 1980, *38*, 783-792.

Storms, M. D. A theory of erotic orientation development. *Psychological Review*, 1981, *88*, 340-353.

Taylor, L. Aspects of the ideology of the gay liberation movement in New Zealand. *Australian and New Zealand Journal of Sociology*, 1977, *13*, 126-132.

Troiden, R. R. Becoming homosexual: A model of gay identity acquisition. *Psychiatry*, 1979, *42*, 362-373.

Warren, C. A. B. *Identity and community in the gay world*. New York: John Wiley, 1974.

Warren, C. A. B. Homosexuality and stigma. In J. Marmor (Ed.), *Homosexual behavior: A modern reappraisal*. New York: Basic Books, 1980.

Weeks, J. *Coming out: Homosexual politics in Britain from the nineteenth century to the present.* New York: Quartet Books, 1977.

Weeks, J. Inverts, perverts, and Mary-Annes. *Journal of Homosexuality*, 1980/81, *6*, 113–134.

Weeks, J. Discourse, desire and sexual deviance: Some problems in a history of homosexuality. In K. Plummer (Ed.), *The making of the modern homosexual.* London: Hutchinson, 1981.

Wegner, D. M., & Vallacher, R. R. *Implicit psychology.* London: Oxford University Press, 1977.

Weinberg, M. S., & Bell, A. (Eds.). *Homosexuality: An annotated bibliography.* New York: Harper & Row, 1972.

Weinberg, M. S., & Williams, C. J. Neutralizing the homosexual label. In M. S. Weinberg & E. Rubington (Eds.), *The solution of social problems: 5 perspectives.* New York: Oxford University Press, 1973.

Weinberg, M. S., & Williams, C. J. *Male homosexuals: Their problems and adaptations.* New York: Oxford University Press, 1974.

Weinberg, T. S. On "doing" and "being" gay: Sexual behavior and homosexual male self-identity. *Journal of Homosexuality*, 1978, *4*, 143–156.

Weis, C., & Dain, R. Ego development and sex attitudes in heterosexual men and women. *Archives of Sexual Behavior*, 1979, *8*, 341–356.

Weltge, R. W. The paradox of man and woman. In R. W. Weltge (Ed.), *The same sex: An appraisal of homosexuality.* New York: The Pilgrim Press, 1969.

Whitam, F. L. The homosexual role: A reconsideration. *Journal of Sex Research*, 1977, *13*, 1–11.

Whitam, F. L. Rejoinder to Omark's comment on the homosexual role. *Journal of Sex Research*, 1978, *14*, 274–275.

Whitam, F. L. A reply to Goode on "The homosexual role." *Journal of Sex Research*, 1981, *17*, 66–72.

Williams, C. J., & Weinberg, M. S. *Homosexuals and the military: A study of less than honorable discharge.* New York: Harper & Row, 1971.

Zavalloni, M. Social identity perspectives and prospects. *Social Sciences Information*, 1973, *12*, 65–91.

Zita, J. N. Historical amnesia and the lesbian continuum. *Signs*, 1981, *7*, 172–187.

Research on Sexual Orientation: Definitions and Methods

Michael G. Shively, MA
Christopher Jones, MA (cand.)
John P. De Cecco, PhD

Center for Research and Education in Sexuality (CERES)
San Francisco State University

ABSTRACT. An extensive survey of the research literature on sexual orientation was undertaken for the purpose of determining how sexual orientation had been conceptually and operationally defined and how research subjects had been identified and selected. Two hundred-twenty-eight articles from 47 different journals were analyzed. Sexual orientation, it was found, was conceptually defined in 28 studies and operationally defined in 168. In 196 studies respondents were identified on the basis of the settings in which they were found. Because of the great variation in both conceptual and operational definitions, it was almost impossible to determine with certainty the theoretical frameworks used in the studies. The wide divergency in the definitions of sexual orientation, the investigators conclude, is symptomatic of an underlying conceptual confusion.

In the course of our research on homosexuality, we became aware of the various ways in which sexual orientation was defined in the research literature and the apparent disparity among these definitions. We were perplexed over the methods by which subjects were identified and selected for inclusion in various studies. It often appeared that sexual orientation was merely assumed by the investigators: it was neither defined nor determined in any systematic fashion. In referring to each other's research, there was often tacit acceptance by one investigator of another's claim to have studied individuals of particular orientations. Although they occasionally quarrelled over the conclusions drawn from their studies, investigators rarely questioned whether the sexual orientation labels assign-

Christopher Jones is presently a graduate student in the social work program at the University of California, at Berkeley.

The authors wish to thank Ellsworth Lund and Wendell Ricketts for their assistance in reading and summarizing the data.

Reprints should be requested from Michael Shively at CERES, San Francisco State University, San Francisco, CA 94132.

ed to particular individuals or groups were validly applied. It was simply assumed, for example, that a group not known to be homosexual was entirely heterosexual.

PURPOSE

To address these definitional disparities and related issues we undertook an extensive survey of the research literature on sexual orientation. The major focus of this effort was to determine whether sexual orientation was defined and how research subjects were identified and selected. We were also interested in the level of definition, whether the definitions were conceptual, and thereby embedded in theory, or simply operational for the study at hand.

METHOD

We compiled a working list of studies in the following manner. First, we examined a number of bibliographies, some of which were published (see Appendix A). We selected those articles with titles which referred to heterosexuality, homosexuality, bisexuality, or to sexual orientation in general. The reference lists of selected articles were then examined in the same manner. To the survey were added studies found in the three journals devoted exclusively to research on human sexuality and published in the United States: *Archives of Sexual Behavior, Journal of Homosexuality,* and *Journal of Sex Research.* Since the *Journal of Homosexuality* was first published in 1974, the search for articles in all three journals commenced with that year. Studies that were published earlier and had appeared in the bibliographies or reference lists were, of course, included in the survey. By utilizing these sources, a survey list of 1,160 unduplicated titles was amassed.

This working list of studies was pruned in various ways to eliminate unsuitable articles. Articles published before 1969, with major exceptions, were excluded since that year historically marked the beginning of the Gay Liberation movement and the proliferation of published research on sexual orientation. We were careful to include articles frequently cited in the reference lists of published articles even though they appeared before 1969, such as those by Bieber, Gagnon, Hooker, and Simon. Foreign language articles were not examined because of the difficulty in obtaining the journals in which they appeared and reliable translations. Reviews of research, philosophical treatises, and position and opinion papers were not included because they lacked respondents. However, five articles devoted to theory were included because they attempted to define sexual orientation. Monographs and books were left out for two reasons: our intention was to survey research published in journals, which we believed reflected the scope and diversity of research on sexual orientation more than the larger works and major book authors, for the most part, were published in the journals. Some articles perforce were omitted because the journals could not be obtained through the libraries utilized for this survey: The Leonard Library at San Francisco State University, the San Francisco Public Library, the library of the University of California at San Francisco, and the libraries of the University of California at Berkeley.

The articles were read and summarized, using a summary data sheet designed for the survey. After recording the authors, titles, journals, and dates of publication, each article was classified for general type of methodology. The size and composition of the sample and the method of selecting respondents were noted. It was then determined whether sexual orientation was conceptually or operationally defined. If definitions appeared they were entered verbatim on the data sheet. Some effort, often difficult, was made to see how sexual orientation figured into the research design. To maintain a high level of reliability in summarizing the relevant information, the articles were read by only three individuals who worked closely together. For consistency, the data for computer entry and analysis were coded by one individual.

The 228 articles ultimately selected and analyzed appeared in 47 different journals. About 55% were published in three American sex research journals: about 30% in the *Journal of Homosexuality*, 15% in the *Archives of Sexual Behavior*, and 10% in the *Journal of Sex Research*. Forty-five percent of the articles were distributed over the remaining 44 journals. (See Appendix B for a complete list of journals.)

These studies were categorized by the general type of methodology used: 85 (37.3%) were field studies, usually involving the collection of questionnaire or interview data; 65 (28.5%) were psychometric studies, involving the measurement of psychological traits, such as femininity or masculinity, and psychological adjustment; 33 (14.5%) were biomedical studies of factors believed to be related to sexual orientation such as hormone levels and patterns of sexually transmitted diseases; 27 (11.8%) were clinical studies involving patient populations or case studies of individuals; 9 (3.9%) were physiological studies in which the response to sexual stimuli was measured using, for example, the penile phallometer; 5 (2.2%) were theoretical articles which attempted to define sexual orientation; and 4 (1.8%) were classified as experimental studies because they contained experimental and control groups, the experimental groups receiving a treatment not given the others.

The data base for these studies was specifically identified: 37.3% (f = 85) used self-administered questionnaires; 24.6% (f = 56) face-to-face interviews; 21.5% (f = 49) existing clinical or medical records; and

12.7% (f = 29) used a combination of questionnaires and interviews. In 3.9% (f = 9) of the studies no data base was mentioned or could be construed.

As in the past, the research on sexual orientation continued to be more occupied with males than females or with one sex to the exclusion of the other. About 56% (f = 120) of the studies included only male respondents, 21.1% (f = 48) included respondents of both sexes, and 14.9% (f = 33) included only females. In 8.3% (f = 19) the biological sex of the respondents was not designated.

RESULTS

One of the first questions addressed in the analysis of the data was how subjects were identified for possible inclusion in the studies. As shown in Table 1, in 86% of the studies respondents were included on the basis of one of the 13 settings in which they were found. The greatest proportion (33.8%) of the studies located respondents in homosexual organizations, 21.8% in clinical settings for homosexual patients, and 11.4% through homosexual friendship networks. When authors did not indicate a setting as a source of respondents (5.7% of the cases), they appeared to use a method of identifying sexual orientation such as self-identification by respondents or a sexual orientation rating scale. In several studies (8.3%) the method of identifying sexual orientation was not reported.

In most studies (42.5%) it appeared that the researchers depended on some authoritative source outside of the research effort to identify potential respondents, such as psychiatrists, institutional authorities or records, other researchers, or some respondents identifying others. Those researchers who recruited respondents from homosexual or heterosexual organizations (36%) appeared to have assumed that all individuals in those organizations were homosexual or heterosexual. This assumption forced reliance on the individual's affiliation. It also presumed that the bases of affiliation were the same for each individual and the same as those of the researcher. If one adds to these percentages the studies in which the investigator directly relied on the self-report of sexual orientation (3.1%), it can be concluded that 81.6% of the studies made no independent assessment of their respondents' sexual orientation for the purpose of inclusion.

A crucial issue in the survey was whether or not sexual orientation was conceptually or operationally defined. We found that it was conceptually defined in 28 (12.3%) studies and operationally defined in 168 (73.7%) studies. In 24 (10.5%) studies, sexual orientation was both conceptually and operationally defined and in 56 (24.6%) it was not defined at all.

In the 28 studies in which sexual orientation was conceptually defined,

Table 1

How Subjects Were Identified
for Inclusion in the Studies (N=228)

	f	%
Through Settings		
Homosexual Organizations	77	33.8
Clinical Homosexual Group	50	21.8
Respondent's Network	26	11.4
Classroom	17	7.5
From Another Study	5	2.2
Researcher's Network	5	2.2
Heterosexual Organizations	4	1.8
Imprisoned Homosexuals	4	1.8
Clinical Heterosexual Group	2	.9
Clinical Pedophile Group	2	.9
Imprisoned Heterosexuals	2	.9
Imprisoned Pedophiles	1	.4
Pedophile Organization	1	.4
subtotal	196	86.0%
Through Scales and Histories		
Self Report	7	3.1
Sex History	3	1.3
Kinsey Rating Scale	2	.9
Other Rating Scale	1	.4
subtotal	13	5.7%
Method of Identification was Not Stated	19	8.3
Total	228	100.0%

a multitude of definitional elements were found. Sixteen studies combined several elements. Since these elements are not mutually exclusive, all conceptual distinctions were noted, resulting in 10 categories as shown in Table 2.

Physical sexual activity was the element appearing in 50% of the con-

Table 2

Elements Appearing in the Conceptual

Definitions of Sexual Orientation(n=28)

	Number of Definitions In Which Elements Appeared	%
Physical sexual activity	14	50%
Affectional attachment (close relationships)	8	28%
Erotic fantasies	6	21%
Arousal (attraction to, psychological response to)	6	21%
Sustained erotic preference for and relations with one sex	5	18%
Self Identification (as bisexual, heterosexual, homosexual, etc.)	3	11%
Motivated by inner necessity (obligatory sexuality)	2	7%
Choice of object of one sex	2	7%
Awareness of attraction to one sex	2	7%
Miscellaneous	5	18%

ceptual definitions. Affectional attachment, fantasies, arousal, and sustained erotic preference appeared about half as frequently. Ambiguity in the terms used made it difficult to determine the possible equivalency of various elements. Arousal, for example, can be physical but it was also referred to as psychological (i.e., mental). "Erotic preference," "choice," and "attraction" can apply to either the physical or mental or to both. "Erotic relations" can be physical or mental (e.g., emotional, fantasized) or both.

The conceptual definitions probably reflected various theoretical beliefs about the origin and nature of sexual orientation. However, since they usually appeared outside of any explicit theoretical context, it was almost impossible to determine what the authors of the studies had in mind. These elements, as they appear in Table 2, suggest that some authors were thinking of etiology ("motivated by inner necessity"), some of observable behavior, and others of enduring mental states ("sustained erotic preference"). While some included only behavior, others included only emotional closeness or fantasy. The linguistic and conceptual confusion is readily apparent. Most definitions were written with homosexuality in mind since 91.6% (f = 209) of the studies contained homosexual samples. There was obvious diversity in how homosexuality was conceptualized in the studies.

In those studies where sexual orientation was operationally defined, there was considerable variation in the method used. The operational definitions were classified into 10 categories, as shown in Table 3. The method used most frequently (f = 42, 25.0%) was self-report in which respondents usually answered a direct question about their sexual orientation. In terms of ordered frequencies, this method was followed by determination of sexual orientation by the investigator from the respondents' sex histories (f = 32, 19%), by use of the Kinsey heterosexual-homosexual rating scale (f = 30, 17.8%), and by inference based on the organizations and settings in which the respondents were located (f = 28, 16.6%).

There was a wide range of methods used to define and assess sexual orientation, with no single method even approaching preponderance. This astonishing variation in operational definitions, ranging from accepting respondents at their own word (self-report) to asking them nothing about their sexual orientation (identification through locales) reflects the great diversity of belief about what sexual orientation consists of. Even those

Table 3

Classifications of Operational

Definitions of Sexual Orientation (n=168)

	f	%
Self Report	42	25.0
Sex History	32	19.0
Kinsey Rating Scale	30	17.8
Organizations and Settings	28	16.6
Penile Phallometer	12	7.1
Other Rating Scales	11	6.7
Clinical Homosexual Groups	9	5.4
Imprisoned Homosexuals	2	1.2
Researcher's Network	2	1.2
Total	168	100.0%

methods that appear most "scientific," the rating scales and the phallometer, stem from different views of sexuality, either as psychological and
therefore preferential or as physical and therefore involuntary.

DISCUSSION

Our initial concern was whether or not sexual orientation was conceptually defined in the research literature. It was defined in only a minority
of the studies and with wide variation in meaning as illustrated by these
examples: "sex object choice" (Milham & Weinberger, 1977, p. 345);
"Pederasty means anal intercourse with a boy" (Tindall, 1978, p. 373);
"Sexual orientation refers to the individual's physical and affectional preference for individuals of the opposite or same sex" (Liljestrand, Gerling, & Saliba, 1978, p. 361); and "True homosexuality, like heterosexuality, is a lifelong process involving the initial development of physiologic
responses and the later expression of overt sexual behavior. The physiologic component is an established pattern to visual, auditory, and tactile
stimulation. The response is an emotional and sexual arousal culminating
in fantasies, dreams, or sexual outlet through masturbation or sexual in-
volvement" (Saghir & Robbins, 1971, p. 503). As a research concept,
sexual orientation clearly has a perplexing array of meanings.

Although the studies in which sexual orientation was operationally
defined were much more numerous, a wide range of methods were used.
In most instances, however, the method of measurement was apparently
operational only for the study at hand. Studies that had conceptual definitions usually had operational definitions.

The conceptual jumble apparent in the research on sexual orientation
cannot, we believe, be resolved with greater methodological rigor. It is
symptomatic of an underlying confusion. Sexual orientation was treated
as if it were a palpable, unitary phenomenon although it was conceived in
divergent and sometimes contradictory ways.

The fact that respondents were selected on the basis of their putative
sexual orientation implies that the researchers were in fact concerned with
sexual identity. The idea of sexual identity, however, provides no more
stable focus of investigation than the amorphous notion of sexual orientation. The single, constant attribute of the concepts of sexual orientation
and sexual identity is the biological sex of partners in sexual relationships.
Both concepts, therefore, imply relationships. The array of conceptual
and operational definitions and the diverse methodologies suggest that the
investigators may have had correspondingly varied notions about what
constituted a sexual relationship. These variations in approach suggest
that some conceived relationships as "physical" and "erotic," while
others saw them as "romantic," "affectional," and "affiliative."

If the focus of research were to shift from the context of sexual identity and orientation to that of sexual relationships, the research approach would also have to change. First, the research focus would have to shift from isolated respondents to their relationships. Second, respondents could not be treated as objects who can be externally assessed. The structure of relationships could only be determined through knowledge of partners' beliefs and attitudes, as we have suggested (De Cecco & Shively, 1983), and how, in fact, they conduct their relationships.

REFERENCES

De Cecco, J. P., & Shively, M. G. From sexual identity to sexual relationships: A contextual shift. *Journal of Homosexuality*, 1983, *9*, 1–26.
Liljestrand, P., Gerling, E., & Saliba, P. A. The effects of social sex-role stereotypes and sexual orientation on psychotherapeutic outcomes. *Journal of Homosexuality*, 1978, *3*, 373–382.
Milham, J., & Weinberger, L. E. Sexual preference, sex role appropriateness, and restriction of social access. *Journal of Homosexuality*, 1977, *4*, 343–357.
Saghir, M. T., & Robbins, E. Male and female homosexuality: Natural history. *Comprehensive Psychiatry*, 1971, *12*, 503–510.
Tindall, R. H. The male adolescent involved with a pederast becomes an adult. *Journal of Homosexuality*, 1978, *3*, 373–382.

APPENDIX A

Bibliographies Used to Initiate Working List of Studies

Brewer, J. S., & Wright, R. W. *Sex research: Bibliographies of the Institute for Sex Research*. Phoenix, AZ: Oryx Press, 1979.
Morin, S. F. *Annotated Bibliography of Research on Lesbianism and Male Homosexuality (1967–1974)*. American Psychological Association Manuscript 1191. Abstracted in the *Journal of Supplement Abstract Service Catalog of Selected Documents in Psychology*, 1976, 6(1), 15.
Bibliography of articles published in *The Journal of Sex Research*, 1965–1977.
Comprehensive Bibliography for Social Work Practice with Sex-Related Problems, prepared by the staff of Social Work Program, University of Hawaii, Honolulu, unpublished, 1978.

APPENDIX B

Alphabetical List of Journals with Frequencies and Percentages

	f	%
Adolescence	1	.4
American Journal of Psychiatry	5	2.3
American Journal of Psychoanalysis	4	1.9
Archives of General Psychiatry	6	2.7
Archives of Sexual Behavior	34	14.9
Australia and New Zealand Journal of Psychiatry	1	.4
Behavior and Research Therapy	3	1.4

Appendix B continued

	f	%
Behavior Therapy	2	.9
Biological Psychiatry	2	.9
British Journal of Psychiatry	12	5.4
British Journal of Venereal Diseases	1	.4
British Medical Journal	2	.9
Comprehensive Psychiatry	1	.4
Dissertation Abstracts International	2	.9
Gerontologist	1	.4
Homosexual Counseling Journal	1	.4
Hormones and Behavior	1	.4
International Journal of Psychiatry	1	.4
Journal of Abnormal Psychology	9	3.9
Journal of Clinical Psychology	2	.9
Journal of Consulting and Clinical Psychology	6	2.6
Journal of Endocrinology	1	.4
Journal of Homosexuality	68	29.8
Journal of Individual Psychology	1	.4
Journal of Marriage and the Family	1	.4
Journal of Nervous and Mental Disease	1	.4
Journal of Personality Assessment (Journal of Projective Techniques)	6	2.6
Journal of Psychology	1	.4
Journal of Research in Personality	1	.4
Journal of Sex Research	23	10.2
Journal of Social Issues	2	.9
Journal of Studies on Alcohol	1	.4
Journal of the American College Health Association	1	.4
Lancet	1	.4
Medical Aspects of Human Sexuality	2	.9
Nature	1	.4
New England Journal of Medicine	3	1.4
Pediatrics	1	.4
Proceedings, APA Annual Convention	1	.4
Psychiatry	1	.4
Psychological Reports	5	2.3
Psychoanalytic Review	1	.4
Sexual Behavior	2	.9
Social Problems	3	1.4
Sociometry (Journal of Research in Social Psychology)	1	.4
Transaction	1	.4
Urban Life (A Journal of Ethnographic Research)	1	.4
	228	**100.0% Total**

Human Sexuality in Biological Perspective: Theoretical and Methodological Considerations

Thomas Ford Hoult, PhD

Arizona State University

ABSTRACT. An increasing number of observers are claiming that a biological model is more appropriate to an understanding of human sexuality than the conventional social-learning one. Such claims have prompted a perusal of the biological literature to ascertain whether the relevant evidence is convincing. The results of this review suggest that claims for the biological model are questionable since the evidence for that model either derives from animal studies (and is thus not generally applicable to human behavior) or is inconclusive, contradictory, or methodologically deficient. It is concluded, therefore, that behavioral scientists are at present on firm ground in using a social-learning, in preference to a biological, model to interpret most aspects of human sexual behavior.

During the last few years an increasing number of scholars, including some social scientists, have asserted that evidence now available is sufficient to justify replacing a social-learning model with a biological model in examining human behavior. Their assertions are sometimes global. Richard Alexander (1979), for example, claims that all behavior of all organisms consists of nothing but direct or indirect attempts to maximize reproductive success. More often, advocates of the biological model narrow the focus to the assertion that the various aspects of human sexuality are largely if not entirely a function of inborn factors.

It is with the latter assertion that the present paper is concerned. The term "human sexuality," as used here, includes sexual actions per se, sexual orientation (erotic object choice), and gender identity (an individual's sense of being either male or female, or a mixture of the two). The underlying question for this paper is: How convincing is the biologi-

Professor Hoult received his PhD in sociology from the University of Southern California in 1951. He has been Professor of Sociology at Arizona State University since 1964. He is the author of *The Sociology of Religion*, *The Dictionary of Modern Sociology*, *The March to the Right*, and *Sociology for a New Day*. Reprint requests may be addressed to Dr. Hoult at the Department of Sociology, Arizona State University, Tempe, AZ 85287.

cal evidence that details of human sexuality are directly due to innate traits and processes?

THE SOCIAL-LEARNING PERSPECTIVE

The preceding paragraph should not be interpreted to mean that behavioral scientists decry the importance of biological influences on human life. To the contrary, behavioral scientists, with few exceptions, accept without question the proposition that the human species, like all others, is the product of a long and complex evolutionary process. Thus, behaviorists do not argue against the idea that the human phenotype, like all phenotypes, possesses a biology that interacts with environment.

If the foregoing were all there was to be said about the matter, biological and behavioral scientists would be in full agreement. But they are not, because many biologists hold that, from an evolutionary point of view, humans and numbers of other animal species are homologous, and therefore that the same principles govern the behavior of all. In contrast, behaviorists characteristically assert that members of the human species are unique because humans alone inherit no important specific behavior patterns. Rather, it is asserted, humans are born with a broad flexibility and potential for learning. This belief gives primary significance not to genes as such but to individual experiences and to the historical era, society, and culture in which men and women happen to be reared.

The behavioral paradigm, applied to sexuality, suggests that humans are born with an undifferentiated sexual drive so malleable that it can be channeled in one or more of a multitude of directions. More specifically, we are born neither heterosexual nor with any other particular sexual orientation. Rather, in social interaction and in accordance with behavioristic principles, we learn our sexual orientation and other facets of sexuality much as we learn our native language. The things we learn are, so to speak, "in the lap of the gods," although cultural pressures and biases incline most people toward that which is popularly defined as "normal."

This view, long dominant in the behavioral sciences, is now challenged by a number of researchers who prefer biological explanations. Behavioral scientists could perhaps ignore such an argument if it were sketchy or advanced by people with questionable qualifications. But neither condition prevails: The challenge is widespread and supported by many important scientists. It therefore behooves all students of human sexuality to look carefully at the evidence cited by the biological school. The present review concentrates on those authors who are most often cited (e.g., Diamond, Kallmann, and Money) or whose data are the most challenging and representative of the genre (e.g., Whitam, Starka, and

Benjamin). Their work is evaluated in terms of well-known methodological standards, as delineated in Gagnon (1977, pp. 41–56) and illustrated in Miller and Humphreys (1980, pp. 172–174.)

MILTON DIAMOND'S THEORY

The essence of the biological model of sexual behavior is described by Milton Diamond, a reproductive biologist. According to Diamond (1968a, p. 418), "sexual behavior in the human is more dependent upon pre- and postnatal genetic-endocrine influences than upon the postnatal environment." More recently, Diamond (1979, p. 554) asserted that a child's self-concept, upon which sexuality is built, rests on an inborn "biased predisposition."

These claims by Diamond are particularly significant because he is often mentioned as the pre-eminent researcher concentrating on the biological aspects of sexual behavior. Yet, in the decade and a half since his first report, Diamond has produced no conclusive research in support of his views. In 1968, he edited a volume (1968b) almost entirely devoted to animal research which, from a behavioral point of view, has little relevance to human life.

Diamond's nearest approach to human data, which he terms "clinical evidence of a sort," consists of a brief reference to a study by Ehrhardt and Money (1967) of ten daughters of mothers given androgenic progestins. Diamond thinks it is significant that nine of the girls were described as "tomboys." But, as Ehrhardt and Money point out (p. 98), their study did not involve sufficient controls or cases to justify any firm conclusion. There was, for example, no attempt to determine if the girls were reared under conditions that might well prompt any child to act in a way traditionally defined as masculine. That such conditions could have been influential is suggested by the fact that two of the mothers of the nine girls were themselves tomboys and that "some of the sisters of the index cases were tomboyish" (p. 96). Finally, Diamond (as did Ehrhardt and Money) notes that the activities of the girls were "within limits acceptable for a female in today's upper-middle class families." Attributing special significance to the subjects' tomboy behavior therefore seems unreasonable.

Yet, with no more evidence than described, i.e., nonhuman animal research and the study of nine tomboys observed unsystematically and inconclusively, Diamond (1968a, p. 427) asserts that "during fetal development hormones can act to organize the nervous system with a sexual bias for future sexual behavior." And a decade later, although no direct evidence had been published in the interim, Diamond wrote two more review articles containing these assertions:

> In the adult individual . . . neural organization . . . is on a broad
> plane and believed to influence: erotic response levels, arousability,
> genital mechanisms, sexual identity, and sex-related biases in the
> spontaneous initiation or acceptance of various activities, as well as
> choice of sexual objects. (1977, p. 38)

> An individual is born with a biased predisposition to interact with
> the world in certain ways . . . . The basic feature is sexual identity.
> (1978, p. 19)

The statements, although acceptable as possible hypotheses, are not supported by data available to date.

Along with stressing the inborn aspects of sexuality, Diamond often refers to the importance of environmental factors; indeed, his 1979 summary article emphasizes the idea that human sexuality is due to the interaction of nurture with nature, rather than to one of these factors alone. However, according to Beach (1977, p. 23), Diamond believes that the principal role of environment is to evoke "the expression of behavioral characteristics which were 'biologically programmed' early in development." Among the elements of this programming, as described by Diamond (1977, p. 41), are "neural tissues," which play a crucial part in developing such phenomena as degree of masculinity or femininity; sexual identity, and sexual object choice. This claim, however, is followed by the remark: "There is as yet little anatomical evidence that separate neural tissues exist for each of these components of sexual behavior." He believes there are only "clinical considerations" that "indeed quite distinct tissues *might* develop and exist" (emphasis added).

THE KALLMANN STUDY

The only evidence that Diamond mentions to substantiate his belief that "homosexuality and transsexualism might fit into this category of genetic-endocrine psychosexual problems" (1968a, p. 438) is that found in Franz Kallmann's two articles (1952a; 1952b) describing what Kallmann believed to be the heritability of homosexuality. The difficulty here is that Kallmann's work was not a scientific endeavor. Indeed, his work was so limited and presented in so strange a manner that it is difficult to analyze it without giving the impression one is indulging in an *ad hominem* attack.

Kallmann claimed (1952a, p. 287) that his approach was based on a "statistically representative sample of predominantly or exclusively homosexual" men who had twin brothers. He gave no indication that his 85 subjects were chosen systematically and could therefore be regarded as possibly composing a representative sample. Thus, one does not know what to make of his findings since they may be due to the subjects' uniqueness.

Even if Kallmann had observed basic scientific standards, his findings would not necessarily support his conclusion. Insofar as it is possible to decipher his reports,[1] he found that the likelihood that both members of a pair of brothers will be homosexual is: (a) least when they are ordinary siblings; (b) slightly more when they are two-egg (dizygotic) twins; and (c) significantly more when they are one-egg (monozygotic) twins (although he specified no criteria for identifying which twins belonged to which type). He concludes (1952a, p. 294) that his data support a "multiple causation" theory of homosexuality, with "inversive tendencies" extending from "an unbalanced effect of opposing sex genes to the equivalent of compulsive rigidity in a schizoid personality structure." It could be argued that the closer same-sex people are related, and the more they resemble one another, the more likely it is they will have similar experiences and evoke similar reactions from others, and thus develop similar personalities. The same caveat applies to a number of other sexuality-of-twins studies (e.g., Martin, 1978).

Given the nature of Kallmann's work, Diamond's assertion (1977, p. 60), that Kallmann had produced an "unchallenged" and "excellent classical study," is difficult to understand. This praise is especially questionable in view of Kallmann's (1960) subsequent criticism of his own research on the grounds that the results could properly be regarded as a "statistical artifact." Further, other researchers (Davison, Brierly, & Smith, 1971; Heston & Shields, 1968; Klintworth, 1962; McConaghy & Blaszczynski, 1980; Rainer, Mesnikoff, Kolb, & Carr, 1960) have reported data that suggest Kallmann's conclusions should be regarded with caution or rejected outright.

THE IMPERATO-MCGINLEY STUDY

A study receiving considerable general publicity was conducted in the Dominican Republic by Julianne Imperato-McGinley and her colleagues. The research was concerned with a number of Dominican citizens—24 in the 1974 report and 38 in the 1979 report. The subjects, although chromosomally and hormonally male, were born with ambiguous external genitalia. A substantial proportion of the total (18 of 24, as described in 1974; 19 of 33 living, as described in 1979) were reared as females. When these children reached the age of puberty, they began to exhibit a male phenotype. All 18 in the 1974 report, or 17 out of 18 on whom data were available in 1979, changed gender identity and had "libido directed toward the opposite sex" (Imperato-McGinley, Guerrero, Gautier, &

Peterson, 1974, p. 1213). It was concluded that the "male sex drive appears to be testosterone related" (1974, p. 1215). In 1979 the investigators theorized that "the extent of androgen (i.e., testosterone) exposure of the brain . . . has more effect in determining male gender identity than does sex of rearing" (Imperato-McGinley, Peterson, Gautier, & Sturla, 1979, p. 1236).

However, other conclusions are equally if not more convincing. Sagarin (1975, p. 331) explained that, in the area where the subjects live, male children with ambiguous external genitalia have been so common for three generations that a special term has been developed to designate them. The term is *guevedoces*, translated as "penis at 12 [years of age]" (Imperato-McGinley et al., 1974, p. 1213) and sometimes *machihembra*, "first woman, then man" (Imperato-McGinley et al., 1979, p. 1235). Villagers know that, although some of their male infants are born with female-looking genitals and are therefore "sort of girls," they are expected to turn into full-fledged males when they reach puberty. Therefore, to claim that these children are reared "unambiguously from birth to puberty as females" is misleading. Sagarin argues that "these people could well be reared *like* girls, being treated as normals who have female-like characteristics in childhood, but who are being prepared to be . . . males." Money (1974a, p. 215), in commenting on a somewhat similar situation in New Guinea, pointed out that if individuals alter their sexual preference concomitant with an apparent gender change at puberty, one need not postulate a hormonal cause if the society in question regularly predicts and, in effect, "commands" such alteration. A hormonal influence is also questionable when, as in the Dominican Republic (and Latin America generally) there is an overwhelming advantage to being a male.

STUDIES BY RABOCH AND SIPOVA, STARKA, KOLODNY, WHITAM, BENJAMIN, DÖRNER, AND BELL

Jan Raboch and Iva Sipova (1974) assert that hormone disorders cause individuals not only to become homosexuals and transsexuals, but also to have higher than normal IQs. Raboch and Sipova point to 85 men in four "pathological groups" who had, on the average, significantly higher IQs than did a control group of 100 men. The experimental groups are described as "17 nonfeminine homosexuals," "24 feminine homosexuals," "24 genetically male transsexuals," and 20 adults suffering from "a hypogonadotropic form of eunuchoidism" (none of the classificatory terms is defined). The control group consisted of married men complaining of sterility. Raboch and Sipova (p. 157) relative to their experimental groups, note that "we may assume that the androgen and/or estrogen level was abnormal in the period of the hypothalamic organizatory phase'' (i.e., the fourth to sixth month of fetal development). They conclude that disorders in the supply of steroid hormones ''disturb, on the one hand, the sexual development, and, on the other, simultaneously increase the mental level of these subjects'' (p. 160). Raboch and Sipova provide no evidence that hormone disorders produce homosexuals and transsexuals; individuals of either type are simply assumed to be the product of such disorders, despite evidence to the contrary (Marmor, 1971; Masters & Johnson, 1979, pp. 403–409). Furthermore, since Raboch and Sipova mention nothing about observational controls (e.g., do some sexual minorities cultivate intellectual development?) and pay no attention to the possible unrepresentativeness of their samples, their findings are of questionable merit.

Starka, Sipova, and Hynie (1975) measured the plasma testosterone of 41 men described as having ''psychosexual disorders.'' Twenty-one of the men were classified homosexual, of which 18 were said to be ''feminine disposed'' and 3 to possess ''virile reactions.'' The 21, regardless of their alleged virility or femininity, were found to have significantly lower testosterone levels than 75 men described as having ''normal somatosexual appearance'' and ''spermiograms within normal range and adequate sexual activity.'' These designations were not defined.[2]

The authors never consider the possibility that ''hormonal change may *follow* psychosexual development'' (Sagarin, 1975, p. 330). Sagarin's contention is mentioned as a possibility by Kolodny and colleagues. The Kolodny group concluded their study of plasma testosterone in male homosexuals with the observation that the depressed levels they observed ''could be the secondary result of a primary homosexual psychosocial orientation, with depressive reaction relayed through the hypothalamus from higher cortical centers'' (Kolodny, Masters, Hendryx, & Toro, 1971, p. 1173). A striking finding was that the more the subjects were committed to homosexuality (Kinsey groups 4 through 6), the lower their plasma testosterone and sperm motility. It was later found that the more homosexual men (Kinsey 5s and 6s) had abnormally elevated levels of urinary luteinizing hormone (Kolodny, Jacobs, Masters, Toro, & Daughaday, 1972). But these seemingly clear results are properly regarded with caution, as the research teams note, because the 30 homosexual men were self-selected volunteers and may therefore have been quite atypical. Further, 10% of the subjects had been treated for gonorrhea and 7% for syphilis (Kolodny et al., 1971, pp. 1171–1172). Their infections and subsequent treatment may have affected the hormonal analyses. Finally, it is worthy of note that Tourney and Hatfield (Note 1) were unsuccessful in their attempt to replicate the Kolodny results.

Frederick Whitam's work is particularly striking because, although he is a sociologist, he has adopted a biological interpretation of sexual orientation. The Whitam studies that reflect this view are not persuasive because they depend on retrospective descriptions of childhood memories, the accuracy of which cannot be verified. In one paper (1977b), Whitam reported that homosexuals more often than not assert that, as children, they played the role of homosexuals before they were aware of their sexual orientation. On the basis of their assertion, Whitam concludes that the homosexual role must, to an important degree, be an expression of some prenatal physical factors. The idea that people can *play* a role before they *take* it (i.e., before they know it internally) is, of course, a contradiction of well-established role theory, a point Whitam acknowledges (1981, pp. 69–71).

Two of Whitam's studies (1977a; 1980) involve two samples of men, one homosexual and one heterosexual, which in demography are vaguely described and which were chosen by means not clearly specified. Clandestine sampling procedures may sometimes be necessary with concealed homosexuals, but such procedures are not ordinarily justified with heterosexuals. Even with homosexuals, since a representative sample is not achievable, the researcher should employ a systematic procedure (as did Bell and Weinberg, 1978, pp. 26–40), that minimizes the bias inherent in interviewing only those whom one casually meets and who are willing to be questioned.

Whitam found that the homosexual males, far more than the heterosexuals, reported, for example, playing with dolls, cross-dressing, and preferring the company of girls. But it is hazardous to take such self-reports at face value, as criticisms of studies by Freud and Hirschfeld indicated long ago. In addition to the problem of faulty recall, there is the all-too-human tendency to "reconstruct our autobiographies in an effort to bring them into greater congruence with our present identities, roles, situations and available vocabularies" (Simon & Gagnon, 1968, p. 734; see also Ross, 1980; Spanier, 1976). In sum, it seems fair to state that Whitam's conclusion—that sexual orientation appears so early in the life span as to suggest a link to biology—is based on questionable data. Moreover, his findings are not replicated by others such as Goode (1981, p. 81) and Troiden and Goode (1980). This criticism of Whitam's conclusion does not mean that there are no early predictors of sexual orientation. Indeed, Green (1974, Chapter 10) describes possible predictors in some detail, but is careful to add that it is an unverified assumption to say that childhood sissies and tomboys will become homosexual.

In 1966 Harry Benjamin (1966/1977) published his study of transsexualism, a condition wherein individuals who morphologically belong to one sex become convinced that they belong to the opposite sex. This phenomenon is interpreted by Benjamin and others (e.g., Diamond,

1978, pp. 17-18) as supporting the theory that sexual-destiny-at-birth is characteristic of humans as well as of other animals. Transsexualism, however, could be viewed as support for the assertion that sexual identity and orientation are learned postnatally. That is, most people are reared as members of their morphological sex. Despite the usually unequivocal nature of such rearing, some individuals reject their sex of rearing or the erotic choice of the opposite sex, thus testifying to broad flexibility in the adaptive capacity of human beings.

In the hormonal research of Günter Dörner and his colleagues, men identified as homosexual, as compared with those designated heterosexual or bisexual, are described as exhibiting a "positive estrogen feedback effect" when they are injected with estrogen. This phenomenon is normally observed in females but not in males. The authors conclude from this finding that homosexual men have a "predominantly female-differentiated brain" (Dörner, Rohde, Stahl, Krell, & Masius, 1975, p. 6). Subjects involved in the Dörner paper cannot realistically be described as representative of homosexual men since all were hospitalized for treatment of sexually transmitted diseases or skin problems. In addition, when the Dörner data are analyzed in detail, it becomes clear that the "positive estrogen feedback" effect was observed in only one-third of the homosexual sample. Seventy-seven percent of the effect was due to the extreme reactions of 7 of the 20 men. On the other hand, 10 of the 20 heterosexual men accounted for all of what may be termed the "negative feedback effect" found in the heterosexual group. The average negative result achieved with the bisexual men was far larger than the average achieved with the heterosexual men. Such results are inexplicable. Surely, if male homosexuality is due to a "predominantly female-differentiated brain," then such a brain should be at least relatively more evident among those who are somewhat homosexual (i.e., bisexuals). The Dörner work, from a scientific point of view, is deficient in sampling as well as in intelligibility of findings.

Finally, the recently published study by Bell, Weinberg, and Hammersmith (1982), like that of Whitam, is based on the childhood recollections of a large number of adult heterosexual and homosexual individuals. On the basis of such data, the researchers conclude that there is no direct link between parent-child interaction and adult sexual orientation. Sexual orientation, they believe, is strongly related to childhood "gender nonconformity." Finding no clear environmental explanation for gender nonconformity in childhood, the researchers speculate that it, and the associated sexual orientation, may be based on a "biological precursor." That is, of course, a legitimate hypothetical assertion, but (as the researchers note) it is not a scientific confirmation of the idea that human sexuality is in general directly shaped by biological conditions.

THE ENIGMA OF JOHN MONEY

John Money is probably today's leading expert on the phenomenon of hermaphroditism. His work is enigmatic because of his advocacy of conflicting theories of human sexuality. On the one hand, he has long been known to support the idea that gender identity and role and sexual orientation are far more matters of social pressure and learning than of biological inheritance. Some years ago Money and his colleagues wrote "it is no longer possible to attribute psychologic maleness or femaleness to chromosomal, gonadal or hormonal origins" (Money, Hampson, & Hampson, 1955a, p. 308). In another article, Money and the Hampsons wrote (1955b, p. 285): "A gender role is not established at birth, but is built up cumulatively through experiences encountered and transacted . . . In brief, a gender role is established in much the same way as is a native language." With reference to what Money terms "gender identity disorders" (1974b, p. 66), he says "the weight of evidence, based chiefly on hermaphroditic studies (summarized by Money and Ehrhardt, 1972), gives priority to postnatal programming." He has also observed about young people in general (1974a, p. 220): "Their romantic imagery and love affairs in adolescence will, as components of their gender identity, be consonant with assignment and rearing"—regardless of their genetic, gonadal, and hormonal state. He also notes (1977b, p. 27): "There is no evidence to date that the XX or XY chromosomal complement directly programs the behavior of children or adults."

Contradicting his endorsement of learning theories, Money has expressed the belief that some basic aspects of human sexual behavior are directly due to inborn factors. He wrote: "The disposition toward one sexual orientation or the other does appear to be inborn . . . as a result of the influence of sex hormones on the development of sexual pathways in the brain" (Money, 1976-77, p. 160). The following year he wrote that transsexualism led him to believe "there may be a special disposition in the organization of the brain toward the acquisition of roles" (Money, 1977c, p. 80), a statement that Beach (1977, p. 253) declares has a "similar ring" to the claims of "biological extremists."

Aside from references to animal studies and largely uncontrolled clinical observations, Money provides no direct evidence to support a biological perspective of sexual behavior. Instead, he engages in what he terms "provocative speculation" (1963, p. 821), the following being typical:

> Whatever the degree of an individual's homosexual commitment, the behavior concerned may be in some degree hereditary, constitutional, and biological in its determinism. (1970b, p. 425)

> In the case of sexuality, the common assumption is that homosexuality is socially induced, postnatally, in the course of infantile and

early childhood development; yet it is also known that the prenatal sex-hormonal environment of the fetus influences brain pathways so as possibly to facilitate or hinder masculine or feminine dimorphism of subsequent psychosexual development. (1977a, p. 231)

It is not unusual that such assertions are unaccompanied by data that are directly supportive. This may be due, according to Rogers and Walsh (1982) to the serious shortcomings of Money's research into alleged biological causes of sexual behavior. When data are described, they are almost invariably equivocal in nature. For example, it is known that certain prenatal hormone levels can feminize or masculinize offspring (Money & Schwartz, 1977). However, as Money points out (1975b, pp. 57-58), the resulting tomboy girls and nonassertive boys usually identify with their gender of rearing and (to the degree that they are sexually active) are erotically attracted to the opposite sex. The ambiguous nature of such findings becomes starkly apparent when one views them in light of Mead's discovery (1950, pp. 170-182) that, in Tchambuli society, the gender identities of the two sexes are to some degree the reverse of those found in Western areas. Would a Tchambuli woman who was "masculinized" *in utero* turn out to be a fluttery Southern belle? Further questions about Money's theories are suggested by androgynous trends in Western society. Females are increasingly involved in violent crime and in activities traditionally regarded as masculine (Warren, 1981). If such trends continue, it will become increasingly meaningless to speak about hormones "feminizing" or "masculinizing" behavior.

In contrast to the paucity of data Money marshals to support a biological perspective, he provides a wealth of information that gives credence to a social-learning view. He repeatedly notes that people born with ambiguous genitalia will customarily develop a gender identity and sexual orientation consonant with their sex of rearing (Money, 1963; 1970a; 1971; 1972; 1974a; 1975a; 1975b; 1975c; Money, Hampson, & Hampson, 1955a, pp. 308-318). Another example, one of Money's best known, concerns an infant boy whose penis was burned off in a surgical mishap (Money, 1975a, pp. 66-71; Money, 1977c; Money & Ehrhardt, 1972, pp. 118-123; Money & Tucker, 1975, pp. 91-98). The parents decided to rear the child as a girl and an appropriate course of surgery was begun. Meanwhile, the child's identical twin was reared in the ordinary way. The combined parental-medical effort ultimately produced two young people who, despite their genetic identity, became quite different, one relatively feminine and the other conventionally masculine. Such cases led Money and Tucker to conclude: "[T]he gender identity gate is open at birth for a normal child no less than for one born with unfinished sex organs . . . and it stays open at least for something over a year after birth" (1975, p. 98).

In 1976 Money and Dalery described seven chromosomal females who, because of a metabolic error, were born with "a clitoral penis indistinguishable from a normal penis" (p. 358). All seven were treated medically in accordance with whether they were to be reared as female or male. When grown, the three reared as males—despite their female gonads and chromosomes—identified themselves as males and perfomed sexually as men with female partners.

The three males appear to exemplify Money's frequently expressed idea that, when it comes to sexual orientation and identity, it is social learning, not biological sex, that is more determinant. However, Money and Dalery (pp. 369–370) contend that each of the three apparent males is a "perfect female homosexual" and therefore it is "reasonable to propose a prenatal hormonally induced component, in the central nervous system, of a bisexual or homosexual gender identity/role in anatomically nonhermaphroditic individuals." Money and Dalery give no evidence for the existence of the hypothetical component. They say that the mysterious element "does not automatically assert itself." It becomes manifest only under the influence of a postnatal factor that "is almost certainly social." If the "social" factor is determinative, it is unnecessary to posit an unidentified and unmeasured biological "component."

EXPERIMENTAL STUDIES AND REVIEWS

In 1973, Yalom, Green, and Fisk reported the results of a "natural experiment" which suggested that boys who are prenatally exposed to female hormones (given to diabetic women to help prevent miscarriage) are significantly less masculine than are non-exposed boys. This finding was impressive because the researchers had designed and used procedures that were in most respects a model of scientific method. They were careful to choose their samples systematically, they compared their experimental groups with control groups, and they used a double-blind format in which neither subjects nor evaluators were aware of the variables being studied.

The research involved two basic comparisons. A group of six-year-old and a group of sixteen-year-old hormone-exposed boys was each compared with a non-exposed group of the same age. On a series of physical and psychological tests, the hormone-exposed sixteen-year-olds, when compared with the non-exposed group, were significantly less stereotypically masculine. Similar differences between the groups of six-year-olds were not found with the tests, but were noted to exist to some degree by their teachers.

Given these findings, the researchers modestly conclude: "While it was not possible to rule out influences other than hormonal which may have influenced results, data suggest that prenatal sex hormone levels may influence some aspects of postnatal psychosexual development in boys" (Yalom et al., 1973, p. 554). Underlying the twice-used "may" in their conclusion are several important factors, only two of which need be mentioned here. One is the fact that the only relevant differences between the groups of six-year-olds were found in the teacher evaluations, and these were at a statistically significant level on just two variables, assertiveness and athletic coordination. On both of these variables, 16 of the 17 control subjects were said to be more assertive and athletic than their class average, suggesting that the control boys were atypically masculine. It seems fair to conclude that no psychosexual differences between the hormone-exposed and non-exposed six-year-olds groups were demonstrated. But if important aspects of psychosexual development stem from prenatal hormone exposure, as the researchers assert, such development should have been more evident among younger boys who have had less time to be socialized in terms of gender norms.

Another important qualification of their findings was stated by the authors:

> A major uncontrolled variable in the study was the state of health of the mothers in the experimental and contrast groups. The mothers of all the experimentals suffered from a chronic illness requiring daily attention. . . . It is possible that chronic illness in the mother induces overprotection of offspring or greater anxiety over health in offspring so as to interfere with aggressive masculine development. (p. 559)

In sum, the Yalom et al. paper, though scientific in procedure and presentation, must be judged "inconclusive."

The same assessment is appropriate for a number of analogous studies described by Gartrell (1982) and by Meyer-Bahlburg (1977; 1979). Meyer-Bahlburg focused primarily on the animal research of several scholars; that research is relevant to the present paper since much of it was intended as a foundation for radical attempts to prevent or eliminate human homosexuality by manipulating hormones prenatally or by "psychosurgery." Even if such goals were desirable or ethical, Meyer-Bahlburg found that the studies he evaluated were so methodologically deficient that they could contribute little, if anything, toward reaching the ends sought.

Furthermore, as Meyer-Bahlburg pointed out, the studies produced conflicting and disconfirming results for a hormonal theory of human homosexuality: "[T]he evidence in favor of an endocrine basis for male homosexuality is very weak. Gross hormonal deviations have practically been ruled out" (1977, p. 318; see also Meyer-Bahlburg, 1980). This conclusion has recently been substantiated by biologists Kirsch and Rodman who state: "There are no convincing data supporting the view that a physiological, hormonal, chromosomal or anatomical anomaly underlies homosexuality" (1982, p. 185). Meyer-Bahlburg believes that the findings

> suggest a model of human sexuality . . . in terms of an habitual sexual orientation originally acquired by classical and operant conditioning. Such a formulation . . . allows for all forms of sexual object choice including fetishism and pedophilia, without requiring a separate hormonal basis for each of these. (1977, p. 320)

In 1979, Meyer-Bahlburg presented his report on all known studies of the interplay between hormones and female homosexuality; only 13 involved humans. Although the available information was limited, Meyer-Bahlburg concluded that the majority of adult lesbians have normal hormone levels. One-third appear to have an elevated androgen level, but there is no evidence that sexual orientation and amount of androgen are causally connected. Even persons with known prenatal abnormalities usually develop a sexual orientation that is conventional for the sex of rearing, Meyer-Bahlburg observed. He concluded: "[O]ne has to assume that prenatal hormone conditions do not determine sexual orientation" (1979, p. 117).

CONCLUSIONS

As this survey indicates, research currently cited in support of a biological model of human sexuality is methodologically deficient, inconclusive, or open to contradictory theoretical interpretations. In addition, much of such research concentrates on animal studies and therefore has little relationship to human behavior which is generally affected by cultural values. Therefore, this paper's basic question is: How convincing is the biological evidence that the details of human sexuality are directly due to innate traits and processes? The answer is that the evidence is far from persuasive. We may conclude that the biological perspective on human sexuality has not yet made a substantial contribution to the "balanced biosocial synthesis" that the Baldwins (1980) have recommended.

This conclusion is not intended to imply that biology has nothing to do with human sexuality (since the two are, of course, inextricably intertwined). It means simply this: The claim that biological factors have an immediate, direct influence on such things as sexual identity, behavior or orientation remains unproven. When biology seems to be critical in such matters, an intervening cultural factor is often more immediate. For example, physiological feminization or ambiguous genitalia in males can affect sexual identity if the culture stresses the value that "real" maleness requires stereotypical male appearance and aggressive action. Such cultural influences do not, of course, play any part in the formation of genitalia and basic sexual drive. For these, all animals are "indebted" to biology alone. What humans do with such biological resources, however, and how they are regarded, appear to be heavily dependent on what is learned in social interaction.

These considerations all suggest that, for the present, when questions are raised about human sexuality, behavioral scientists can reasonably adhere to a social-learning model. This conclusion may seem to be the bland verbal equivalent of carrying coals to Newcastle. However, it will not seem innocuous to those who have participated in recent debates on sexual behavior at some of our learned social science conclaves. At these gatherings, it has become evident that a surprising number of social and psychological scientists are adopting a biological perspective in explaining human sexuality. That view is widely popular, as Ross, Rogers, and McCulloch (1978) point out, because it is consonant with some basic societal expectations.

In contrast, evidence for a social-learning model, as applied to human sexuality, is amply supplied in a number of works: Mead (1949), on the part that learning plays in sexual differentiation and the development of social sex roles; Ford and Beach (1951), on sexual behavior in a variety of cultures; Gagnon and Simon (1967; 1973), on the social sources of sexuality and on variant forms of behavior; Henderson and Gagnon (1975), on trends in sexual behavior; Weinberg and Williams (1974), on the problems and adaptations of male homosexuals; Bullough (1976), on variant sexual attitudes and practices through history; Gagnon (1977), on sexuality in general; Herdt (1981), on a society where virtually all males are first exclusively homosexual and then mainly heterosexual; and Weinrich (1982), on homosexuality as a natural form of behavior. All of these studies add to the evidence that the human species has evolved to the point where humans have tremendous adaptability and few significant inborn behavior patterns. As Margaret Mead expressed the point (1949, p. 185): "[O]ur humanity rests upon a series of learned behaviors, woven together into patterns that are infinitely fragile and never directly inherited."

NOTES

1. At one point (1952b, p. 139), Kallmann mentions "112 single-born index cases with fully recorded sex and family data and with a plainly homosexual history after adolescence." In his Table 3 (p. 142), however, he shows no single-born cases and explains, "brothers and half-brothers have

been omitted because of incompleteness." Then he adds, describing Table 3: "Generally speaking, the homosexuality rates of the brothers and dizygotic cotwins of homosexual index cases do not seem to differ significantly."

2. They were not explained because, says Dr. Starka in a personal communication, "these terms are clear for the andrologists." (Andrology is the medical specialty concerned with diseases peculiar to males.)

REFERENCE NOTE

1. Tourney, G., & Hatfield, L. *Androgen metabolism and schizophrenics, homosexuals, and normal controls.* Paper presented at the Annual Meeting, Society of Biological Psychiatry, 1972.

REFERENCES

Alexander, R. D. *Darwinism and human affairs.* Seattle: University of Washington Press, 1979.
Baldwin, J. D., & Baldwin, J. I. Sociobiology or balanced biosocial theory? *Pacific Sociological Review,* 1980, *23,* 3-27.
Beach, F. A. (Ed.). *Human sexuality in four perspectives.* Baltimore: Johns Hopkins University Press, 1977.
Bell, A. P., & Weinberg, M. S. *Homosexualities: A study of diversity among men and women.* New York: Simon & Schuster, 1978.
Bell, A. P., Weinberg, M. S., & Hammersmith, S. K. *Sexual preference: Its development in men and women.* Bloomington IN: Indiana University Press, 1981.
Benjamin, H. *The transsexual phenomenon.* New York: Warner Books, 1977. (Originally published, 1966.)
Bullough, V. L. *Sexual variance in society and history.* New York: John Wiley, 1976.
Davison, K., Brierly, H., & Smith, C. A male monozygotic twinship discordant for homosexuality. *British Journal of Psychiatry,* 1971, *118,* 675-682.
Diamond, M. Genetic-endocrine interactions and human psychosexuality. In M. Diamond (Ed.), *Perspectives in reproduction and sexual behavior.* Bloomington IN: Indiana University Press, 1968. (a)
Diamond, M. (Ed.). *Perspectives in reproduction and sexual behavior.* Bloomington IN: Indiana University Press, 1968. (b)
Diamond, M. Human sexual development: Biological foundations for social development. In F. Beach (Ed.), *Human sexuality in four perspectives.* Baltimore: Johns Hopkins University Press, 1977.
Diamond, M. Sexual identity and sex roles. *The Humanist,* 1978, *38,* 16-19.
Diamond, M. Sexual identity and sex roles. In V. L. Bullough (Ed.), *The frontiers of sex research.* Buffalo, NY: Prometheus Books, 1979.
Dörner, G., Rohde, W., Stahl, F., Krell, L., & Masius, W. A neuroendocrine predisposition for homosexuality in men. *Archives of Sexual Behavior,* 1975, *4,* 1-8.
Ehrhardt, A. A., & Money, J. Progestin-induced hermaphroditism: IQ and psychosexual identity in a study of ten girls. *Journal of Sex Research,* 1967, *3,* 83-100.
Ford, C. S., & Beach, F. A. *Patterns of sexual behavior.* New York: Harper & Row, 1951.
Gagnon, J. H. *Human sexualities.* Glenview, IL: Scott, Foresman, 1977.
Gagnon, J. H., & Simon, W. (Eds.). *Sexual deviance.* New York: Harper & Row, 1967.
Gagnon, J. H., & Simon, W. *Sexual conduct: The social sources of human sexuality.* Chicago: Aldine, 1973.
Gartrell, N. Hormones and homosexuality. In W. Paul, J. D. Weinrich, J. C. Gonsiorek, & M. Hotvedt (Eds.), *Homosexuality: Social, psychological and biological issues.* Beverly Hills, CA: Sage, 1982.
Goode, E. The homosexual role: Rejoinder to Omark and Whitam. *Journal of Sex Research,* 1981, *17,* 76-83.

Green, R. *Sexual identity conflict in children and adults.* New York: Basic Books, 1974.

Henderson, B., & Gagnon, J. H. (Eds.). *Human sexuality: An age of ambiguity.* Boston: Educational Associates (Little, Brown), 1975.

Herdt, G. H. *Guardians of the flutes: Idioms of masculinity.* New York: McGraw-Hill, 1981.

Heston, L. L., & Shields, J. Homosexuality in twins. *Archives of General Psychiatry,* 1968, *18,* 149-160.

Imperato-McGinley, J., Guerrero, L., Gautier, T., & Peterson, R. E. Steroid 5 α -reductase deficiency in man: An inherited form of male pseudohermaphroditism. *Science,* 27 December 1974, *186,* 1213-1215.

Imperato-McGinley, J., Peterson, R. E., Gautier, T., & Sturla, E. Androgens and the evolution of male-gender identity among male pseudohermaphrodites with 5 α -reductase deficiency. *New England Journal of Medicine,* 1979, *300*(2), 1233-1279.

Kallmann, F. J. Comparative twin study on the genetic aspects of male homosexuality. *Journal of Nervous and Mental Disease,* 1952, *115,* 283-298. (a)

Kallmann, F. J. Twin and sibship study of overt male homosexuality. *American Journal of Human Genetics,* 1952, *4,* 136-146. (b)

Kallmann, F. J. Research note. *Psychosomatic Medicine,* 1960, *22,* 258-259.

Kirsch, J. A., & Rodman, J. E. Selection and sexuality: The Darwinian view of homosexuality. In W. Paul, J. D. Weinrich, J. C. Gonsiorek, & M. Hotvedt (Eds.), *Homosexuality: Social, psychological, and biological issues.* Beverly Hills, CA: Sage, 1982.

Klintworth, G. K. A pair of male monozygotic twins discordant for homosexuality. *Journal of Nervous and Mental Disease,* 1962, *135,* 113-125.

Kolodny, R. C., Jacobs, L. S., Masters, W. H., Toro, G., & Daughaday, W. H. Plasma gonadotrophins and prolactin in male homosexuals. *Lancet,* 1972, *2,* 18-20.

Kolodny, R. C., Masters, W. H., Hendryx, J., & Toro, G. Plasma testosterone and semen analysis in male homosexuals. *New England Journal of Medicine,* 1971, *285,* 1170-1174.

Marmor, J. "Normal" and "deviant" sexual behavior. *Journal of the American Medical Association,* 1971, *20,* 165-170.

Martin, N. G. Genetics of sexual and social attitudes in twins. In W. E. Nance, G. Allen, & P. Parisi (Eds.), *Twin research, psychology and methodology.* New York: Liss, 1978.

Masters, W. H., & Johnson, V. F. *Homosexuality in perspective.* Boston: Little, Brown, 1979.

McConaghy, N., & Blaszczynski, A. A pair of monozygotic twins discordant for homosexuality: Sex dimorphic behavior and penile volume responses. *Archives of Sexual Behavior,* 1980, *9,* 123-131.

Mead, M. *Male and female: A study of the sexes in a changing world.* New York: William Morrow, 1949.

Mead, M. *Sex and temperament in three primitive societies.* New York: Mentor Books (The New American Library), 1950.

Meyer-Bahlburg, H. F. L. Sex hormones and male homosexuality in comparative perspective. *Archives of Sexual Behavior,* 1977, *6,* 297-325.

Meyer-Bahlburg, H. F. L. Sex hormones and female homosexuality: A critical examination. *Archives of Sexual Behavior,* 1979, *8,* 101-119.

Meyer-Bahlburg, H. F. L. Homosexual orientation in women and men: A hormonal basis? In J. E. Parsons (Ed.), *The psychobiology of sex differences and sex roles.* New York: Hemisphere, 1980.

Miller, B., & Humphreys, L. Lifestyle and violence: Homosexual victims of assault and murder. *Qualitative Sociology,* 1980, *3,* 169-185.

Money, J. Cytogenetic and psychosexual incongruities with a note on space-form blindness. *American Journal of Psychiatry,* 1963, *119,* 820-827.

Money, J. Matched pairs of hermaphrodites: Behavioral biology of sexual differentiation from chromosomes to gender identity. *Engineering and Science,* 1970, *33,* 34-39. (a)

Money, J. Sexual dimorphism and homosexual gender identity. *Psychological Bulletin,* 1970, *74*(6), 425-440. (b)

Money, J. Sexually dimorphic behavior, normal and abnormal. In N. Kretchmer & D. N. Wallcher (Eds.), *Environmental influences on genetic expression, biological and behavioral aspects of sexual differentiation.* Fogarty International Center Proceedings No. 2. Washington, D. C.: U.S. Government Printing Office, 1971.

Money, J. Phyletic and idiosyncratic determinants of gender identity. *Danish Medical Bulletin,* 1972, *19*(8), 259-264.

Money, J. Psychologic considerations of sex assignment in intersexuality. *Clinics in Plastic Surgery*, 1974, *1*, 215-222. (a)

Money, J. Two names, two wardrobes, two personalities. *Journal of Homosexuality*, 1974, *1*(1), 65-70. (b)

Money, J. Ablatio penis: Normal male infant sex-reassigned as a girl. *Archives of Sexual Behavior*, 1975, *4*(1), 65-71. (a)

Money, J. Nativism versus culturalism in gender-identity differentiation. In E. Adelson (Ed.), *Sexuality and psychoanalysis*. New York: Brunner/Mazel, 1975. (b)

Money, J. Sex education and infertility counseling in various endocrine-related syndromes: The juvenile and adolescent years. In L. I. Gardner (Ed.), *Endocrine and genetic diseases of childhood and adolescence*. Philadelphia: W. B. Saunders, 1975. (c)

Money, J. Statement on antidiscrimination regarding sexual orientation. *Journal of Homosexuality*, 1976/1977, *2*, 159-161.

Money, J. Bisexual, homosexual and heterosexual: Society, law and medicine. *Journal of Homosexuality*, 1977, *2*, 229-233. (a)

Money, J. Destereotyping sex role. *Society*, 1977, *14*(5), 25-28. (b)

Money, J. Human hermaphroditism. In F. Beach (Ed.), *Human sexuality in four perspectives*. Baltimore: Johns Hopkins University Press, 1977. (c)

Money, J., & Dalery, J. Iatrogenic homosexuality: Gender identity in seven 46, XX chromosomal females with hyperadrenocortical hermaphroditism. *Journal of Homosexuality*, 1976, *1*, 357-370.

Money, J., & Ehrhardt, A. A. *Man and woman, boy and girl*. Baltimore: Johns Hopkins University Press, 1972.

Money, J., Hampson, J. G., & Hampson, J. L. An examination of some basic sexual concepts: The evidence of human hermaphroditism. *Bulletin of the Johns Hopkins Hospital*, 1955, *97*, 301-319. (a)

Money, J., Hampson, J. G., & Hampson, J. L. Hermaphroditism: Recommendations concerning assignment of sex, change of sex, and psychologic management. *Bulletin of the Johns Hopkins Hospital*, 1955, *97*, 284-300. (b)

Money, J., & Schwartz, M. Dating, romantic and nonromantic friendships, and sexuality in 17 early-treated adrenogenital females, aged 16-25. In P. Lee, L. P. Plotnick, A. A. Kowarski, & C. J. Migeon (Eds.), *Congenital adrenal hyperplasia*. Baltimore: University Park Press, 1977.

Money, J., & Tucker, P. *Sexual signatures: On being a man or a woman*. Boston: Little, Brown, 1975.

Raboch, J., & Sipova, I. Intelligence in homosexuals, transsexuals and hypogonadotropic eunuchoids. *Journal of Sex Research*, 1974, *10*, 156-161.

Rainer, J. D., Mesnikoff, A., Kolb, L. C., & Carr, A. Homosexuality and heterosexuality in identical twins. *Psychosomatic Medicine*, 1960, *22*, 251-258.

Rogers, L., & Walsh, J. Shortcomings of the psychomedical research of John Money and co-workers into sex differences in behavior: Social and political implications. *Sex Roles*, 1982, *8*(3), 269-281.

Ross, M. W. Retrospective distortion in homosexual research. *Archives of Sexual Behavior*, 1980, *9*, 523-531.

Ross, M. W., Rogers, L. J., & McCulloch, H. Stigma, sex and society: A new look at gender differentiation and sexual variation. *Journal of Homosexuality*, 1978, *3*, 315-330.

Sagarin, E. Sex rearing and sexual orientation: The reconciliation of apparently contradictory data. *Journal of Sex Research*, 1975, *11*, 329-334.

Simon, W., & Gagnon, J. H. On psychosexual development. In D. A. Goslin (Ed.), *Handbook of socialization theory and research*. Skokie, IL: Rand McNally, 1968.

Spanier, G. B. Use of recall data in survey research on human sexual behavior. *Social Biology*, 1976, *23*, 244-253.

Starka, L., Sipova, I., & Hynie, J. Plasma testosterone in male transsexuals and homosexuals. *Journal of Sex Research*, 1975, *11*, 134-138.

Troiden, R. R., & Goode, E. Variables related to the acquisition of a gay identity. *Journal of Homosexuality*, 1980, *5*, 383-392.

Warren, M. Q. *Comparing male and female offenders*. Beverly Hills, CA: Sage, 1981.

Weinberg, M. S., & Williams, C. J. *Male homosexuals: Their problems and adaptations*. New York: Oxford University Press, 1974.

Weinrich, J. D. Is homosexuality biologically natural? In W. Paul, J. D. Weinrich, J. C. Gonsiorek,

& M. Hotvedt (Eds.), *Homosexuality: Social, psychological and biological issues.* Beverly Hills, CA: Sage, 1982.

Whitam, F. L. Childhood indicators of male homosexuality. *Archives of Sexual Behavior,* 1977, *6,* 89-96. (a)

Whitam, F. L. The homosexual role: A reconsideration. *Journal of Sex Research,* 1977, *13*(1), 1-11. (b)

Whitam, F. L. The prehomosexual male child in three societies: The United States, Guatemala, Brazil. *Archives of Sexual Behavior,* 1980, *9*(2), 87-99.

Whitam, F. L. A reply to Goode on the homosexual role. *Journal of Sex Research,* 1981, *17*(1), 66-72.

Yalom, I. D., Green, R., & Fisk, N. Prenatal exposure to female hormones. *Archives of General Psychiatry,* 1973, *28,* 554-561.

Sexual Orientation, Sociobiology, and Evolution

Douglas J. Futuyma, PhD
State University of New York, Stony Brook

Stephen J. Risch, PhD
University of California, Berkeley

ABSTRACT. Sociobiologists have proposed evolutionary explanations of homosexuality. Such hypotheses assume that the homosexual orientation is a distinct, reifiable trait, rather than an expression of universal sexual and emotional drives. For homosexuality to constitute an evolved trait, it must have a genetic basis. However, there is no reliable evidence that homosexual and heterosexual orientations are caused by genetic differences. On these and other grounds, we find sociobiological explanations of homosexuality to be implausible and unsupported by evidence. Evolutionary theory provides no guide to morality or ethical progress, nor for appropriate social attitudes toward homosexuality.

An extraordinarily vast literature addresses the question of why some people are homosexual. Much of it fails to meet even modest scientific standards. Much of it is motivated by the general antipathy Western society shows toward homosexuality and by the desire for its prevention. To find discussions of the causes of homosexuality that accept homosexuality in a liberal spirit ought to be a signal of theoretical progress. Unfortunately, socially progressive theories are not necessarily valid ones; they, too, must be tested. Science is not science unless its conclusions are examined as critically when they conform to our personal beliefs as when they oppose them.

The notion that homosexuality may have a genetic or biological basis

Douglas Futuyma is Professor of Ecology and Evolution at the State University of New York at Stony Brook, New York 11794. He received his BS at Cornell and his MS and PhD at the University of Michigan, Ann Arbor, in zoology. He is the author of *Evolutionary Biology* and *Science on Trial: The Case for Evolution*, the co-editor of *Coevolution*, and currently is editor of the journal, *Evolution*. His research and technical publications are primarily on the evolution and ecology of insects and plants. The second author, Stephen Risch, is Professor of Entomology at the University of California, Berkeley. He also received his PhD at the University of Michigan in Ecology and Evolutionary Biology. From 1979-1983 he was Professor of Ecology and Evolution at Cornell University. He has published articles on ecology and the interaction of science, technology, and society. Reprint requests may be addressed to the senior author.

The authors wish to thank Gar Allen, Davydd Greenwood, Simon Levin, Paul Sherman, Barry Strauss, Warren Wagner, and an anonymous reviewer for helpful criticisms of the manuscript.

has long been one of the chief etiological theories (for reviews see Weinberg & Bell, 1972; Weinrich, 1976). In the last few years, this notion has re-emerged in sociobiological form. Sociobiology, proclaimed a "new synthesis" by E. O. Wilson in 1975, purports to offer a rigorous theoretical framework for understanding the evolution of behavioral interactions among all social animals, including humans. However, sociobiological theory, as applied to humans, has met with vigorous criticism not only from social scientists but also from many evolutionary biologists. Still, sociobiology continues to have wide appeal to many who see it as a paradigm for explaining puzzling behavioral phenomena.

Among these phenomena is homosexual behavior. Wilson offered a sociobiological hypothesis to explain homosexuality both in his scholarly book (1975) and in his more popular *On Human Nature* (1978). He theorized that homosexuality might be a biologically adaptive "normal" trait "that evolved as an important element of early human social organization" (p. 143). Moreover, "homosexuals may be the genetic carriers of some of mankind's rare altruistic impulses" (p. 143).

It is not surprising that Wilson's speculations were warmly received among many gay liberation advocates. An excerpt from his book (1978), and an enthusiastic review, appeared in a major gay periodical, *The Advocate* (May 3, 1979). One sociobiologist, J. D. Weinrich, has argued in *Christopher Street* (Stein, 1978) and in his doctoral dissertation (Weinrich, 1976) that the average homosexual is more intelligent than the average heterosexual. In the pages of this *Journal*, Ruse (1981) has offered a detailed exposition and defense of sociobiological theories of homosexuality.

We find these evolutionary theories of human sexual orientation to be unsupported by even the most rudimentary data. Moreover, it is hard to see how some of these theories could ever be subjected to proper scientific testing; in our judgement, they cannot be considered even valid scientific hypotheses. The thrust of this article will be a criticism of sociobiological theories of sexual orientation, followed by a brief remark on the relationship between biological theory and normative social values.

GENETICS, EVOLUTION, AND SOCIOBIOLOGY

Wilson, Weinrich, and Ruse, assuming that human homosexual behavior is an evolved trait, seek to explain how it could have evolved. To suppose that a particular trait has evolved is to imply that (1) there are genes that, under suitable environmental circumstances, program individuals to develop the trait and (2) that over the course of generations, these genes have replaced alternative genes, which do not code for that trait. For example, Kettlewell (1955) reported that a gene for black coloration increased in frequency within English populations of the peppered moth over the course of about 100 generations. At first constituting less than 1% of an otherwise gray population of moths, black moths increased gradually over the generations, until they reached almost 100%. This increase was caused by the natural selection of an initially rare mutation (the black form). The superior capacity for survival and for reproduction of black moths over gray moths was due to the greater ability of black moths to escape predation by birds. During the period of gene replacement, both forms of moths were present, so the peppered moth population may be described as *polymorphic* (having more than one genotype). It is now a *monomorphic* population, consisting essentially of one genotype with respect to coloration.

One of the tasks of evolutionary biology is to identify the evolutionary changes that have occurred; another is to determine why they have occurred. The first task includes demonstrating that a trait has a genetic basis. The second task includes identifying the selective factors responsible for the superior survival or reproduction of one type over another (in the case of moths, showing that the two forms face differential predation).

Both tasks are difficult and can be successfully performed only by following proper procedural protocols. What does it mean to show that a characteristic has a genetic basis? Any biological characteristic has a *genetic* basis, in the trivial sense that it could not develop unless the organism has information in the DNA that permits the potential development of the trait. However, any trait likewise has an *environmental* basis, in that the organism cannot develop the trait unless it has the right environmental input (e.g.; sufficient food, proper temperature). Humans have genetic information for developing five fingers on each hand and five toes on each foot. Still, we know nothing about how many genes are involved, whether they are dominant or recessive, or even whether the genes for fingers are different than those for toes. Fingers and toes might not be different traits, in a genetic sense: There may be simply genes for digits. In addition, the genetic information for digits will not be expressed unless the organism has an environment in which to develop. As long as a species is monomorphic for a particular trait, we can say nothing about the trait's genetic basis.

It is only when the characteristic varies that the genetic or nongenetic sources of the variation can be explored. Variation may be due entirely to genetic differences among individuals, entirely to differences in their environments, or to both. For example, humans are sometimes polydactylous, a condition in which there are extra fingers and toes. Since the polydactylous condition may be either dominant or recessive, it can be caused by several different genes; since the condition affects both hands and feet, it can be inferred that fingers and toes are not genetically independent traits. Because the gene for polydactyly is not always expressed, it shows that both genetic and nongenetic factors affect the development of the digits. Other variations, such as differences in language, have no genetic basis at all. No one would deny that humans have a genetic capacity for language, but the particular language the individual speaks is not determined by genes. We know nothing about the genetic basis for the *capacity* for language, because it is a monomorphic condition.

Before explaining why a trait has evolved, one must first know that the trait actually exists as a genetic entity that is capable of evolving independently of other parts of the organism. It would be meaningless first to ask what is adaptive about having five fingers and then to ask why five toes are adaptive, if fingers and toes are genetically so highly correlated as to be two aspects of the same trait. Instead, it is more proper to ask why five *digits* are adaptive. It is also meaningless to look for evolutionary explanations of why the French speak French and the Germans speak German: These linguistic differences have not evolved as genetic differences. It would be biologically meaningful, however, to ask what selective factors caused humans to evolve the capacity for language.

It is possible, but often difficult, to determine the selective reasons for evolutionary change even if a characteristic is polymorphic. To do so, one must first see if individuals with different traits differ in their average capacity for survival or reproduction, and then try to determine why. When a characteristic is monomorphic, however, it is even more difficult to demonstrate the actual selective reasons for its evolution. It was long supposed, for example, that snakes and lizards have scales because scales tend to reduce water loss through the skin, an advantage in dry environments. Although the theory was plausible, it proved to be erroneous: An aberrant gopher snake born without scales suffered no more water loss than normal gopher snakes (Licht & Bennett, 1972).

Thus, many adaptive explanations may be plausible but lack empirical support. This is one of the chief criticisms of many sociobiological theories (Gould & Lewontin, 1979; Lewontin, 1976). For example, Trivers (1972) argues that, in many animals, including humans, it would be advantageous for males to be promiscuous and females to be more "coy" and choosy in selecting a mate. Trivers presumes that promiscuous males will pass on more genes for promiscuity if they father as many offspring as possible, whereas females will fail to transmit their genes unless their offspring survive. Chances for survival of offspring are best if they have high quality genes inherited from a high quality male who is carefully chosen by the female for his superior attributes (Barash, 1977). This is a plausible theory, but one unsupported by evidence. It is equally possible to erect a counter-theory that would show how it would be advantageous for males to form a pair bond and thereby to assure the survival of their offspring (hence, of their genes) by careful nurturance.

What does all this have to do with homosexuality? In evaluating any evolutionary hypothesis of the origin of homosexuality, we must address these issues: (1) Is homosexual behavior a distinct trait or is it simply one manifestation of a more generalized trait, such as sexual behavior? One possible theory is that the human population could be genetically uniform for two sets of genes—one for heterosexual behavior and another for homosexual behavior—with the different sets of genes expressed under different conditions. If this theory were correct, sexual orientation in humans would resemble a condition in some birds (e.g., warblers), which have one set of genes for bright colors during the breeding season and, presumably, another set for dull coloration during the winter. The other possibility is that humans could be genetically uniform for a single set of genes for sexual behavior, which is expressed as either heterosexual or homosexual orientation, depending upon the social circumstances. That is, are variations in sexual orientation inherited, or are they reactions to different social conditions? There is no point in explaining the prevalence of genes for homosexuality *per se* if no such genes exist. (2) If genes for homosexuality exist, is the adaptive explanation for them based on evidence or conjecture? The necessary evidence requires the demonstration that the average individual with a capacity for homosexual behavior is more capable (or at least as capable) of passing on her or his genes than an individual with only a heterosexual capacity.

We now examine the major evolutionary hypotheses of homosexuality in light of these questions using Ruse's (1981) arguments as a framework.

EVOLUTIONARY HYPOTHESES OF HOMOSEXUAL BEHAVIOR

Evolutionary theorizing on homosexuality stems from the difficulty that, if there were a gene for exclusive homosexuality, it would be infrequently passed on to subsequent generations, and so would never exist except in a small percentage of the population. If heterosexuals reproduce more than homosexuals, a likely but uncertain assumption, genes for heterosexuality (if they exist) would replace those for homosexuality (if they exist). If genes for homosexuality are to exist in more than a very small percentage of the population, there must be some counteracting advantage of homosexuality. Although not all the hypotheses to explain the advantage of "homosexuality genes" are sociobiological, despite Ruse's (1981) sweeping inclusion of all of them under the umbrella of sociobiology, we shall consider each hypothesis in turn.

Heterozygous Advantage

The first hypothesis is that of the eminent ecologist, G. E. Hutchinson (1959), who postulated that individuals who are heterozygous, i.e., those who inherited one gene for heterosexuality from one parent and one gene for homosexuality from the other, might survive or reproduce better than those who have inherited genes only for heterosexuality or only for homosexuality. The heterozygotes would be heterosexual but, by successfully reproducing, would maintain a high frequency of homosexual genes in the population. The analogy is sickle cell hemoglobin: In parts of Africa, heterozygous individuals with a "normal" hemoglobin gene and a sickle-cell gene survive better than either those with only "normal" genes (who are more subject to malaria) or those with only sickle-cell genes (who are more likely to be anemic).

There is, however, not a shred of evidence that people whose ancestry includes both heterosexual and homosexual individuals differ in any way from those with an exclusively heterosexual ancestry (if such ancestries exist). Moreover, the sickle-cell hemoglobin analogy is forced, since it is the only well-documented case of heterozygous superiority of a single gene in any species (Lewontin, 1974).

In this connection it is necessary to ask if there is any evidence whatsoever of the genetic basis for heterosexuality and homosexuality. Despite Wilson's (1975, 1978) and Ruse's (1981) assertion that such evidence exists, what they cite is very unconvincing. Showing that a trait "runs in families" does not prove there is a genetic basis (Lewontin, 1975): Wealth, religious affiliation, and social attitudes also run in families. The only evidence for a genetic basis, in the absence of controlled genetic crosses, must come from adoption studies which show that the offspring of parents with trait A develop that trait even if reared by parents with trait B, particularly in the case of monozygotic (genetically identical) twins reared apart. If reared together, monozygotic twins cannot provide evidence of genetic inheritance because they are subject to the same environmental influences. To our knowledge, there are no adoption studies of twins or any other relatives that focus on their sexual orientation.

There are two major twin studies that pertain to sexual orientation. The most extensive is by Kallmann (1952a, 1952b), who claimed that the monozygotic twins of 40 male homosexuals were homosexual in every case, whereas the incidence of homosexuality in the dizygotic (fraternal) twins of 26 male homosexuals was no higher than in the male population in general. Kallmann even claimed that the monozygotic twins in his sample obtained the same ratings on the Kinsey, Pomeroy, and Martin (1948) scale of sexual orientation and that they tended to be *"very similar* in . . . the part taken in their individual sex activities" (p. 291, emphasis in the original). Kallmann's report has been widely questioned. Rosen and Gregory's (1965) textbook on abnormal psychology, for example, states that most investigators have not accepted Kallmann's conclusion that homosexuality has a hereditary basis. His research has many faults: (1) There is no evidence that the twins were reared apart. (2) Kallmann does not describe how he determined which twins were monozygotic and which were dizygotic; the methods in use at the time the study was undertaken are subject to as much as 30% error (Gregory, 1968). (3) The sex ratio among the "dizygotic" cotwins (31 males to 14 females) is so skewed as to suggest misclassification or an undetermined source of sampling bias. (4) He claims that the vast majority of his subjects were emotionally and socially maladjusted which, if true, raises the question (Gibbens, 1967) of whether the sample is at all representative and whether the homosexual behavior may have been a manifestation of psychopathology rather than a simple expression of sexual orientation. (5) Despite his claim that the monozygotic twins provided evidence of the high heritability of homosexuality, there was no evidence of a higher incidence of homosexuality either among the twins' fathers or dizygotic cotwins. Finally, (6) Kallmann implies that he obtained sexual information from the twin brother of all but 8 of the 71 homosexual individuals, and these 8 were "deceased or otherwise unavailable" (p. 290). It is almost inconceivable, given the need for homosexuals to hide their sexual orientation, that Kallmann should have obtained such extraordinary cooperation. It should also be pointed out that Kallmann's major work, on the genetic basis of schizophrenia, has been severely criticized (Pastore, 1949) for bias and carelessness, including diagnosis of schizophrenia from hospital records more than 25 years old and from purely anecdotal information.

A second twin study with a small sample (five monozygotic and seven dizygotic male twin pairs, plus one sibship of one heterosexual and two homosexual concordant pairs of monozygotic twins), is by Heston and Shields (1968). The twins in this study were also reared together. In any case, the sample is so small that there is no statistically demonstrable correlation between zygosity and rate of concordance. Thus there are no satisfactory data existing for concluding that variation in sexual orientation is inherited.

Kin Selection

One of the foundations of sociobiological theory is the principle (Hamilton, 1964) that a gene that reduces the chances of survival or reproduction of the individual who carries it may, despite this apparent disadvantage, increase and become the prevalent gene in the population by a process known as kin selection. Because relatives share some of the same genes through common inheritance, an individual can promote the propagation of its own genes by fostering the survival and reproduction of copies of those genes that are carried by relatives. Thus, a female bird can endanger its own survival by foraging for food for its young, but it propagates genes for parental care that have been inherited by its offspring, whose survival is benefited by its actions. The same principle holds for other relatives, such as siblings. A gene that causes sterility (as in the case of exclusive homosexuality) could increase if homosexuals, by helping relatives to reproduce, contribute even more genes to subsequent generations by fostering the survival of nieces and nephews than by reproducing offspring of their own. Thus Wilson (1975, 1978), Weinrich (1976), and Ruse (1981) argue that the genetic disadvantage of homosexuality could be more than offset by altruism of homosexuals toward relatives.

The fundamental assumption of kin selection is that human kin groups are formed along strict genetic lines. This assumption frequently does not accord with ethnographic data. Sahlins' (1976) survey of the relevant anthropological literature has shown that, in many groups, individuals may act altruistically toward members of a kinship group because of group bonds, even though they are not related by descent.

In addition to this basic flaw, there are a number of special problems in applying kin selection theory to homosexuality. First, it assumes that the average homosexual individual, throughout human evolution, reproduced less than heterosexual individuals. There are, as far as we know, no data to support this conjecture. Ruse (1981), following Weinrich (1976), tries to show that homosexuals may have a low expectation of successful reproduction, and therefore adopt altruism toward relatives as an alternative strategy of indirect reproduction. He cites data to show that homosexual men are physically slighter than heterosexual men and that men in preliterate societies who adopt a feminine sex-role have been traumatized. If homosexual men are really slighter than heterosexuals, is it because they abandon physical competition or because they have adopted homosexuality? If it is the former, the physical differences are a consequence of behavior that may reduce reproduction, not a cause of reduced reproductive potential. If, as Weinrich claims, the adoption of feminine sex-roles is caused by early trauma, it may be the trauma, and not the homosexuality, that reduces the prospect of reproduction. In any case, Weinrich presents no evidence that homosexual behavior in preliterate societies is associated with reduced reproduction. There is, however, much contrary evidence from cultural anthropology that both heterosexuality and homosexuality are parts of many individuals' sexual repertoire in a great many societies (Ford & Beach, 1951).

Weinrich and Ruse argue that the benefit conferred on relatives by homosexuals may have been large throughout human history: Homosexuals (or at least men who adopt a feminine sex-role) often occupy privileged positions (e.g., priests, shamans) in preliterate societies, which may economically benefit themselves and their extended families. However, this pattern is far from universal (Ford & Beach, 1951): In many societies, homosexuals do not enjoy special privileges that could aid their relatives. Moreover, there is no evidence of how economic privilege may be translated into increased reproduction or survival. Entirely lacking is evidence that increasing reproduction by relatives quantitatively compensates for the reproductive cost of exclusive homosexuality and none suggesting that privileged positions, such as the priesthood, are bestowed on the many homosexual men these societies presumably harbor. Furthermore, the kin selection argument also fails to explain homosexuality in females, who generally have not been privileged. Sociobiologists are left to argue, therefore, that homosexuality in females is an incidental genetic by-product of homosexuality in males.

In our opinion, the kin selection argument is extended to the extreme by Ruse and Weinrich when they postulate that homosexuals may be better actors (Ruse) and more intelligent (Weinrich) than heterosexuals because these abilities enable homosexuals better to play their privileged roles and to reap benefits for their families. Whatever data such claims are based upon probably derive from a highly biased selection of homosexuals who have the psychological strength to come out. Even if it were true that a random sample of homosexuals could be shown to be more intelligent, altruistic, or artistic than a random sample of heterosexuals, such traits could very well be a *consequence* of homosexuality (developed, perhaps, as a protection against oppression) rather than a genetic correlate. Indeed, from a genetic point of view, if there is genetic variation in intelligence or altruism (which has been questioned in the case of intelligence; see Kamin, 1974; Lewontin, 1975), it is very likely that the genes for these traits would not be those for sexual orientation and that the two traits would not be correlated. It is hard to imagine that the same genes that hypothetically determine sexual orientation would also make a substantial contribution to variation in intelligence.

The kin selection argument for the evolution of homosexuality constitutes at this stage little more than a plausible theory. Showing that homosexuals are nice to their relatives and are in a position to help them does not provide the needed evidence. People without children of their own will of course help take care of their relatives if they are socialized to do so.

Parental Manipulation

Ruse's third sociobiological speculation about homosexuality invokes the notion of parental manipulation, a Freudian notion dressed up in evolutionary trappings. According to this theory (originally suggested in Trivers, 1974), parents might actually propagate more of their genes to future generations by influencing some of their children to become homosexual so that (somehow) their other children will be more successful in reproducing. Ruse cites no evidence, except anecdotes of cases of parents in certain societies who encourage their children to take on privileged positions that entail change of gender role. Ruse does not suggest that consciousness of economic benefit, rather than unconscious striving for reproductive benefit, might motivate parents to encourage some children to forego their reproductive roles.

We view parental manipulation as a prime example of unverifiable sociobiological speculation: Even if one could show, as certain researchers have repeatedly tried to do (see Bell, Weinberg, & Hammersmith, 1981), that the development of homosexuality is associated with certain kinds of parental behavior, how could one hope to demonstrate that this reflected an adaptive behavior of the parents? If the psychoanalytic etiology of homosexuality were true, how would one determine if parental behavior was adaptive, unconscious manipulation, or, as the psychoanalysts would have it, pathological? One of the weaknesses of sociobiology is that it sees almost every aspect of behavior as adaptation. But organisms display a wealth of nonadaptive (neutral), and even maladaptive, characteristics (Futuyma, 1979, Chapter 17; Gould & Lewontin, 1979). Showing that behavior is adaptive is never easy and, in some cases, it is nearly impossible.

SOCIAL, POLITICAL, AND ETHICAL IMPLICATIONS

To many sociobiologists, homosexuality is apparently an aberration or idiosyncrasy that cries out for explanation. For us, homosexuality is one example of the immense flexibility of human behavior. It requires no more explanation than a preference for blondes or brunettes or for music or sports. It may be plausibly argued (as Ruse does) that homosexuality presents an evolutionary paradox, the resolution of which is a matter of intellectual interest. The paradox exists, however, only if it is assumed that homosexuality has evolved as a definable, reifiable trait. As we have noted, there is no evidence that the homosexual orientation is genetically dissociable from the heterosexual orientation. Just as the evolution of toes is one aspect of the evolution of digits, homosexual orientation, in our opinion, is one manifestation of universal sexual and emotional drives. If this is so, evolutionary theory should seek to explain the origin of human *flexibility* in sexual needs. This flexibility, we believe, is a monomorphic trait of all humans. As we have noted, it can be extraordinarily difficult to demonstrate the adaptive value of a genetically uniform trait, whether it be the scales of snakes or the flexibility of human sexual behavior.

Sociobiological speculation about homosexuality may be prompted by intellectual interest in evolutionary paradoxes; but it is hard not to suspect that it is sometimes motivated by the belief that homosexual behavior is pathological. Sociobiological arguments can be evaluated for *scientific* content as we have done, whether they are couched in normative or non-normative terms. But the form of the argument, as well as its content, is subject to evaluation.

Most of the psychological and medical literature on homosexual behavior concerns ways to prevent or to "cure" it. We object not only to blatant statements of this kind of bias, but also to insinuations in what purports to be scientific literature that homosexuality is abnormal or pathological. The tenor of much recent sociobiological literature on homosexuality, in contrast, is liberal. But whether invoked to justify oppression or acceptance of homosexuals, the biological argument is specious. Appeal to biology is based on the untenable presumption that what is biologically "natural" is also good. Natural selection and evolution, it is clear, can neither define nor guide us toward standards of morality and ethical progress.

REFERENCES

Barash, D. P. *Sociobiology and behavior.* New York: Elsevier, 1977.
Bell, A. P., Weinberg, M. S., & Hammersmith, S. K. *Sexual preference: Its development in men and women.* Bloomington, IN: Indiana University Press, 1981.
Churchill, W. *Homosexual behavior among males: A cross-cultural and cross-species investigation.* Englewood Cliffs, NJ: Prentice-Hall, 1967.
Ford, C. S., & Beach, F. A. *Patterns of sexual behavior.* New York: Harper & Row, 1951.
Futuyma, D. J. *Evolutionary biology.* Sunderland, MA: Sinauer, 1979.
Gallup, G. G., Jr., & Suarez, S. D. Homosexuality as a by-product of selection for optimal heterosexual strategies. *Perspectives in Biology and Medicine,* 1983, *26*, 315-322.
Gibbens, T. C. N. Sexual deviation. In A. Allison (Ed.), *The biology of sex.* Middlesex: Penguin Books, 1967.
Gould, S. J., & Lewontin, R. C. The spandrels of San Marcos. *Proceedings of the Royal Society of London (B),* 1979, *205*, 581-598.
Gregory, I. *Fundamentals of psychiatry* (2nd ed.). Philadelphia: W. B. Saunders, 1968.
Hamilton, W. D. The genetical evolution of social behavior: I, II. *Journal of Theoretical Biology,* 1964, *7*, 1-52.
Heston, L. L., & Shields, J. Homosexuality in twins: A family study and a registry study. *Archives of General Psychiatry,* 1968, *28*, 149-160.
Hutchinson, G. E. A speculative consideration of certain possible forms of sexual selection in man. *American Naturalist,* 1959, *93*, 81-91.
Kallmann, F. J. Comparative twin study on the genetic aspects of male homosexuality. *Journal of Nervous and Mental Disease,* 1952, *115*, 283-298. (a)
Kallmann, F. J. Twin and sibship study of overt male homosexuality. *American Journal of Human Genetics,* 1952, *4*, 136-146. (b)
Kamin, L. J. *The science and politics of IQ.* New York: Wiley, 1974.
Kettlewell, H. B. D. Selection experiments on industrial melanism in the Lepidoptera. *Heredity,* 1955, *9*, 323-342.
Kinsey, A., Pomeroy, W. B., & Martin, C. E. *Sexual behavior in the human male.* Philadelphia: W. B. Saunders, 1948.
Lewontin, R. C. *The genetic basis of evolutionary change.* New York: Columbia University Press, 1974.
Lewontin, R. C. Genetic aspects of intelligence. *Annual Review of Genetics,* 1975, *9*, 387-405.
Lewontin, R. C. Sociobiology: A caricature of Darwinism. *Philosophy of Science Association Journal,* 1976, *2*, 22-31.
Lewontin, R. C. Sociobiology as an adaptationist program. *Behavioral Science,* 1979, *4*, 5-14.
Licht, P., & Bennett, A. F. A scaleless snake: Tests of the role of reptilian scales in water loss and heat transfer. *Copeia,* 1972, 702-707.
Pastore, N. The genetics of schizophrenia. *Psychological Bulletin,* 1949, *46*, 285-302.
Rosen, E., & Gregory, I. *Abnormal psychology.* Philadelphia: W. B. Saunders, 1965.

Ruse, M. Are there gay genes? Sociobiology and homosexuality. *Journal of Homosexuality*, 1981, *6*, 5-34.

Sahlins, M. *The use and abuse of biology: An anthropological critique of sociobiology.* Ann Arbor, MI: University of Michigan Press, 1976.

Stein, D. Why gays are smarter than straights: Homosexuality and sociobiology. *Christopher Street*, 1978, *3*(1), 9-14.

Tripp, C. A. *The homosexual matrix.* New York: McGraw-Hill, 1975.

Trivers, R. L. Parental investment and sexual selection. In B. Campbell (Ed.), *Sexual selection and the descent of man.* Chicago: Aldine, 1972.

Trivers, R. L. Parent-offspring conflict. *American Zoologist*, 1974, *14*, 249-264.

Weinberg, M. S., & Bell, A. P. *Homosexuality: An annotated bibliography.* New York: Harper & Row, 1972.

Weinrich, J. D. *Human reproductive strategy: The importance of income predictability, and the evolution of non-reproduction.* Unpublished doctoral dissertation, Harvard University, 1976.

Wilson, E. O. *Sociobiology: The new synthesis.* Cambridge, MA: Harvard University Press, 1975.

Wilson, E. O. *On human nature.* Cambridge, MA: Harvard University Press, 1978.

Index